Exploring Nature with Your Child

by Dorothy Shuttlesworth

Harry N. Abrams, Inc., Publishers,
New York

For Mel
and Lee Ann and Rich, and Mary Lynn
and Gregory and their young explorers

Photo research and editing by
Anthony A. Long and Pieter van Delft.
Design and art direction by
A.D.M. International bv., Amsterdam.
Line illustrations by
Piet Eggen.

Created by:
Plenary Publications International, Inc.
300 East 40th Street
New York, N.Y. 10016

ISBN 8109-0895-6
Library of Congress
Catalog Card Number: 77-72010

Printed and bound in the United States

Contents

Exploring Nature in a Changing World   6
Understanding the Birds   14
Mammals, Large and Small   40
The Sea and the Shore   66
Fishes–from Sunnies to Sharks   84
Snakes, Frogs, and Their Relatives   106
Exotic Zoo Animals   136
Popular Pets and Their Origins   156
The Misunderstood Spider   172
The Kingdom of the Insects   182
Plants, Trees, and Flowers   214
Index   238
Acknowledgments   240

Exploring Nature in a Changing World

Children are natural explorers. They have the true explorer's interest in faraway places as well as in their immediate surroundings, and they are eager to know why the things that they encounter are as they are.

As a parent, you will be able to think back to your own early years when you were thrilled to see a bird building its nest or to watch rival colonies of ants fighting each other. Perhaps you planted seeds and experienced deep-felt wonder when the green shoots began to push through the soil. As time passed, the keen pleasure in such simple discoveries may have dimmed. But with your child this sense of wonder can be rekindled, and when that happens, life becomes richer and more meaningful for the entire family. In your relationship as fellow explorers your own role is likely to be that of the guide traveling along the highways and byways of nature, even as you help your child to find direction in the bewildering world that people have made. It is a rewarding partnership. Fortunately nature exploring does not have to depend on expeditions to distant places such as the plains of Africa or the jungles of Asia. Delightful discoveries can be made in your own back yard, in city parks and suburban gardens, along forest trails where you may hike, and by the shores of ocean, lake, or stream where you may vacation. In a suburban area you may look out of the window in the morning and see a woodchuck nibbling its breakfast in a dewy field or a rabbit scampering across the lawn, purposefully headed for the vegetable garden. You may watch spiders spinning silken traps or see a tug-of-war between a robin and an earthworm. In family expeditions to woodlands and meadows, to zoos and museums, there is even more to be observed.

The question is sometimes asked, What is the best way to pursue nature exploring with children? Actually there is no 'best' method, because children vary in their approach to nature's activities just as they differ in countless other ways. One child is full of curiosity about plant and animal life from the time he or she is an infant. Another is absorbed in fanciful ideas, while still another has a mechanical bent, remaining oblivious to the wonders of nature until you bring them to the child's attention. Nature exploring is not always a simple matter. It is not just 'knowing the answers,' perhaps pointing out each tree or bird that you see, giving names and a few pertinent facts. A background of informa-tion is invaluable, to be sure, but you must pass it on in such a way that you do not overwhelm the child's own modest discoveries. Awareness is essential, but it should not be carried to a point where your child considers you slightly eccentric. On the whole, the successful approach lies in encouraging inquisitiveness and providing opportunities to satisfy curiosity.

Children with a practical turn of mind enjoy hearing about ways in which people have put nature's 'inventions' to use. Outstanding among these is camouflage, which effectively gives protection to many birds and other animals. This principle pointed the way for the change from army uniforms, which made soldiers conspicuous targets, to the deceptive, neutral earth-and-leaf tones used today. Another debt we owe nature is the inspiration of bird flight, which was carefully studied in advancing our own conquest of the air. Fish benefit from streamlining: another principle we put to good use. Wasps were adept at making paper from wood fiber centuries before people developed the technique. The 20th-century invention of radar is an old story to bats, which have a comparable system for getting their bearings as they fly sightless through treacherous passageways. These are only a few of the lessons that children enjoy having pointed out to them as they become acquainted with nature's ways.

Exploring nature teaches the child to overcome many baseless fears. Occasionally you find a boy or girl showing more timidity than enjoyment in encounters with animals. It may be difficult to trace the reason for this since a child sometimes has experiences of which his parents are unaware. I saw a case in point recently in a woodsy stretch of a city park where children were playing unsupervised. A big boy, one hand closed and outstretched, started to chase a little fellow, and was fairly hissing with menace: 'Spider! Spider!'

The smaller child was screaming with fright. My curiosity aroused about the creature inspiring his terror, I went up to the older boy and asked if I might see the spider. He gave me a delighted conspiratorial smile and showed me what was in his hand. It was a small flower!

'I just wanted to scare him,' he explained. 'He didn't come close enough to see what I really had.'

Meanwhile something remarkable was happening. The younger boy had stopped crying, and he was coming slowly

▷ Nature explorations lead to many habitats, including the 'in-between' world of the amphibians—animals like this bullfrog, which begin life as water babies and later become land creatures. It is best not to collect or disturb such examples of wildlife, but simply observe them in their natural settings. The bullfrog is a giant among North American frogs; one may grow to a length of eight inches or more.

▽ The association of insects and flowers is one of the most colorful aspects of nature study. Butterflies and other insects are recognized as allies of plants, though some insect species are destructive. A child who plants a tree (left) takes a personal interest in its growth and in protecting it. To some people dandelions may be common weeds, but to a young rabbit (right) they are excellent food, especially the tips.

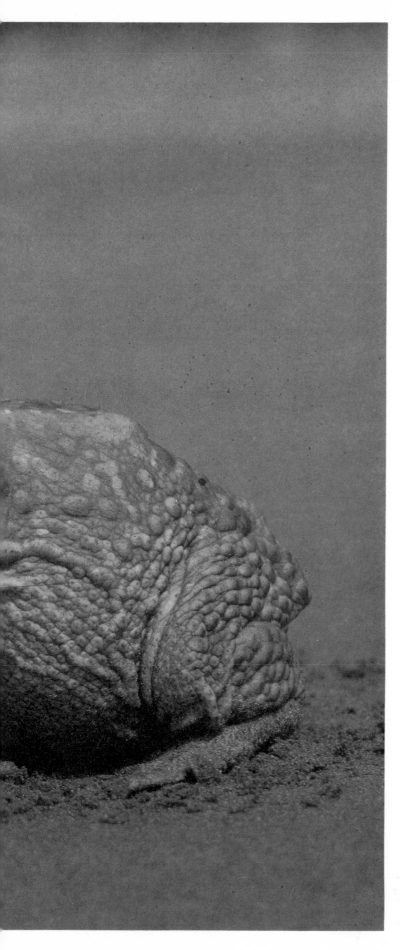

toward us. My interest in what he thought was a spider had aroused his curiosity and was giving him courage to see what the dangerous creature looked like. This was strong evidence of the influence, whether advantageous or detrimental, that older people can have on a youngster. As we spend time with children, we become aware of the fears they may have of creatures unfamiliar to them. Once we realize that these fears exist, it is usually not difficult to set at rest a timidity that is really baseless. The remedy is simply to give the youngster an understanding of the dreaded animal. Adults, too, carry many baseless fears from childhood days, and it is surprising how often in the course of nature exploring that a child can return the favor and help dispel them in the true scientific spirit of detached curiosity.

We contribute a great deal to a child's future happiness by creating a sympathetic acquaintance with as much wildlife as possible. Although it was a number of summers ago, I can still remember the time that a woman whose usual haunts were in New York City visited our woodland cabin. All day she had been enjoying the sights of trees and flowers, the river, and glimpses of bird life; but in the evening a screech owl's tremulous, wailing whistle suddenly shattered the quiet. Our friend was quite unnerved by the sound, which admittedly is strange, even weird, and we immediately did our best to explain about the attractive and harmless little owl. There was no way to reassure her. It was obvious that she could hardly wait to return to what, to her, was the calming environment of a big city. A few evenings later another visitor, this time a small boy of no more than five years old, heard the wail of the screech owl.
'What was that?' he asked.

We told him, hastily thinking of interesting facts that might dispel his fears. But we need not have bothered. As soon as he heard that it was an owl, he said wistfully, 'I wish he would come close so I could hold him and pat him.' It was pleasant to think how rich life would be for this child, growing up with an acceptance of the sounds and sights that have a rightful place in nature's scheme. Of course he had not come by this attitude through chance. His parents had already given him some knowledge and understanding of wildlife. They had told him true stories about animals and taught him nature lore and hobbies that widened his view of the world, which made his experiences more enjoyable.

▽ Bats have their own 'radar' system. Flying, they emit shrill squeaks; when the sound hits a solid object it bounces back to the bat, giving a 'sound picture' of the surroundings, even picking up flying insects—bat food.

▽ ▽ The great bowl of a communications radar in Alaska is comparable to the bat's ears—it picks up a wide range of reflected sounds from which it interprets complex information about far distant objects.

11

Modern schools have excellent programs of nature study, but even the best programs cannot take the place of family participation in nature interests. On the other hand, a child whose parents enjoy nature with him finds this of real help with his schoolwork. He will readily discuss ideas he encounters at school when he knows that his mother and father are interested.

Actually it is not always easy to keep up with the rapid strides made by children. It seemed I had barely stopped smiling over my three-year-old's comments, such as, 'I know bees make honey, but I don't see *how* they get it into jars,' when he was coming home from the first grade asking, 'What is the difference between rodents and other kinds of animals?' A year later he was likely to interrupt lunch with such posers as, 'If dinosaurs were so powerful, why did they all die?' Suddenly we had arrived at questions that are still a puzzle to scientists.

As a matter of fact, many parents are discovering in our rapidly changing world that their children have become leaders rather than followers in nature appreciation and in understanding the vital need for conservation of natural resources, particularly in the future.

Recently the word 'ecology' has become a vital part of our language, and now many school children are made aware of its meaning and importance before their parents become involved. The word derives from the Greek *Oikos,* a house, and refers to the study of the connecting relationships between energy, plants and animals. Just as a house is the sum total of the skills and experience of many builders, and can exist for only as long as the people within maintain it properly, so it is in the 'house' of nature.

We cannot afford to continue to exploit natural resources, including animals, without some thought as to their origins, uses and replacements. This requires an understanding of nature. In the modern, technological world when so much of the earth has been abused, and the cities grow ever-larger, it is all too easy to forget our collective responsibility to nature. As a guide and a companion in a family, a parent can rediscover the fascination of nature's ways, then perhaps remember and pass on that we humans, too, are part of the animal and plant kingdom.

Many children grow up in big cities and
rarely have a chance to go into the country,
but it is a mistake to think that the city
contains no wildlife. Many creatures such
as pigeons (below) have adapted to thrive
in urban surroundings. An early contact
with animals and birds will often develop
into a keen interest in nature (opposite),
which may well last for a lifetime.

Understanding the Birds

As soon as they are old enough to take an interest in their surroundings, most children delight in birds. A bundle of feathers with bright eyes and a perky air of self-confidence is an appealing figure, whether trilling on a spring day or seeking food in wintry gales.

The maturing youngster may look more inquiringly at the graceful songsters and one day may startle you with the question: 'What makes a bird a bird?'
Taken off guard, you might answer: 'A bird has feathers and wings and is able to fly.'
But there you stop, confused. Some birds, such as the ostrich and penguin, do not fly. A fuller explanation will take this into account: 'Birds are warm-blooded, feathered, egg-laying animals that have backbones and wings, although the wings do not always serve as flying aids.'
Of course you will have to expand this definition to make it clearer to a child, but the definition will fit the tiny, speedy hummingbird as well as the earthbound ostrich, the majestic eagle, and the comical puffin. It will fit the feathered creatures of woodlands, prairies, oceanic islands, mountain slopes, lakes, deserts, jungles, and barnyards. It will stand up under a challenge such as I had from a three-year-old:
'But, Mommy, you called the chicken a bird. It's a chicken!'
By strongly emphasizing feathers, I finally persuaded her that even the stalwart barnyard fowl deserves to be ranked with the birds. Feathers are about the only feature that birds do not share with any other kind of animal.

The Importance of Feathers
Bird plumage often is so beautiful that we are likely to overlook its practical value. What clothes are to people, feathers are to birds: raincoat and undergarments in one. If you watch a chicken caught in a storm, you will see how it droops its wings and tail, thus making the best use of its feathers. Rain flows off as it does from your slicker. Examining a feather, you will find it has three distinct parts: the quill (or central stem); flat barbs attached to the major part of the quill; and soft fluff at the base. This fluff, close to the body, functions as the warm underclothing.

Feathers also provide camouflage. While we quickly recognize this in many wild birds, the protective coloring of chickens is less obvious when we observe them in a barn-

yard. Were a hen living in a natural state, wandering in thick woodlands with her chicks, her neutral color would blend in with the surroundings. It is the rooster that is decorative, having lovely, iridescent tail feathers and often colorful neck plumage.

Wild birds offer many convincing examples of safety through camouflage. The female Baltimore oriole, for example, is a dull orange yellow while her mate is a brilliant combination of orange, black, and white. Among the cardinals, the male is a rich red; the female's plumage is light brown with only the faintest tinge of red. The name rose-breasted grosbeak is appropriate only for the male of this species. He displays a deep rose patch on his white breast, but his mottled yellow, brown, and white mate looks rather like an overgrown sparrow.

In each of these cases we see the same principle at work. Since the female bird must look after the eggs and young, the less attention she attracts the better. The arrestingly colored male can remain at a distance from the nest, distracting potential enemies.

You may notice an interesting phase of protective coloring in birds that are molting. When the males of a certain species lose their bright feathers after the mating season, the new ones they grow are of somber hues. By fall the male scarlet tanager is the same dull yellow green as his mate. Both male and female bobolink become sparrowlike in appearance. The bright yellow body feathers of the goldfinch give way to others of dull yellow brown. Thus garbed, the male birds are fairly inconspicuous until the following year, when the time comes again for them to be brightly attractive to the females.

New Feathers for Old
If late summer happens to be the time that your family shows more than a casual interest in birds, the subject of molting is a particularly interesting theme to explore. Some species lose their worn and faded feathers in August, and by September the birds have completely new plumage. Among the exceptions to this schedule are waterfowl, which begin to molt in June. By September they have passed through two molts, during which they have taken on and discarded a dull plumage.

Many kinds of birds undergo plumage color changes as they grow from chick to adult. Also, many change color with changing seasons each year. On ptarmigan (most northern members of the grouse family) the change is dramatic. These birds molt twice a year, completely altering color. Summer plumage is black, brown, and white; winter's is snowy white. An intermediate stage is seen in late spring. As a result the bird is almost constantly camouflaged from predators.

15

Unless there is a definite change in a bird's coloration during molting, the process is not easy to observe. A gradual change starts with one feather, usually the innermost primary wing feather, and it continues over the wings until all are replaced. The new feathers of some species of birds develop all over the body at the same time, while on others the development occurs in patches. Ducks, grebes, loons, and other swimming birds that do not depend on flight as their only means of locomotion molt all feathers at the ends of the wings within a very short time.

The growth of feathers is made possible by their having a continuous supply of blood. Each feather has its start in a small hollow in the bird's inner layer of skin, which is equipped with feather-producing cells and a tiny vein and artery. Blood flows through these as the feather grows longer and broader. When the feather is fully grown (the proper size for a particular species of bird), the artery and vein seal off. With no more blood coming through, no more nutrition reaches the feather and it stops growing. Months later it simply drops away from the bird's body, and the process of growing a new feather begins immediately.

Feathers do not grow haphazardly over a bird's body; they are arranged in definite lines or patches (called feather tracts) between which are bare areas. However, the overlapping of feathers of the adjacent tracts keeps the skin completely covered in healthy birds.

Most birds molt only once a year, but the brilliantly colored males that have dull winter coats must change again to regain their beauty in the spring. Some birds, such as the scarlet tanager and the goldfinch, undergo a spring (before nesting) as well as a fall (after nesting) molt. In these cases, however, the spring molt usually is not complete; the same wing and tail feathers serve both plumages.

Some birds change between winter and spring without undergoing a second molt. This happens because of what is called feather wear; the feather tips, which have given the general tone to the winter plumage, wear away and expose the bright colors of the breeding plumage. The robin is a notable example. Its breast becomes redder as spring advances because the gray feather tips are wearing off. Yellow, brown, and gray most frequently edge the feathers of the winter plumage of many birds. As these colors disappear, black, brown, or red is revealed. Molting draws heavily on a bird's energy reserves, for much body tissue – feathers – must be built in quite a short time. While growing a new set of feathers, a bird is 'too tired' to sing or fight. It stays in seclusion except when it must seek food. For this reason, rather than because of an early departure for southern climes, you see few birds in late August and early September. As soon as the birds have completed their molting, they regain their vitality and are ready to migrate or to face the rigors of a northern winter.

Versatile Beaks
The child who is always wondering about the 'why' of things will be fascinated by the endless variety of bird beaks. In almost every case the beak formation gives us a clue to a bird's eating habits, its diet, and even its surroundings. The duck, for example, has a wide, flat bill that is suitable for feeding on water plants, water insects, and shellfish. After seizing food in its beak, the duck holds it there until the water strains out of its sievelike edges. Given the same watery conditions, the sharp horny beak of a chicken would be quite useless. The chicken's beak resembles a pick rather than a scoop. It strikes efficiently into the soil for insects and seeds. The sparrow is another bird with a sharp seed-eating beak. As for the woodpecker, its beak is virtually a chisel. You may hear a woodpecker hammering for insects, or you may simply discover the evidence that it has been there in a series of holes in a tree trunk.

These are but a few examples of the close relationship between the style of a bird's beak and the kind of food it eats. Children will get the point at once if you tell them the Aesop fable of the stork and the fox. The stork, having been served soup in a shallow dish by his host, a fox, gets his revenge by inviting the fox to dinner and serving food in a narrow-necked vessel, which suits his own beak perfectly, but from which the fox cannot lap the soup.

The beak has many uses other than getting food. It is used for feeding young birds. It is a tool for gathering nesting material and digging nesting sites. It often serves as a weapon for attack or defense. It also enables many birds to do an effective job of preening and smoothing their plumage and keeping it clean.

To find cormorants, an explorer does well to look along seacoasts, though some species frequent inland waters. These birds are famed for their diving ability. When wings are outstretched, the plumage can dry quickly.

If the hen you watched during a storm could be observed after the rain stopped, you might see her using her beak to oil her feathers. There is an oil gland on the back, just at the base of the tail feathers. She presses this gland with her beak to force out oil and then rubs the beak over and through her feathers. Now her 'oilskin slicker' is ready for the next downpour. A number of other birds, including waterfowl, use this same method for oiling.

A parrot's curved bill is unique in construction and use. It is an excellent piece of equipment to use in climbing. The upper mandible, or upper bill, is movable, being connected to the bird's skull by a hinge. When the parrot climbs, it uses this as a hook to support its body while its feet find a new resting place.

Feet Are Versatile Too

Birds depend on their feet in a variety of ways. Waders, such as flamingos and herons, have extremely long toes, which distribute the bird's weight and keep it from sinking into soft mud. Short-tailed birds, the murres, for example, use the feet as rudders during flight. Diving birds, such as grebes, use their feet to propel them underwater. When you notice a bird scratching for food, you are witnessing another use for the feet. Birds of prey, such as eagles and hawks, seize their victims in their long, powerful talons.

Many birds use their feet to gather nesting material and put it into place. For some birds the feet are fighting weapons. A parrot uses its foot to grasp and bring food to its mouth in much the same way as we use a hand.

Sharp Eyes and Ears

Are the bright eyes of a bird as efficient as the alert and shining appearance would lead us to believe? They really are. Birds are much more sharp-sighted than people. They have remarkably keen vision, and some are especially well adapted for viewing objects both far away and at close range. Thus a hawk flying so high it would appear as a mere speck to us, can look down and spot a rabbit, or even a mouse, on the ground. This bird has two centers of vision – one for all-round observation, the other to judge distance – and as it swoops down from the heights, its vision shifts from one center to the other. In this way its eyes are adjusted for short-range work when it seizes its prey.

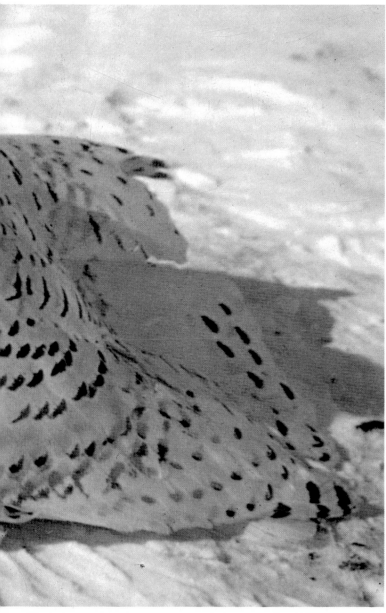

Most birds, despite their sharp eyesight, do not have the bifocal vision of the hawk. As a result they often misjudge such obstacles as telephone and power lines and are injured or killed by colliding with them.

The color of birds' eyes varies considerably. The iris may be brown, grey, blue, yellow, white, pink, purple, green, and even red. The 'red-eyed vireo' takes the first half of its name from this striking feature. The hen, that ideal bird for study, has a yellow iris. It is equipped with an eyelid that shuts out vision; this lid comes up from the bottom of the eye, rather than moves down from the top. It also has another feature that is also like a lid. This is a film that moves across the eye from the inside corner to the outer side.

You may escape being questioned about the hearing ability of birds because their ears are fairly well hidden. Then suddenly this very fact may be the basis for a query from your young observer:
'How can that bird hear? I don't see any ears!'
Except for some owls, which have noticeable ear tufts, the ear of a bird is no more than a hole, rather well covered with feathers, on the side of the head. Yet a bird's hearing, like its sight, is remarkable. As you walk in a field or woodland, you may notice how the snapping of a small twig will startle and put to flight birds that are a considerable distance away. When you see a robin cocking its head and you realize that it is listening for an earthworm moving underground, you develop considerable respect for the hearing ability of birds.

How Birds Fly

'How *do* birds fly?' is a question many children ask, perhaps accompanying the query with a leap into the air with arms outstretched. There is always the faint hope that they, too, can take off. It will help the inquisitive child to understand the mechanics of flight if you point out that a bird's streamlined form is of great advantage in flying. Another important consideration is the bird's structure, which is extremely light. Its bones and the shafts of its feathers are hollow, and, as is easily observed, the size of the wings is greater in proportion to the body than an arm is to the human body. It might be helpful to compare the child's framework to the bone and feather structure of the bird, which has one bone corresponding to the child's upper arm and another to the bone between the elbow and wrist. Have the child extend the thumb upward, hold the first and second fingers in a horizontal position, and fold the other two into the palm. This affords a rough comparison with the structure of a bird's wing. The bird has a winglet corresponding to the thumb, and a second and third digit similar to the extended fingers. These are sometimes extended upright, but they may also be held horizontally. While the child's arm, hand, and fingers are covered only with skin, the bird has flight feathers, one sheath on the 'forearm,' and another series on the 'hand.'

There are four types of bird flight: flapping, gliding, static soaring, and dynamic soaring. In the flight pattern known as flapping, the 'arm' wings help to lift the bird into the air, while the 'hand' wings produce propulsion through the air. Forward motion and speed are obtained on up-and-down strokes. In this up-and-down motion the wing tips move through a much greater arc than the wrists would. In small birds, such as the finch, the whole wing flaps as a unit, producing lift and speed at the same time.

Birds use their wings differently for different kinds of flight, such as horizontal, soaring, gliding, hovering, taking off, and climbing. Various types of birds have wings of different shapes and proportions.

An important part of the flying mechanism is a sinew with elastic qualities which is between the joints of a wing. On the downward thrust the sinew holds the feathers in a tight overlapping position. When the wing comes up, the tension of the sinew relaxes and the feathers separate and twist. This allows air to flow between the feathers, another significant aid for flight.

The Mystery of Migration
There is no more fascinating way of arousing interest in flight than to catch sight of migrating birds, perhaps a flight of geese in 'V' formation or a close-massed flock of grackles racing like a dark, windblown cloud. Even after years of research, scientists sometimes speak of the mystery of bird migration, for it is still not completely understood. Puzzling as such migrating may be, it is no more puzzling to me than the way my daughter took note of it before she reached her second birthday. On two different occasions we were having a late-afternoon walk along streets brightening with electric lights and alive with homebound traffic, when the little girl in the stroller looked up and pointed in great excitement:
'Look, birdies!'
There they were – large flocks of them, high above the city's hubbub, traveling in steady and sure flight toward their winter residence. The wonderful instinct that keeps birds on their course during such long-distance travel has been called a sixth sense, and it seemed that a sense beyond those that ordinarily serve people must have prompted my daughter to take her eyes from the excitement on the ground at exactly the right time to catch the nature news high in the sky. A few years later we began to have fun deliberately watching for 'birdies.'

Not all birds migrate. Some you will know as permanent residents in your neighborhood. The migratory birds arriving in the spring and remaining through the warm months are summer residents. Fall migrants that remain through the cold season are winter residents. Other birds you may see only briefly as they pass through your area to nesting grounds or winter quarters, and these are transients. Migratory birds are different things to different people, since your summer residents are winter residents in other regions, and your transients somewhere become winter and summer residents.

A confusing fact about migration is that certain well-known migrators do not travel as far south or north as we think. According to popular belief, the robin, that noted herald of spring, winters in the warm comfort far to the south. In the United States it is therefore a bit disconcerting, when taking a winter walk, to see a robin looking for food among frozen surroundings, especially if the child with you asks:
'Don't robins go south in winter?'
The majority of them *are* enjoying southern sunshine. Many have settled along the Gulf Coast or are in Mexico and in Florida, feeding on holly and mistletoe berries. But some choose to remain in northern climes with only friendly evergreens to shield them. A proportion of other so-called spring species – such as the bluebird, song sparrow, meadow lark, redwing blackbird, and cedar waxwing – also brave the northern winter.

To spear or to scoop? Various are the fishing techniques of water birds, even among those having especially long bills. While a stork and an egret poke and pry in search of small fish, a pelican twists its neck to use its bill as a scoop. Pelicans' unusual bills, whose pouches are actually elastic skin, were once believed to serve as a storage place for extra food. But their real purpose is catching fish. When a pelican plunges its open bill into a school of fish, the bill acts as a scoop: fish and water are taken in; then water runs out and fish are gulped down. Bills are also useful in caring for young ones. Babies push their bills into a pouch for predigested food.

▽ *Ducks are among the most accessible, and interesting, birds to observe. Often they can be persuaded to come close if food is offered (bottom right). A good look at their beaks may tell you their favorite foods; the flat bill of the mallard duck is excellent for tearing up weeds and other vegetation, while the broad bill of the shoveler is adapted to strain off tiny animals and plants from the surface layers of the water. Eider ducks have very strong beaks which can crack open the shells of the shellfish which make up their diet. The backward-pointing teeth on the edges of the bill of the merganser duck help it to keep hold of the fish it catches to feed on.*

Sky Lanes of the Birds

Because the expressions 'traveling north' and 'flying south' are used repeatedly, children are likely to think that birds unfailingly migrate in these directions. This is not an accurate picture, however, because some fly southeast, others southwest. Certain species have followed fixed travel routes until these routes have become well-defined sky lanes for these particular species. Some travel north by one route and return south by another, perhaps leading over an entirely different part of the country. One route may be overland and the return route over water. The golden plover is an interesting example of a bird that has a double migration route. In the spring it travels from South America to Labrador in as direct a line as possible, through the middle of the North American continent. In the fall it goes eastward to the Atlantic, and much of its return flight is over water. On this longer course it flies about twenty-four hundred miles.

There are also variations in the hours for migratory flights. Some birds are on the wing by day, others by night, while still others are active day and night. Warblers, thrushes, and woodcocks are among the night flyers. Geese, crows, swallows, robins, hummingbirds, blue jays, and bluebirds are a few of the daytime travelers. As for ducks, you may see them on the wing day or night.

Birds were once credited with speeds approaching those of the pioneer airplanes flying at that time. The theory was that most birds carried out the greater part of their journey in one continuous push. But in recent years the speed of many birds has been clocked accurately, and we now know that a hundred miles an hour is an exceptionally fast rate, achieved by only a few species such as certain swifts. Most birds during migratory flights apparently move at a rate somewhere between twenty and fifty miles an hour. The great journeys made by some species are accomplished by the birds moving for long hours at a steady rate rather than by great bursts of speed over short distances. When we compare the speed of an individual bird with the time it takes a flock of that same species to complete its migratory journey, we realize that the birds do not fly continuously day after day or night after night. They may pause for extended rests or if storms make flying very uncomfortable, and they must wait for favorable weather conditions.

mallard

shoveler

eider

merganser

hornbill

parrot

Everglade kite

godwit

The beak for the job: the hornbill feeds on large soft fruit and some insects. Godwits find food by probing mud. Parrots specialize in cracking nuts and seeds, while the Everglade kite uses its bill as a precision snail picker.

Altogether we may sum up some of the puzzling aspects of bird migration by saying that in its simplest form migration is a journey away from, and back to, a nesting ground, which makes possible a food supply throughout the year.

Being a Good Neighbor to the Birds

There are a number of ways to bring wild birds close to your home where you may study their ways and enjoy them. One of the most effective overtures of friendship is to provide a birdbath. Songbirds usually are attracted by water and some of them even relish a bath when it is raining. During hot, dry spells when many natural sources of water dry up, your birdbath will serve a really essential purpose. At such times the birds may have trouble finding drinking water. A simple way to provide a birdbath, or drinking fountain, is to set a shallow pan on a post or ledge and fill it with water. When placing the pan, keep in mind the danger from cats; these natural enemies of birds must not have a nearby hiding place from which to launch a surprise attack. A birdbath of concrete is excellent because its dull surface blends well with the greens, browns, and grays that surround it, and its rough surface makes perching easy.

You can also attract birds by building houses and shelters for them, but probably the greatest service you can render is to furnish food in the winter. Though completely self-reliant in warm weather, during the cold winter months birds are often desperate for food. They have an exceptionally high body temperature, and so long as they have sufficient food to keep this temperature normal, they do not suffer from the cold. If the body temperature is lowered because of a lack of food, they suffer severely and may even freeze to death if bad weather persists.

You can provide food for them in several ways. If you have a yard, simply trample down the snow in a suitable spot and sprinkle crumbs and seeds. Or you may tie pieces of suet to trees or posts. A feeding tray fastened to a window makes a good, safe feeding station; it also gives you a fine opportunity to watch birds at close quarters. You may even photograph them there. Cut a circular hole near the bottom of a board that fits into the window frame where you have placed the feeding tray. To take pictures, raise the window, insert the board barrier, and direct your camera through the hole. Sit quietly as you wait.

◁ The feet of different kinds of birds show amazing diversity. Here is a tree creeper whose widely spaced claws make possible a strong grip as it scurries up and down tree trunks in search of food.

▽ The jacana has such long, widely spread toes it can run across delicate water plants without sinking.

Bird wings suit varying functions. The Galápagos cormorant (top) cannot fly at all but swims well. Swans (below) fly strongly but have some difficulty reaching takeoff speed. Hummingbirds (right) can dart, hover, and even fly backwards. The Anna's hummingbird shown here measures around four inches from beak to tail.

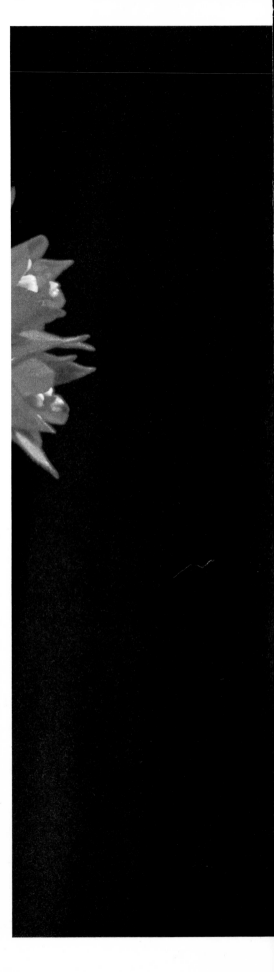

Bird Flight

Man has always envied birds' ability to fly and has tried to imitate them. His own first efforts seem comical by today's standards. Hundreds of years ago, men tried to put big feathers on their arms; later, the feathered 'wings' were attached to enormously heavy engines that vainly flapped them. These attempts failed miserably.

It was not until this century that certain secrets were discovered: first and foremost, a wing must have a special shape to give it 'lift.' Looked at from the side, it must be flat below, curved above. Thus, air traveling over the upper surface has farther to go and so exerts less pressure. The wing tends to rise. The inner part of a bird's wing is shaped in this way, providing lift. The second requirement is lightness and strength of materials. A bird's bones are honeycombed with air spaces, so they are very light. Also, for its weight, a feather is the strongest structure in nature.

The final requirement of a wing is to propel the flying creature. In a bird that flies by flapping, propulsion is mainly provided by the long feathers at the outer half of the wings—the primaries. As the wings rise, these twist to allow the air to flow past. As the wings descend, they fold over one another to form an 'air valve,' which pushes against the air and drives the bird in the direction desired.

Using these few basics, the birds have adjusted their manner of flying to their way of life. A vulture on the plains, for example, must soar aloft for hours in quest of a meal —usually a dead animal. If the bird had to flap constantly to travel, it would lose more energy than the meal could provide. The vulture economizes by soaring on rising currents of hot air, scarcely beating a wing from dawn to dusk while it coasts over miles of territory.

In contrast, small birds that chase insects or follow the season's seeds and berries must be fast and maneuverable, not only to find food but to evade their enemies, such as hawks. They are the flapping specialists. Swifts, for instance, are so often seen in the air that it was once thought they had no legs. Flapping reaches its height of perfection among the hovering birds. Hummingbirds are the masters of this art, swiveling their wings back and forth at a rate that defies the eye as they hang in front of flowers to sip the nectar. Some small hawks, too, can ride the air currents and hover for short periods, although not with such skill.

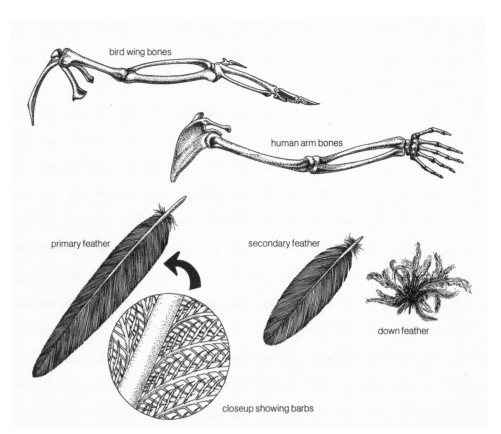

bird wing bones

human arm bones

primary feather

secondary feather

down feather

closeup showing barbs

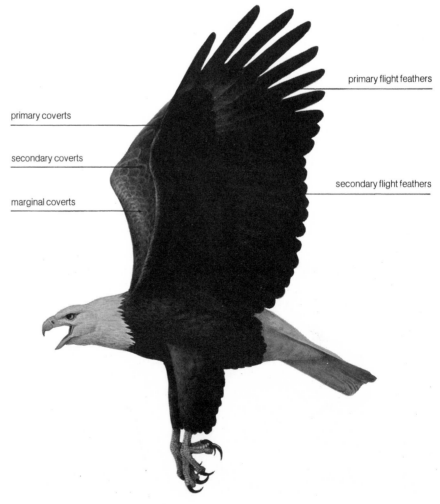

primary flight feathers

primary coverts

secondary coverts

secondary flight feathers

marginal coverts

28

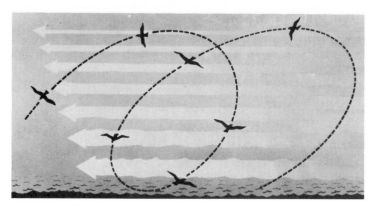

△ *Dynamic soaring: the air flow is much faster a hundred feet above the ocean. Seabirds on long journeys dive from a height with a following wind helping. The wind's push adds to the speed of the dive, so when the birds turn back into the wind, the high total air speed gives them a powerful boost upwards.*

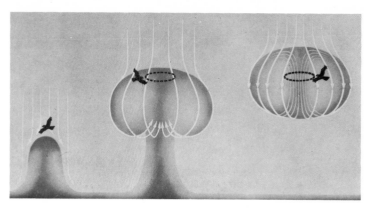

△ *Static soaring: big birds such as vultures, which live in hot areas, use this method to save energy. Air rises over hot spots on the land. Cold air rushing in to replace it helps form a bubble. Birds with the large wings needed to soar can stay within this bubble to get a free ride to great heights.*

◁ *Cliffs and hills create powerful upward drafts of air that birds can ride; seagulls are particularly good at using them. On the far left, the onshore wind is simply directed upwards. At left, the seagulls are using a complicated eddy of air in the lee of a cliff during an offshore wind.*

▽ *A study in wings: the hovering and fast-flying tern (left) has slim, pointed wings. The gliding gull has broader, blunter ones.*

Migration is an intriguing subject for nature study. How do birds find their way on seasonal journeys? How do they sense when to move from their summer feeding and nesting grounds to a warm winter home, where conditions will be better for a few months? Geese are especially noted for their travels. Here a mass of snow and blue geese rests in South Dakota during their journey. Blue geese travel southward some twenty-four hundred miles. Their return route is six hundred miles longer.

The When and Why of Birdsongs

Spring is the time to enjoy the music of birds, for it is during the nesting season that their singing is at its finest. Most of it is instinctive, and probably it is an attempt on the part of the male to intimidate other males. This is a surprising explanation to anyone who thinks the male's song is a serenade to his mate. Yet you will notice that the males of some species reach their nesting grounds well ahead of the females and begin singing then. Singing is also characteristic of certain caged birds, whose only companionship is that of human beings. Then there are species that have a second singing period after the post-breeding molt. This, however, lasts only a few days. Frequently I have been asked by children: 'Do birds sing when they are flying?' Unfortunately it is not possible to give a simple answer. As a rule, singing takes a bird's undivided attention; but some birds, the bobolink, for one, do sing while flying as well as when perching. Other birds, besides singing from a perch, occasionally indulge in ecstatic songs as they bound into the air and seem about to burst with their hurried, twittering notes. The meadow lark and goldfinch are simply two of the species that carry on in this delightful fashion.

Identifying Songs

'What bird is that?' is a question frequently asked by youngsters becoming interested in identification. If you are able to recognize the songs of various species, you have a good clue to the right answer.

Some songs are as characteristic as the bird's physical appearance. The interested listener and observer can soon recognize such tunes as the *conk-a-ree-e* of the redwing blackbird and the rollicking medley of the bobolink. The best time of year to begin your study of birdsongs is very early spring. Migrants are arriving then, but not in such great numbers that their songs become a confused medley. Morning hours or in the late afternoon are the best times of day to listen and look. Concentrate at first on the songs of the more common, therefore more familiar, birds of your region. This will make it easier to distinguish individual calls and melodies later at the height of the singing season.

Certain birds make recognition quite simple by calling their own names: it was their calls that gave them their names to begin with. Among the better known of these are the bobolink, chickadee, phoebe, bobwhite, and whippoorwill. While you may not be able to write out birdsongs in musical notation, you should find it easy to jot down many songs in words or syllables. This is instructive, even though any two listeners may arrive at two different interpretations of the same song. Here are three versions, for example, of the song of the white-throated sparrow: *Old Sam Peabody, Peabody, Peabody*, or *Sow wheat Peverly, Peverly, Peverly*, or *Sweet Canada, Canada, Canada*.

Some interpretations have been published so often that they are now accepted by bird lovers as standard. The scarlet tanager is credited with saying *chip-churr*, and the nuthatch *ank, ank*. Though the American robin has a variety of sweet-sounding songs, its early morning serenade is *wake up, cheer up, cheerily-up, wake up*. A cardinal may join in with a shrill *whoit, whoit, whoit, whit, whit, whit, whit*. The song sparrow suggests a lyrical mood: *maids, maids, put on your teakettle, ettle, ettle, ettle*. The greenfinch in Great Britain is said to sing *twitter, twitter, twitter chow, chow, chow, chow, chow jeerrrrr*; while the goldcrest is credited with *I twist, and twist, and TWIST my nest together*.

An excellent way to become familiar with birdsongs is through recordings, which may be found in many stores and libraries. Ambitious students of nature often enjoy learning to imitate birdsongs and birdcalls, but success requires a great deal of patient practice. The chickadee is fun to imitate, as it is a particularly responsive bird.

Other Bird Sounds

Besides its song a bird can produce other meaningful sounds. The young call to their parents from the nest with a definite hunger alert. Some babies that walk behind the parent when in search of food make a peeping sound, which helps keep the family together and prevents the chicks from getting lost. Certain birds develop a vocabulary of some variety as they mature. There is a call, especially useful during migration, which keeps each in touch with the group. There is also a call of alarm and one of warning. While some birds have won a reputation as excellent songsters, others, such as the brown pelican, are noted for being virtually silent. There are birds which make sounds that take the place of song; for example, the ruffed grouse with his drumming. The male produces his 'music' by

◁ House martens, close relatives of swallows, gather on power lines before migrating south for the winter. The grouping takes a few weeks. At first, only a few birds perch. As the numbers grow, they race up and down the countryside in excited, twittering flocks catching the swarms of late summer insects for food to nourish their tiny bodies during thousands of miles. Finally, as if on a signal, they are gone.

△ A map showing the extremes of migration of the American barn swallow: not all travel this far; they pick up the route at various points. The method used by the birds to navigate is still something of a mystery. They probably guide themselves by a combination of sun position, star positions, and landmarks. Navigation involves very complicated instruments for human beings, but swallows seem to have a built-in 'map.'

standing stiffly erect, his tail down, fanning the air with his wings so rapidly a muffled drumming sound is produced. He may select a certain location, such as a log, for performing, going to the same spot and facing in the same direction every time he drums. This habit reminds us of songbirds that become greatly attached to favorite perches from which they sing.

When you hear children trilling happily at play, you may tell yourself with some satisfaction that they are 'singing like birds.' Such a comparison, however, is not accurate. The human voice is produced in the larynx. A bird's voice comes from a different organ called the syrinx, located at the base of the windpipe. (In Greek mythology Syrinx was a nymph who was transformed into a tuft of reeds, and from these the god Pan made his pipes.)

Variety in Eggs

There is an almost endless variety of birds' eggs. There are big eggs and small eggs; white, colored, and spotted eggs; eggs that differ in shape and the length of time needed to hatch. You need considerable information to answer the apparently easy query: 'How many eggs does a bird lay?' There is no unconditional answer. Each species has a usual number that makes a full set; yet there are differences even among species. A northern thrush, for example, normally lays four eggs, while a tropical thrush lays only two or three. If a nest is robbed, the bird may lay additional eggs to replace the stolen ones. There is a historic case of a flicker that laid seventy-one eggs in seventy-three days! Fantastic as this may sound, it points up the fact that constant nest-robbing has turned domestic fowls into virtual egg-laying machines. A domestic hen may lay hundreds of eggs a season if they are promptly taken away. On the other hand, if the eggs are left untouched, her production will cease after fifteen or twenty eggs.

'Which bird lays the biggest eggs?' and 'Which lays the smallest?' are welcome questions because there are definite answers to them. The ostrich, largest of birds, produces the largest; the hummingbird, smallest of birds, lays the smallest. However, it does not always follow that the larger bird lays the larger egg. Those birds whose chicks hatch in a well-developed state lay relatively larger eggs than a bird whose chicks are less well-developed.

Among the well-developed babies are those of our friend the chicken as well as the grouse and the spotted sandpiper. When they hatch, they are already covered with soft down. Their eyes open immediately, and in no time at all they can toddle about, following their mother. Very soon they learn to pick up and eat their own food. This type of bird is called precocial, which is related to the word *precocious*. Birds that hatch in a more helpless state are naked or at best have a scant covering of down. They are blind at first and are dependent on their parents for food for at least a week but usually much longer. Such birds are known as altricial. This is derived from the Latin word that means 'nourishers.'

Bringing Up a Feathered Family

The length of time needed for incubation varies with different species. The English sparrow takes twelve or thirteen days; the robin needs thirteen or fourteen days; the fish hawk about four weeks. In some families the duty of sitting on the nest is shared by both parents; in others it falls entirely to the mother. In the phalarope family there is a reverse situation. Once the eggs have been laid by the female phalarope, they become the sole responsibility of the male. He incubates the eggs unaided, although the mother stays nearby and shows continued interest in her family.

Helpless baby birds require an extraordinary amount of care, and children seem to enjoy hearing about this, perhaps because it gives them a warm feeling about parental devotion. How proud a mother hen seems of her chicks as she struts about the barnyard clucking loudly! In the wilds, where danger is ever present, a mother bird's behavior may be quite the opposite; she does everything possible to make her brood inconspicuous. A grouse, sensing an intruder, will go to the extreme of chirping pitifully and thrashing along the ground as if hurt. This serves two purposes: her cry warns the young to remain quiet, and her movements divert attention from her young family.

Baby birds have enormous appetites, and until they are able to care for themselves, their parents must find and bring them large quantities of food. The fledglings usually feed on insects: even though many of them will grow up to be seed eaters, they need the animal protein for growth. In species where the young are least developed – the mourning dove, for example – the parent first swallows the food and

then feeds it to them in a partly digested form. Occasionally children have the good fortune to watch baby birds being fed; often they see pictures of the birds at feeding time. They may notice that feeding techniques vary with different birds. The most common method is for the parent to push its bill down the baby's throat. With pelicans and certain other species that regurgitate food, the baby puts its head in its mother's throat pouch or takes food from her bill.

Parents often continue to feed the young after they have left the nest, but then the feeding methods are no longer as painstaking. Swallows are particularly interesting at this stage of development. While in the nest, the young bird has food carefully placed down its throat. But once it is able to hop a short distance from the nest, it must be on the alert with bill opened upward, since the parents merely drop food to it without pausing in their flight. The 'proper manners' usually taught to children are out of place in the bird world. There the aggressive baby – the one that stretches its neck farthest and cries the loudest – as a rule is the first to be fed. However, when taking care of a nestful, a parent administers a kind of rough justice. It looks into each youngster's mouth rather quickly after a feeding, and if a morsel has not yet been swallowed, it is snatched back and given to another baby.

Leaving the Nest

Even babies that are covered with down and are able to run about when newly hatched are given careful attention. The parents may keep them under their wings to protect them and keep them warm – that is, brood them – very often for as long as five or six weeks. Some species of birds brood while the babies are in the nest but never after they have started to fly. Brooding protects the young ones from the cold and from excessive heat in a nest unprotected from the sun.

As the baby birds develop feathers, their responsibilities grow. They preen their feathers and begin to exercise, concentrating on stretching their wings. Sometimes they practice taking off before actually leaving the nest. Although birds fly by instinct, the first flight often requires some parental coaxing. It then may be no more than a flutter to a nearby limb or it may be, as in the case of swallows, a sustained and graceful performance. Some birds, such as song sparrows, are ready to try their wings as soon as a week

after hatching, while the wandering albatross has to be forced out by its parents to make room for a new brood – nearly a year later. Because of the solicitous care of their parents – whatever amount of time is involved – young birds develop steadily until able to survive on their own.

How to Keep a Bird Calendar

If you live in a region where the four seasons are clearly defined by sharp weather contrasts, the keeping of a bird calendar becomes an especially enjoyable hobby. There are a number of interesting aspects to consider in studying bird neighbors. For example, some birds, such as chickadees and crows, migrate short distances, yet such species may be near you all winter. Actually they are not the same families that were there in summer; the summer chickadees and crows move southward in the fall, being replaced by others from points farther north.

However, a bird calendar can be simply made with a large ruled sheet of paper, divided into four columns. Head the first column DATE, the second BIRD'S NAME, the third WHERE SEEN, the fourth TIME OF DAY. You may fill in information about only the birds that come near your home, but the record becomes far more lively when you widen the range of observation by means of bird walks.

Building Birdhouses

One of the most satisfying outlets for the energies of young carpenters is building birdhouses, using tools to get a practical grasp on the essentials of construction work. Later, if the youngsters see birds using a house they have provided, they will experience feelings of pride and protective concern. To avoid disappointment to those involved in a birdhouse project, it should be remembered that birds are often very choosy. They may inspect and pass up, or simply ignore, an ideal-looking residence planned just for them. Instead they nest nearby in a hollow stump, post, or tree. It does help if you become familiar with the habits and preferences of the birds you wish to attract. However, you can still expect surprises, for birds like to do things their own way. One summer a neighbor of mine proudly drew my attention to wrens settling in a home he had built for them. The following year he sheepishly pointed out that the wrens of the current season were using the house merely as a foundation. They had built their home on its roof!

▽ The swallow builds its nest in the angles of barns and sheds and makes hundreds of journeys a day to find insects for its hungry brood. This swallow is using both wings and tail to steady its flight as it brings the eagerly awaited food.

▽▽ Naked and ugly at first, these sparrow young will quickly grow. As the parent lands on the edge of its nest, the young birds instinctively open their beaks for the food.

▷△ A bird bath-drinking fountain is a most effective way to bring wild birds close to a home. A shallow pan filled with water and set on a post or ledge will serve, but more elaborate styles enhance many a garden. The rough surface of concrete makes possible easy perching.

▷ A feeding station may be a tray fastened to a windowsill, a mesh sack hung on a tree, or a well-built bird feeder.

Nesting House

Materials

1″ pine boards:
2 of 5$\frac{1}{2}$″ × 4$\frac{3}{4}$″
1 of 4$\frac{3}{4}$″ × 7$\frac{1}{2}$″
1 of 4$\frac{3}{4}$″ × 4$\frac{3}{4}$″
1 of 4$\frac{3}{4}$″ × 3$\frac{1}{3}$″
1 of 9$\frac{3}{8}$″ × 6$\frac{3}{4}$″
1 of 1$\frac{5}{8}$″ × 13$\frac{3}{4}$″
Eighteen 1$\frac{3}{8}$″ screws
Asbestos paper
Thumb-tacks
Preservative
Two 1$\frac{1}{4}$″ screw hooks
Two 1$\frac{1}{4}$″ screw eyes

Garden Birdhouse

Materials

1″ pine boards:
2 of 6$\frac{3}{4}$″ × 10$\frac{3}{4}$″
2 of 4$\frac{3}{4}$″ × 10$\frac{3}{4}$″
1 of 6$\frac{3}{4}$″ × 6$\frac{3}{4}$″
1 of 8$\frac{1}{4}$″ × 8$\frac{1}{4}$″
1 of 1$\frac{5}{8}$″ × 13$\frac{3}{4}$″
Two hinges (leaf 1$\frac{1}{4}$″)
Small hook and eye
Two 1$\frac{1}{4}$″ screw hooks
Two 1$\frac{1}{4}$″ screw eyes
Twenty 1$\frac{3}{8}$″ screws
Five $\frac{3}{8}$″ screws
Preservative, wood glue

Nesting House

Tools

Backsaw, drill with a $\frac{1}{8}$″ bit, sandpaper, brush.

Draw a line along one 5$\frac{1}{2}$″ side on both identical boards, 1$\frac{5}{8}$″ from the edge. Draw intersecting lines along one shorter side, 2$\frac{3}{4}$″ from the edge. Cut out the 1$\frac{5}{8}$ × 2$\frac{3}{4}$″ rectangle that has been created. Prepare the 4$\frac{3}{4}$ × 7$\frac{1}{2}$″ board by drawing lines along the 7$\frac{1}{2}$″ sides, $\frac{1}{2}$″ from the edge. Drill three holes on each line: one in the center and one in each corner. Glue the ends of the side boards and screw them to the bottom. Repeat for the roof, but draw the lines 1$\frac{3}{8}$″ from the edges and use four screws to attach it to the sides. Screw the front and back to the frame following the same procedure. Sand the nesting house and treat it with preservative. Cover the roof with asbestos paper and attach it with thumb-tacks. Construct the hanging device as described under Garden Birdhouse.

Garden Birdhouse

Tools

Scroll saw, drill with a $\frac{1}{8}$″ bit, protractor, brush, sandpaper

Place the board vertically before you on the work table. Draw a horizontal line 9$\frac{3}{8}$″ from the bottom. Mark the center and draw a 1$\frac{1}{4}$″ circle. Drill a hole inside it. Insert the scroll saw and cut out the circle. Draw a vertical line on both sides, $\frac{1}{2}$″ from the edge. Drill holes in the center of these two lines and near the corners. Repeat for back board. Glue the ends of both side boards and position them between the front and back boards. Screw them into place. Draw lines on the bottom boards, $\frac{1}{2}$″ from the four edges. Drill holes where these lines intersect and in the center of them. Screw the bottom to the frame. Use two hinges to attach the roof to the front board, with an overlap on all sides except the back. Use a hook and eye to serve as a lock. Sand the birdhouse and treat it with a preservative. Attach the screw hooks to the remaining board, leaving 8″ between them. Attach the screw eyes to the back of the birdhouse, one at the top, one at the bottom of the exact center, leaving 8″ between them. Tie the board to a tree about ten feet from the ground, using tree-tape or strips of inner tubing and hook the birdhouse on it.

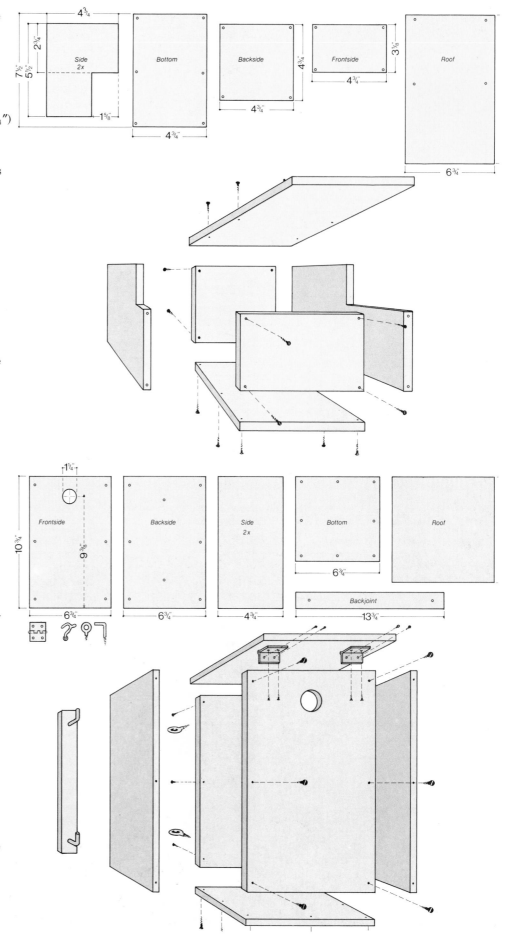

▽ Many birds survive the winter without help from human friends, but well-stocked feeders can be important to the survival of some, and a birdhouse can be valuable at nesting time.

▷ A family interested in providing birdhouses should learn the needs and habits of any species they wish to attract before building. The blue tit pictured seems to be looking with favor at a new house.

Mammals, Large and Small

Big mammals are exciting. Their size is impressive. Although they suggest danger and adventure to children who have read hair-raising stories about vicious wild animals, in recent years much has been learned about big beasts that has changed our feelings toward them. We now know that in their natural surroundings, gorillas are peaceable, even shy. Although some tigers have become man-eaters, they did so because of exceptional circumstances, such as famine caused by drought. In conflicts between people and tigers, people usually have been the aggressors, slaughtering them until these great cats have almost been wiped out of existence. Hunters have been killed by a charging elephant, but only because the powerful mammal first scented danger to itself or its young. Today we can look at wild animals, particularly the great ones of jungles and forests, with understanding and sympathy rather than dread and the desire to kill them.

Mammals and Other Animals

Childrens' curiosity is likely to be aroused when they are told that mammals are just one kind of animal. Birds, fish, insects and other creatures also are animals, but what is it that sets the mammal apart?

To be classified as a mammal, an animal must have three qualities: (1) it must be warm-blooded, which means that its blood remains at nearly the same temperature no matter how hot or cold its surroundings become; (2) it must have hair or fur on its body; (3) a baby mammal is always nourished by milk furnished by its mother. Sometimes the definition is hard to accept because an adult elephant, a rhinoceros, and several other kinds of beasts seem almost hairless. However, if you look closely at their hide, you will see a bit of hair, and the young are covered with a fuzzy coat.

Since there is an almost endless variety among mammals, a helpful way to clarify their differences is to group them into their chief divisions. One group consists of flesh-eating mammals, such as wolves, foxes, lions and tigers. A second group is made up of rodents, mice, squirrels, beavers, and most other animals with long, sharp front teeth. A third group, the hoofed mammals, includes deer and cattle.

All toothless mammals, such as the anteater, are included in a group. Another group, the marsupials, are made up chiefly of mammals with pouches in which to carry their babies. The opossum is the one American representative of this group, but the kangaroo of Australia is perhaps the most widely known of the pouched animals.

Water mammals known as manatees and dugongs are in a class by themselves. So are the flying mammals known as bats. Whales are probably the best known of the water-dwelling group known as cetaceans.

On the basis of their food habits mammals may be divided into two general classes: there are plant eaters (herbivores) and flesh eaters (carnivores). In trying to distinguish one from the other, a child would usually take for granted that the flesh eaters are larger and stronger, but that is not always the case. Teeth and claws are a better basis for distinguishing the two groups. You can point out that the flesh eater has sharp, enlarged canine teeth, shearing side teeth, and strong, sharp claws.

Meat Eaters and Others

Perhaps you have noticed a tendency on the part of a young child to label certain animals 'bad' and others 'good.' If you discuss this, you are likely to find that the 'bad' animals are those which eat other animals. This habit may well be frightening if one does not understand and appreciate the needs of a carnivorous animal, which devours prey in order to sustain life. It is worthwhile to point out that the food habits of both flesh eaters and plant eaters are inborn rather than a matter of choice, and that flesh eaters seldom kill except when they are hungry or defending themselves from attack.

Watch a dog gnaw a bone and you have an excellent illustration of a carnivorous mammal in action. Not only are his incisors sharp and the canine teeth long and strong, but also the molars are especially suitable for cutting.

All members of the cat family are meat eaters. You can study the hunting tactics of tigers at close range when you watch a house cat stalking a bird. The cat does not run down its prey as a dog would; instead it creeps along stealthily until it is within striking distance, when it takes a final leap. The hunting technique of the big wild cats is exactly the same.

The ferocious expression of the Scottish wildcat (with eyes and mouth wide open and ears flat) is an indication of its nature; it is quite untamable. Its relaxed charm is deceptive. Wildcats of Europe have relatives in North America, commonly known as bobcats. They, too, are considered fierce and frightening.

The weasel offers solid proof that you cannot judge an animal's eating habits or its disposition by its size. Though small and slender, this is one of the most aggressive and ferocious of flesh-eating animals. Completely fearless, it sometimes kills animals several times larger than itself and may satisfy its appetite merely by lapping up their blood.

How Mammals Talk

Most children get their first inklings of animal communication when they become familiar with the sounds made by dogs or cats. The dog barks and squeals with pleasure, growls to threaten, whines when afraid, and howls seemingly for the sheer pleasure of hearing its own voice. The cat mews in friendly conversational tones; it purrs with contentment and yowls when it is hurt; it screams and spits in a fight. To the human ear its love serenade sounds shrill and agonizing.

The mammals of forests and plains duplicate some of these sounds, but they have other kinds of vocal expression as well. Some mammals roar, some whistle, some scream, some yap, some bleat, others are virtually silent.

One of the unusual sounds is sufficiently well known so that even children hear about it. This is the call of the moose. Many hunters practice it diligently in the hope of luring one of these massive creatures within gun range. The hunters learn to imitate the female, whose call is like the bawl of a domestic cow. The bull moose, for all his size and strength, usually emits nothing more than a feeble, coughing grunt.

It is quite touching to note that frequently the calls and cries of wild animals serve to alert their family to danger. When the little marmot, standing like a sentinel at a lookout post, gives its shrill warning whistle, not only the marmots but mountain sheep and other creatures take cover as well. Shrill, also, is the whistle of the marmot's cousin, the woodchuck. With more abandon than good sense it whistles and grinds its teeth while trying to escape from an enemy. Gray squirrels give alarm with a kind of flat rasping bark, finally prolonged into a whining snarl.

Even customarily silent mammals find their voices when they are wounded. The scream of a whitetailed deer struck by a bullet can be heard a half-mile away, and a rabbit often gives a piercing squeal when hit. Mammals do not always depend on their voices to express emotion. The cottontail rabbit thumps the ground with a hind foot when it senses danger. The beaver slaps the water with its tail. As for deer and sheep, they stamp with a forefoot when they are frightened, to warn their neighbors.

How Mammals Fight

Fighting in the animal world is not a matter of sporadic outbreaks when a creature decides to attack its neighbors. It is the need for food that drives meat eaters to prey on other animals; few kill for the sake of killing. Among some groups, the males fight it out to win a mate or establish themselves as leader of a herd. The most dramatic battles among mammals are those between animals that bear antlers or horns, such as moose, deer, elk and goats.

The instinct that children have for pounding and pummeling each other seems mild indeed compared to a clash between two bull moose. Hostilities may start with a moose striking its antlers against small trees in a way that broadcasts his defiance. Another male rushes out to accept the challenge, and the battle is on. Heads lowered, the two giants rush at each other. The impact of the collision may knock one down; if he regains his footing, they charge again.

Each moose tries to stab his enemy with a sharp brow tine, which can be the most vicious part of the antler. The wide, flattened areas are useful for defense in warding off blows. Sometimes it is a fight to the death for one of the contenders; yet the ending can be tragic for both. Their antlers may become so firmly locked together that the animals are unable to free themselves, and death by starvation is their fate.

Mountain lions, jaguars, and other members of the cat family have four long pointed teeth (canines) that are used as weapons; they also have sharp claws, which can be withdrawn into the fleshy foot pads when they are not needed. When your child sees a fight between two tomcats, he can feel that he has witnessed jungle warfare; they use their teeth and claws in the same way as the big cats. It is interesting, however, to note that those animals with the most vicious potential weapons – large claws, sharp teeth

The hippopotamus has the largest mouth of any mammal except the whale and displays this feature frequently as it yawns widely. This is a gesture of communication rather than boredom; by showing its immense teeth it makes a mild threat. Disputes over social rank are often settled by yawning and pushing.

and others – seldom, if ever, fight to the death. Squirrels, woodchucks, rats, and other rodents have dependable weapons in their chisel-like front teeth, though rabbits rely chiefly on their strong hind legs with which they can kick savagely. When rabbits fight, each one tries to leap on top of the opponent and kick downward. A deer avoids trouble, but if cornered, it defends itself by striking at the enemy with its front hoofs. The bucks also fight with their antlers.

Horses, burros, and some other hoofed mammals are able to kick with both front and back feet and can also make good use of their large teeth. The grizzly bear has strong, sharp teeth, and its huge front paws can be deadly to an enemy.

Some mammals have specialized defensive weapons. The skunk can discharge a notoriously evil-smelling scent that repels the enemy with nature's poison gas. Foxes, wolverines, weasels, and some other animals have scent glands more or less like the skunk's and also use odor as a defense weapon. But none of these scents is so potent as that of the black and white wood pussy.

Porcupines, like skunks, are not aggressive; they are slow-moving and stupid. Their quills, however, are splendid equipment for defense. Trapped by an enemy, the porcupine contracts its skin muscles, causing the quills to stand erect. Then it bunches itself up, raises its tail, flails anything within reach, and drives many of its shafts into the flesh of opponents. Contrary to a popular belief, the porcupine never shoots or throws its quills.

Surviving the Winter
The rigors of cold weather and the scarcity of food create hardships for mammals in wintertime. However, this is unlikely to impress us as much as the plight of the birds, because generally mammals are not in evidence all year.

Among the few we are likely to see during all four seasons are squirrels. On cold winter days children can appreciate the practical value as well as the beauty of this creature's fur coat. It is often seen scampering over the snow; only on the most frigid days does it curl up in the hollows of a tree.

Even hardier than the squirrel is the cottontail rabbit, which has no cozy retreat. A pile of brush is usually the

only protection it seeks. When grass is no longer available, cottontails nibble dead leaves, the tender bark of small trees and shrubs, and weed and flower stalks.

Deer also endure rugged times. The winter home of the whitetail is a reasonably sheltered area in a wood. A group of a dozen or more band together and choose a suitable spot called a yard for their headquarters. From this home they make paths to places where they can find tender bark and shrubs, or food which they dig from under the snow, such as lichens, acorns and moss.

Wild Mammal Neighbors
Of all the four-footed animals of wildlife, the squirrel is probably the one most commonly observed by children. They live not only in wooded regions, but also in city parks and suburban areas. In fact, these attractive rodents sometimes seem to prefer the hazards of civilization to the dangers of the wilds, and their habits remain much the same whether they live in town or country. Their range is worldwide. They are found on all continents except Australia.

Among the most commonly known are the gray squirrels and red squirrels of North America and the pine squirrel of Europe. These are 'tree' squirrels. The bushy tail serves to balance the body, as when the squirrel leaps from one branch to another. It is fun to watch the little acrobats go up a tree: usually they gallop, alternately using the fore and hind feet in pairs. Coming down, they progress more slowly and cautiously; they descend head first and move the feet individually.

Baby squirrels, born in the spring, are blind and hairless. Hair soon appears, and in about six weeks the young can climb around tree branches and nibble at buds and leaves. At eight or nine weeks they have a full coat and are about half grown. In a year they have achieved almost full growth. The mothers nurse their babies and care for them with devotion. If danger threatens, they may carry them one by one to a safer location in a nearby tree.

During cold weather squirrels generally live in a hollow tree trunk, but in warm seasons they find a suitable spot in the crotch of a tree and construct a nest of such materials as dry leaves, sticks, moss and bark. Unlike a bird's nest with

▽ The killing habits of flesh-eating animals may seem distasteful to many people, but all carnivores must hunt and devour prey in order to sustain life. Weasels are among the smallest of flesh-eaters. This one is eating a fish, but rodents are often victims.

▽ ▷ Lions are sociable creatures; members of a pride do not fight over food.

▽ ▽ Bears may eat meat on occasion but, except for polar bears, they eat anything available—grasses, roots, nuts, fruit, insects, eggs, and fish. The great brown bears of the Far North feast on great numbers of migrating salmon when the fish ascend rivers to spawn.

▷ The red fox is considered an enemy by many farmers because of its fondness for poultry. But the truth is, these foxes are friends rather than foes because their normal livelihood comes from catching rodents rather than from stealing chickens. A fox father is a good provider, patiently hunting food to bring to his mate and their cubs.

a flattened top, the top of a squirrel's nest is rounded. That of a pine squirrel looks something like a crow's nest, but it is roofed over and has a side entrance.

There are many varieties of squirrels that do not live in trees. Some are known simply as ground squirrels. Others have popular names such as chipmunk and suslik. Most of them are sociable creatures that make their homes in underground communes.

As you watch a squirrel bury a nut in the ground, you may with good reason ask yourself: will this ever be found again? It would be a mistake to think that all the nuts that are buried get dug up afterwards especially in the wild, where food is plentiful. For this reason the squirrel makes a valuable contribution to replanting the forests. In regions where winter food is scarce, this clever rodent makes more of an effort to recover the stored nuts. It is believed that the squirrel is guided to the right locality by memory and to the exact spot by a keen sense of smell, which can penetrate through several inches of snow.

Aside from nuts, squirrels enjoy mushrooms, corn, wheat and the seeds from apples, pears and other fruit. Sometimes they rob birds' nests of eggs or fledglings, but it is the red squirrels that are most guilty of this practice. An overabundance of peanuts is unhealthy for squirrels, although a few added to tree nuts and other foods are a nourishing addition to their diet.

Rabbits – A Survival Story
If you are familiar with the ageless story of Peter Rabbit's adventures in Mr. McGregor's garden, you have an excellent basis for understanding this creature's fate in life. He is the pursued; his daily routine is one escape after another. In addition to being a victim of almost every flesh-eating mammal and bird, he is also a target for sportsmen.

Although they are the prey of countless enemies, rabbits are fast breeders and continue to exist in great numbers. Observing them, we immediately notice two features that help account for their survival: long ears, which detect the enemy's approach from a distance; and long, muscular hind legs, which propel a rabbit away from danger with remarkable speed. A further aid to the rabbit's flair for self-

preservation is its extremely keen sense of smell. Its nostrils twitch constantly to catch every scent in the air. The rabbit's whiskers serve as trusted feelers and its eyes are large and bright. It has strong front cutting teeth and with its split upper lip makes efficient use of them.

In summer the rabbit's fondness for cabbage and lettuce plagues gardeners. It also feeds on grass, clover, and herbs. During the winter, when green leaves are scarce, it gnaws bark from trees and nibbles buds from shrubs.

There are many varieties of rabbits. Aside from those living in the wild state, there are thousands raised by people either for a hobby or for extra income. I once knew a rabbit (it was a large Belgian hare) that began his career as an Easter pet. Later on his young owner kept him at the family's store, where the rabbit was trained to snip with his front teeth the cord used to tie packages. This novel performance stimulated business considerably.

It is sometimes confusing, especially to a child, to hear a rabbit called a hare. Presumably 'hare' is just another word for the rabbit. Actually this is not the case. Rabbits resemble hares in appearance, although they differ in some of their habits. Another difference is that hares are larger. Rabbits are born blind and hairless and completely dependent on their mother's care. She pulls fur from her own body with her teeth and paws to line the nest. When she goes foraging for food, she covers the young with fur and grass, which serves as a blanket and also as camouflage. The babies of the hare are born with their eyes open and are able to take care of themselves in three weeks or less. The jackrabbit is a hare, despite its common name.

Mice and Rats – Pets and Pests
Among parents and children there are two schools of thought about mice. As far as adults are concerned, these rodents are pests to be exterminated. As a child sees it, mice may be engaging, clever pets which can be kept without entailing a great amount of work for their owner. The house mouse is responsible for much of the dislike visited on the whole tribe. Because the mouse, originally a native of Asia, was able to stow away wherever food was kept, this creature infiltrated into Europe and later continued on to America. Although it usually makes its home in houses or

barns, it sometimes nests under cornstalks or in grain fields.

Indoors it uses the space between plaster and outer walls for runways; it also travels in the space between ceiling and upper floor. With its strong gnawing teeth it can easily cut through wood, cardboard, or almost any obstacle except metal. The mother mouse makes her nest out of cloth, paper or whatever pliable material she can find.

A very attractive and interesting wild member of the rodent family is the white-footed mouse. It is native to North America and may be found in many woodlands and even on prairies. Its looks are charming; it could be a model for one of those delightful cartoonlike animal characters that children enjoy so much. The soft fur on the back is brown or buff, while it is pure white underneath. Its eyes are large, round, and black, its ears well developed, and its whiskers long. Because of their raids on crops, white-footed mice are not popular with farmers. However, to some extent they make up for this destruction by eating great numbers of harmful insects.

In the Old World from the British Isles across the European continent and eastward to Japan the wood mouse more or less occupies the niche held by the white-footed mouse of the New World. It is among the most common of European rodents. It, too, has soft fur of tan or brown, big dark eyes, and large ears and it lives in woodlands, fields, hedgerows and gardens, as well as among rocks. In Britain its preference for open ground gives it the local name of field mouse.

Because of the great variety of mice and their close relatives, the rats, a study of this animal family can be fascinating. There's the dormouse, made famous by the sleepy one at the Mad Hatter's teaparty in Lewis Carroll's book *Alice in Wonderland*. (Dormice really are great sleepers.) There is the giant rat of Africa, which measures from twelve to eighteen inches in head and body length, and the dwarf mouse of Europe and the Far East, so tiny that it can sit comfortably on top of a stalk of wheat. Large or small, these rodents have one thing in common: they reproduce their kind in amazing numbers. As a result they furnish an important food supply for many larger animals. On the other hand, they can be health hazards for people where their numbers get out of control.

Red squirrels (below and right) are most often found in northern evergreen forests. They are more noisy and frolicsome than the gray type and, when angered, one will stamp its feet, jerk its tail, and chatter furiously. A female may find a hollow in a tree to use as a nest, or make a bulky home among tree branches. They eat a variety of foods such as tree bark, fruit seeds, corn, mushrooms, and nuts.

Gray squirrels (below, bottom, and opposite page) afford fine opportunities for people to observe wildlife in suburbs and cities, for these rodents are undaunted by civilization. Though they may become tame enough to accept food from friendly fingers, they never lose their alert watchfulness and scurry away if they become suspicious. They do not always run to a tree, but may scamper to a cavity in the ground.

The Remarkable Beaver

Beavers are rodents that everyone can admire. They are in-
dustrious, have strong family relationships, and are expert
craftsmen, building dams and homes with much the same
skills as human engineers, carpenters and masons.

If you are exploring nature in a country area, you may
catch sight of a rounded mass of sticks and mud rising like a
miniature island out of a lake. This is a beaver home! If you
were able to look inside, you would see that the home is
made up of either one large room or several smaller ones. In
either case you would notice openings in the floor. The
beaver comes and goes through these openings, reaching
land by an underwater route. Because the areas in the lodge
around the floor openings are wet and cold, the main floor
is slightly raised above the water level, somewhat like a
step. The sleeping quarters are snugly lined with finely
chewed wood fibers or with grass. In winter the mud plaster
of the lodge freezes, and the walls become so strong that
even a bear cannot break through.

A popular myth about the beavers' building techniques is
that they use the large flat-ribbed tail as a trowel to pat
down mud. Actually work is done with the forefeet – sometimes with the side of the head – to push and poke mud into
place. Another misconception about beavers is that they
use their tails as 'trailers' to convey grass, earth and stones
to the building site; such claims have never been proved.
We do know that beavers carry these materials in their
front paws or in the mouth. The tail does seem to be useful
in helping a beaver steer and propel its body in the water.
There is another practical use for the tail: by slapping it
against the surface of the water, the beaver is able to warn
his companions of approaching danger.

Beavers form sociable family circles. They appear to enjoy
being together, and when the family outgrows its lodge,
they may construct new homes along nearby shores until a
large settlement develops. If overpopulation results in a
food shortage in the immediate neighborhood, the genera-
tion of two-year-olds starts off in search of a building site
for a new colony. When young beavers are not occupied
with learning the serious business of tree cutting, engi-
neering, and building, they like to play and frolic, sometimes getting underfoot while the adults are at work.

Industrious Muskrats and Playful Otters

Muskrats also use mud in building their homes, but they
mix it with roots and the stems of plants, for they live in
marshes and shallow water areas. Muskrats construct a
lodge in shallow water by piling layer upon layer of rushes
and mud until the heap is large and reaches a height of four
or five feet above the surface of the water. Then the muskrat, working underwater, chews and digs into this stack
from the bottom, until he hollows out a space above the
waterline large enough to house himself and his family.

You are much more likely to run across muskrat homes
rather than beaver lodges near towns and villages. Muskrats seem to be undisturbed by the sights and sounds of
civilization, whereas the more retiring beaver prefers
wilder regions. In North America, their natural habitat,
they are extremely valuable to the fur trade.

Few creatures are as wary of man as the otter. Even exploring nature far beyond cities and towns, you may fail to
catch a glimpse of this attractive animal. However, you can
still find evidence of their whereabouts by looking closely
along the banks of streams and lakes; there will be footprints in the mud that borders their favorite fishing waters.
Yet young otters are anything but born swimmers. They
live quietly at first, feeding on their mother's milk. When
they are old enough, she takes them for their first swimming lesson. By way of encouraging a baby she has it climb
on her shoulders; then she dives into the water, often swimming with the baby still clinging to her. Lessons may continue throughout the summer until the young otters are as
big as cats. Painstaking practice finally turns the pupils
into first-class swimmers.

An otter family stays together for at least a year and all its
members, parents as well as youngsters, know how to have
fun the way boys and girls do. One pastime they enjoy, for
example, is for two of them to pull at opposite ends of a
stick, tug-of-war fashion. They romp and roll like puppies,
clawing up the turf and throwing the clods about. Their
greatest fun comes from sliding. They love to chute-the-
chute on their stomachs down steep river banks into the
water, and they often continue this in one place until it becomes very slippery. In wintertime they use snow-covered
hills as slides.

Otters are among the most playful of animals. Young ones frolic together in and out of water, and a favorite otter pastime is coasting down slides, using mud banks in summer and snowbanks in winter. A whole family may participate, following each other in quick succession. The sea otter, nibbling at a clam, is carrying a rock on its chest on which to smash the hard clam shells it collects. Sea otters are a different species from the otters of lakes and rivers (top); long ago they spent part of their time on land. They were gentle and trusting, but as they were relentlessly killed for sport, they learned to stay in water, often surrounded by great beds of brown seaweed. Before they were completely exterminated, conservationists took up their cause; however, they are still endangered animals.

The construction of a dam is hard work, even for a beaver. Made to endure, dams may last for many years. They may be fairly small or hundreds of feet long, and often hold back thousands of tons of water. Not all beaver live in lodges. Instead they may burrow into holes along a river bank.

The beaver is a builder that wastes no bit of material. It first eats the bark from a tree it has felled, then cuts up the trunk, using the pieces to construct a dam or lodge. The lodge often is built in a pond, and mud is used to plaster over the wood frame. A small air hole is left in the top; an entrance tunnel is made beneath the water's surface.

Bears in Fiction and Fact

Age-old children's stories present an appealing picture of the bear. There is for example the tale of 'Goldilocks and the Three Bears,' with Mama Bear, Papa Bear, and Baby Bear living together as a well-knit family group. In truth, however, Papa Bear takes no part in such a close relationship. By the time cubs are born, he is off by himself, taking no responsibility for feeding, protecting, or training the young. But the cubs are not handicapped by his absence because the mother takes care of all this competently.

At birth the twin cubs of a black bear are blind, almost hairless, and not much larger than rats. By the time they leave the winter retreat – a cave – in which they were born, they have become saucy, fun-loving creatures with fluffy hair and sharp claws. They box and wrestle, play hide-and-seek, and try all sorts of tricks on their mother. Sometimes she loses patience with them and boxes their ears. For all that, she guards them jealously and the only time she is really dangerous to humans is when her cubs are with her.

One lesson cubs learn well in the wilderness is to be ever wary of humans and other potential enemies. The mother teaches them to swim and climb trees to escape danger. She shows them how to tear apart rotted stumps and mop up swarming ants with the tongue. She demonstrates how to catch mice, how to slap a frog out of water, and how to raid a tree in which bees have stored honey.

Bears are noted for being gourmets. Black bears live chiefly on vegetables, but they also dig for roots and bugs and catch grasshoppers and crickets. They enjoy all kinds of fruit, blueberries being their favorite, and like all bears, they are so fond of honey that they will risk the vengeance of furious swarms of bees to tear open and rob a bee tree. Some black bears add meat to this diet, but when other food is plentiful, they do not show the slightest interest in freshly killed animals.

Family Life among Mammals

Mammals care for their young more closely than do any other group of animals. Such close bonds of family life start with the fact that all mammals supply food to their infants in the form of milk from the mother's body. As well as food, the mother usually provides warmth and protection for her offspring. Finally, as mammal social life is often highly organized and quite complicated, the young must learn how to deal with the various situations that will confront them in adult life: feeding, evading enemies, and caring for their own young when the time comes. All this education takes some time.

Some young mammals are born blind and helpless; others can stand and run with their parents within a few hours of birth. This difference depends on the way of life of the animal, its surroundings, and the dangers that may be present at the place and time of birth.

As a general rule, those animals that are naturally fierce and well-armed with tooth and claw—the meat-eaters—have helpless babies. The plant-eaters, however, are constantly hunted and are therefore in the greatest danger while giving birth, when the mother and baby could be easy pickings for a passing predator; their babies are born in an advanced state.

As hunters, the big cats, such as the cheetahs, have few equals and little to fear from other animals. The cheetah's litter of two to five cubs weigh only eight or nine ounces each at birth, and their eyes do not open for two weeks. The male cheetah provides for the family while the mother is suckling, but it is the mother who has the task of caring for and teaching the young how to hunt during the next year or more.

In contrast, the zebras and giraffes are the victims of such hunters. The six-foot giraffe baby can walk within an hour of birth; both mother and child return to the protection of the herd at that time. Young giraffes are cared for by all the adults in a herd, rather than staying close to their parents. Zebras, on the other hand, stay in families within a herd.

Of all the herding animals, the elephants are probably the most organized. Even in birth, the mother is guarded and possibly helped by another female. The baby then becomes the 'property' of the herd; it can suckle from any nursing female. Discipline is kept by young females who restrain the calves from putting themselves into dangerous situations.

◁◁ *The tiny fennec fox of the Arabian and African deserts digs a long burrow in which to bear its young. The large ears are for heat radiation rather than for exceptionally keen hearing.*

◁ ▽ *Elephant herds have very strong family ties. Mothers go to great lengths to protect their offspring and are always ready to charge—as shown—any intruder.*

▽ *The grizzly bear lives a solitary life. The mother gives birth to her tiny young during her long winter hibernation. She will spend the next two or three years with her cubs teaching them to forage for all kinds of animal and plant food—including, of course, honey.*

Learning in childhood is well illustrated by the apes, for in many ways they are similar to humans. Chimpanzee babies, for instance, rely entirely on their mothers for the first two years of life. The standard of baby care varies according to the mother's experience. When a chimpanzee has her first child, she does not seem to understand right away what is to be done with the demanding little bundle that is her baby. However, she soon starts to attend to it closely, carrying it first on her breast, later letting it ride piggyback. Some chimps are ideal mothers, while others 'spoil' their young with too much attention; but on the whole there is little bullying and the babies are obedient. The baby stays with the mother for four years or more, even after the appearance of a younger sister or brother. Throughout this time, the protection by the chimpanzee group keeps the youngster safe, while it learns the tricks and skills necessary for survival.

◁◁ *A family of zebras (foals right and second from the left) stays together for many years. This group demonstrates the function of the black-and-white-striped camouflage: it is difficult for a predator to tell where one zebra ends and the next one begins.*

◁ *Giraffes form smaller groups than zebras; this herd is composed of calves of various ages under the eye of a tall adult bull.*

◁▽ *Chimpanzees forage on the ground for all types of food, both plant and animal. Groups of mothers with young search separately from the males, but if one group finds a ripe fruit tree, its members will yell, scream, and bang branches to attract their tribal friends.*

▽ *A cheetah mother relaxes with her cubs. This family will stay together for some time, while the parents teach the young their methods for hunting game at high speeds.*

Red deer stags, timid and elegant in demeanor most of the year, become tough fighters during the mating season in fall, dueling with their antlers. The fights, however, are often only a trial of strength and seldom end in serious injury or death. The two rivals lock antlers, then twist and push. The weaker opponent admits defeat by trying to break away and run.

Close Family Ties

Unlike the bears, foxes remain together in family groups. While the young are growing up, both parents take care of them in their underground den. The red fox digs its own burrow, often supplementing the living room with a pantry and then building a tunnel to connect the food storage room with the main burrow. Though a fox family leaves its cozy home during warm weather, it may return to the same winter address year after year. Gray foxes do not regularly dig homes; they dwell in natural cavities in rocks or in hollow trees.

Wolves lead a model family life. When a male and female mate, they are devoted to each other and cooperate in finding, or digging, a den to shelter their expected pups. After the young have been born and are being weaned from the mother's milk, the father is the provider. He brings home small game, such as rodents, as well as carrion and fruit, in fact almost anything edible. Such offerings are eaten by the mother who then regurgitates the partly digested food to give to the young ones, and gradually the cubs change from a milk diet to a solid one. The male meanwhile keeps watch over the family. If he senses danger, he warns his mate and then moves away from the den, yelping as he goes to draw attention away from the family and towards himself. Wolves have quite large families – anything up to fourteen cubs in a litter, although seven is more usual. They are born between March and May.

Deer and Their Antlers

Deer, like bears, have a public image that is largely based on popular writings. As with the bears, some of it is misleading. Reindeer, for example – since they are associated in song and story with Saint Nicholas and Christmas activities – are thought of as friendly sociable creatures. Actually they are not particularly good-humored, and during their mating season the males fight savage battles for the supremacy of a harem. On the other hand, the classic story of Bambi gives a sympathetic picture of a white-tailed deer's devotion to her fawns, and this is quite authentic.

As infants, deer are weak and wobbly, but they can see immediately after birth and before long they are anxious to explore their surroundings. The mother, or doe, scolds them, warning against such activity; if necessary, she bunts them on the head to make them stay put. The fawn's spotted coat blends effectively with its surroundings, providing a natural camouflage. Once the mother has taught her fawns to lie still for protection, she can leave to seek food; but she returns several times a day to nurse them. If an enemy is nearby, she attracts attention to herself to save the fawns.

Probably the most fascinating aspect of deer is their antlers, the solid bony growths that develop on the frontal bones of the skull. Antlers are shed each year and replaced by a new set. With most species only the male has them, but there are exceptions, for example, the caribou. With a few species neither sex has them.

What happens to all the antlers that are shed in forests and woodlands during midwinter or early spring? Because of their mineral content many are eaten by small animals such as mice, rabbits, and porcupines. Others simply disintegrate after sufficient weathering.

Expert Excavators – Moles and Prairie Dogs

You do not have to go far afield for evidence of moles. All too often, unsightly ridges appear in your garden or lawn, which proclaim that these strange, near-blind underground mammals have been tunneling there. Although they live near human dwellings, moles are seldom seen. This endows them with a rather mysterious quality for a child, who quite naturally wonders how an animal can dig up the ground while actually under it.

When the mole is digging, it braces itself with one of its short, powerful front paws while the other pushes the soil upward. This is how the ridges, which disfigure a lawn, are created. To make deeper tunnels, it scoops the earth under its body and pushes it as far back as possible with its back feet. Every now and then it turns a somersault and then proceeds in the opposite direction, shoving the accumulated pile of dirt along until it comes to a vertical tunnel excavated on a previous occasion. Here the mole forces the dirt up into the open, forming the proverbial molehill.

Do not look for moles in far northern regions where the ground freezes to a great depth in winter. Neither are they to be found in tropical or desert areas; very dry soil does not support enough life to sustain the hard-working moles.

Chubby rodents known as prairie dogs are also remarkable excavators. We do not have a clear picture of just how they carry out their elaborate digging operations, but we know that each prairie dog family has a burrow of its own consisting of a main shaft, which goes straight down about fourteen feet. Horizontal tunnels branch out from the shaft to the animals' sleeping quarters. Other vertical shafts rise from some of the horizontal tunnels and are probably used as safety zones in case the lower levels are flooded. The burrows are grouped together in large colonies, sometimes called towns. There is reason to believe that long ago in the midwestern United States some of these towns had a million or more inhabitants.

Another ground-dwelling rodent is the marmot. Its range is not limited to North America as is that of the prairie dog, but includes the European Alps and mountainous areas eastward to China. The woodchuck, or groundhog, a species native only to the United States, has won wide fame as a weather forecaster. According to folklore the groundhog comes out of its den every year after winter hibernation, on the second day of February: if the sun is shining so that the animal can see its own shadow, there will be another six weeks of cold weather; but if the day is cloudy, winter is over and there will be an early spring. The same delightful (though unfounded) story is told in Europe, but there the badger or the hedgehog is cast as weather prophet.

The skunk also is a mammal whose reputation has traveled far beyond its own home ground. This is an animal that can effectively defend itself without fighting. The evil-smelling fluid it can eject is discouraging enough to turn away almost any enemy. This ammunition is shot out as a fine spray from two large musk glands located at the base of the tail. When a skunk feels threatened, it contracts muscles surrounding the glands. The spray may be shot more than nine feet, and in a strong wind the disagreeable smell may carry half a mile.

There are two species of skunk, and each delivers its defence spray in characteristic fashion. The striped skunk does a hand-stand so that its tail falls out of the line of fire. The spotted species simply turns its back to the intruder. These postures at least give the threatened animal – perhaps yourself – time to turn tail.

Identifying Mammal Tracks

When your child becomes interested in the activities of wild mammals, you can join him in a fascinating hobby: hunting for footprints and identifying them. Long ago many primitive people were expert trackers – but for them it was not a hobby. The game they secured by their expert knowledge of tracking often meant the difference between starving and having enough to eat. Today a knowledge of animal tracks is no longer needed for survival, but it can help satisfy the child's desire to play at nature detective.

You may start track hunting by going to places such as muddy stream banks and finding them there, identifying them later. Or you may first obtain a background for field study from books and observations near to home. In your own back yard you may find the tracks of dogs, cats, and squirrels, and watching the animal cross soft ground can give an idea of the order in which the feet are placed. A dog's tracks practically duplicate those of a wolf or coyote except that wolf tracks are usually larger. Except for size the tracks of a cat are similar to those of the wildcat and mountain lion. Bears, skunks and raccoons make plantigrade tracks, which means that they are practically flat-footed, and the greater part of the foot shows in the tracks. Deer, sheep, moose and elk make hoofed tracks. Another clue for the identification of mammal tracks is that tree-climbing animals normally place their front feet side by side when they jump, whereas animals that stay on the ground rarely show the front feet paired in this way. However, the hind feet of both tree-climbing and ground-living animals are generally paired.

Raccoon tracks are particularly intriguing, for the hind foot of this animal is long with a well-marked heel and five comparatively short toes that make an impression remarkably like that of a small human foot.

Tracks can reveal dramatic incidents, such as a fox overtaking a rabbit, or a weasel pouncing on a squirrel, or they may depict peaceful animals wandering in search of shelter and food. After a fresh snowfall tracks are particularly clear and easy to follow. Altogether, tracking helps furnish an answer to your child's question: 'What do mammals do?' It becomes apparent that securing food and raising families are their major concerns.

The mole has been called an underground
bullet; not for its fighting ability, but for its
digging speed. Using its short, powerful
forelegs, one may excavate a hundred-yard
tunnel in twenty-four hours. Each day a
mole eats its own weight in worms and
insect grubs. It digs by bracing itself with
one front paw and pushing soil with the
other. To go deep it scoops dirt under its
body, then heaves it back with its hind feet.

Mammal Tracks – in Snow and Mud

To understand something of the world of tracks, one must first look closely at feet and consider what happens when a print is made. A child's footprint when walking, for instance, will show a fairly accurate picture of the whole sole of the foot. As he accelerates to run, traces of the heel begin to disappear, until at full speed only the balls of the feet are leaving an impression. On the beach or in a play area of sand, try running, jumping and turning quickly. The tell-tale heaps at the edges of a print, the little slides at the end of a jump, will all be duplicated in some way in the signs of the animals you track.

Perhaps the most common track is that of the dog. It can be told from that of the fox by the larger pads, set close together, and the fact that a line taken across the tops of the pad marks at the side of the print will touch the pad marks in the front. At low speeds – just trotting – the fox leaves a curious 'left-right' trail, a little off-center. This is because it runs at a slight angle to the path it is taking (see illustration). In snow, however, it leaves a straight trail like that of a dog. Both fox and dog leave very similar paw marks at higher speeds.

The brown bear is far more slow and steady, leaving a 'pigeon-toed' trail of massive prints with its flat-footed progress. One has only to watch a bear in a zoo to see how it swings the feet across at each step to create such clumsy signs of its progress.

In contrast, cats walk 'on their toes,' leaving their typically round prints with four distinct toe pads and a large, three-lobed main pad. The trail is very similar to that of the fox, but of course the spacing between marks is smaller, and the prints themselves are very different. The line around the cat's paw in the illustration shows the true wildcat's larger paw.

One of the most easy tracks to identify is that of the otter – which is lucky, because this is often the only sign that this elusive creature is in the area, apart from the distinct whistles of the dog-otters in early summer. There are five toes on each foot, joined by a web. The front paw-print is almost circular, while the back one is elongated. Otters usually jump along, leaving a trail of groups with a body slide in between. In snow, you may come across one of their toboggan runs down a slope. The deer leave 'slots' for tracks, and some practice is needed to know one type from the next: among the easiest are those of the roe deer, because they are so small and pointed; and those of the moose, because they are so large.

Rabbit tracks are easy to identify, but a little difficult to interpret until one realizes that the hind legs sweep forward for hopping progress, leaving their elongated track ahead of the rounded forepaws.

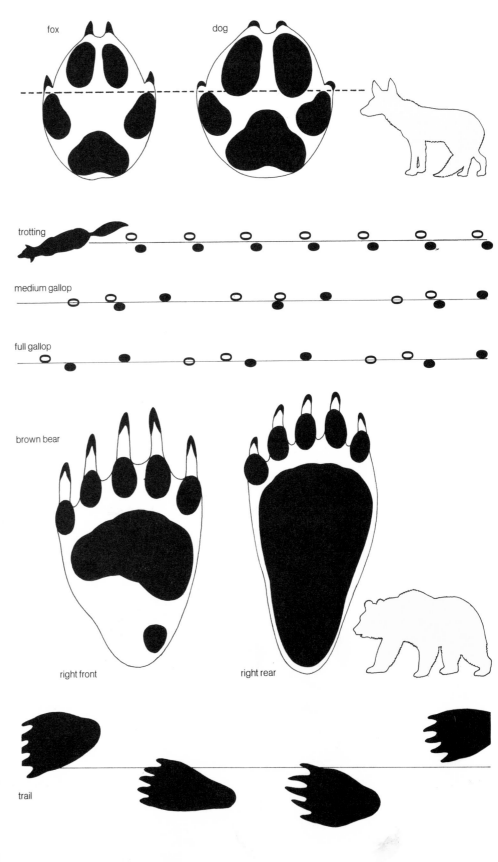

fox

dog

trotting

medium gallop

full gallop

brown bear

right front

right rear

trail

64

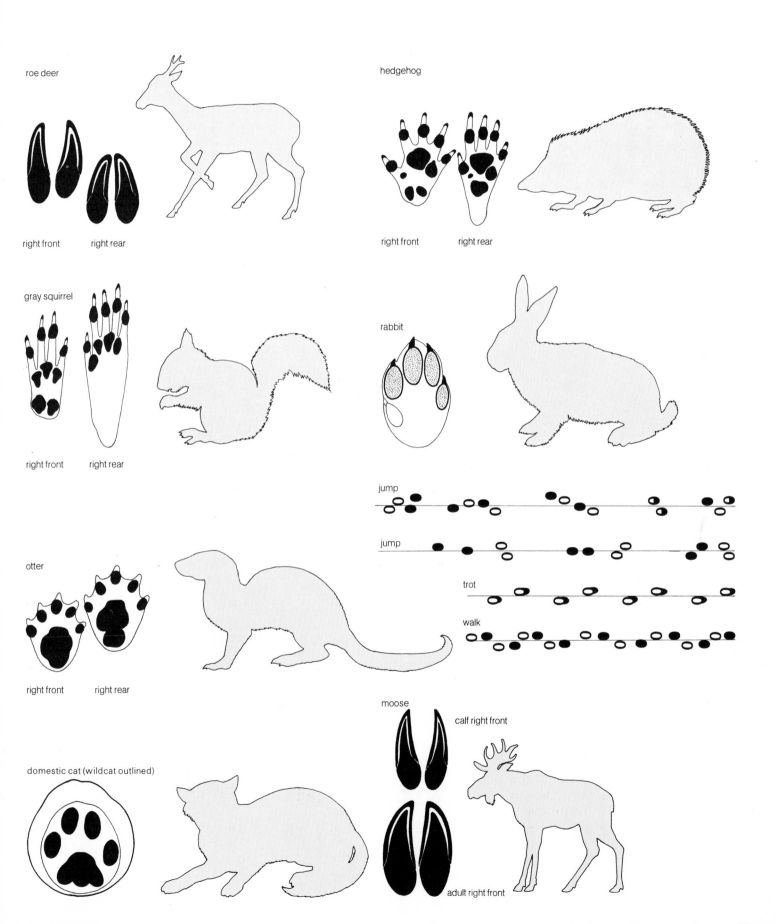

roe deer

right front   right rear

gray squirrel

right front   right rear

otter

right front   right rear

domestic cat (wildcat outlined)

hedgehog

right front   right rear

rabbit

jump

jump

trot

walk

moose

calf right front

adult right front

The Sea and the Shore

Whales are the biggest animals in the world. A fully grown whale may weigh ten times as much as an elephant! This enormous size is certain to impress children. They may be equally impressed by the fact that although whales are mammals, they live in water. A youngster who has recently learned how fish breathe may be puzzled because a whale does not have gills. 'How do they breathe in the ocean? Are you sure it's a mammal?' you may be asked.

One proof that whales are mammals is the fact that a whale baby is born alive and is nourished by its mother's milk. Its size depends on the species and on the size of the parent. Occasionally it has been possible to record birth weights, and there is a record of an eighty-foot blue whale that bore a four-ton baby. A mother whale nurses her calf by means of a special compressor muscle. Using this muscle she injects milk – which looks like cow's milk – into the baby's mouth.

Like land-dwelling mammals, whales are warm-blooded – that is, the blood remains at approximately the same temperature regardless of how warm or cold the surroundings may be. But what about hair, which is also a requirement for a mammal? Although a whale seems to have bare skin, it does have some hairs, just a few, sprouting under its chin. Its ancestors of long ago doubtless had much more hair.

How Whales Breathe

As with land mammals, whales must take oxygen into their lungs, and their features are adapted to make this possible. With nostrils at the top of its head a whale can manage a quick intake of air whenever it comes to the water's surface. When it is below the surface, special muscles close the nostrils firmly so that water cannot enter. There is also a passageway at the back of the mouth which connects the nose passage with the windpipe so that water cannot reach the lungs even when the mouth is open. Ordinarily a whale comes up for air every few minutes, but it can stay underwater twenty minutes or more by making use of the oxygen stored in its blood.

During an ocean voyage you might see the last phase of the whale's unique breathing operation. The exclamation 'There she blows!' on board ship calls attention to one or two fine sprays, which look like steam erupting from the water; these sprays indicate the spot where a whale has just risen to the surface and exhaled. The blast of air sent out of its nostrils is very warm and is saturated with water vapor. The water condenses as it strikes the colder air and forms a column of spray, which has led to the common misconception that whales spout water.

Looking at a picture of a whale that shows its whole body, your child should be able to detect an important difference between the whale's tail and the tail fin of a fish. The whale's tail flattens out into a broad paddle, lying in a horizontal plane. This is just the opposite with the fish's tail, which is always expanded vertically. While the fish moves itself forward by lashing its tail to the right and left, the whale propels itself forward with an up-and-down motion.

What Whales Eat

After hearing the biblical story of Jonah and the whale, a child may ask, 'Do whales really eat people?' Strangely enough this largest of creatures lives on very small animals; only one species – the sperm whale – is even capable of swallowing a man whole. Others would be apt to choke on large prey. The sperm whale usually has teeth only on the lower jaw; its diet consists chiefly of fish and squid.

The so-called killer whale has teeth; but the largest whales are equipped, instead, with enormous strainers. These strainers are made of whalebone plates, which, despite their name, are not bone at all but are material resembling that of human fingernails. The whalebone plates, bordered with a horsehair-like fringe, grow from the roof of the mouth. The whale swims with its mouth open, taking in quantities of shrimp and other small creatures. The whale closes its mouth; the water is forced out but the victims cannot escape from the trap.

The Inspirations for Mermaids

Fairy tales, cartoons, and even decorative motifs introduce most children to the fantastic lovely ladies known as mermaids. Many primitive peoples the world over have legends about mermaids. Only a century ago the famed circus man P. T. Barnum featured in his sideshow what was called a stuffed mermaid. The inquiring mind of a child is naturally intrigued with the idea of a mermaid. Even if these creatures do not exist now, did they ever exist? If not, why were mermaids thought up?

▽ The killing of the great whales is not only bringing them to extinction, it is also a very expensive way for man to obtain food. The diagram below shows the 'pyramid' of life in the cold southern oceans. At the bottom is the plant plankton—microscopic plants and algae which grow in enormous quantities in the sunny top layers of the water. In the row above are shown some of the tiny animals which feed on the plant plankton; among these is the krill, a shrimp-like animal (left of row) which is the main diet of baleen whales. These creatures (third row from bottom) include the blue whales, the largest animals that ever existed on earth. They support their huge bulk by filtering tons of krill, like a thick soup, through the baleen plates in their mouths. At the top of the pyramid is man, the greatest predator the world has ever known. It takes about 1,000 pounds of plankton to make 100 pounds of krill; this can produce about 10 pounds of whale, which, when eaten, may only add one pound to a man's weight. If a way could be found for people to harvest and eat the masses of plant and animal plankton, instead of the few whales, there would be less depletion of the sea's reserves.

▷ Seals and sea lions are perhaps the most appealing of the marine mammals. Their streamlined shape is perfect for swimming, and they have a thick layer of fat under the skin to keep them warm in cold sea-water. Every year they gather in huge groups on the seashore (here, on the Váldez Peninsula in South America, are southern sea lions) to give birth to their young and mate for the next season.

▷▷ This Californian sea lion and her cub are on the Galápagos Islands in the Pacific. The mother sea lion is very attentive to her cub, suckling it with her rich milk and staying very close to it as she teaches it to swim and hunt fish in the rough waves.

▷▽ This sleeping Weddell seal is a picture of peace. Unlike sea lions, seals do not have external ears.

man

dolphin and whale

animal plankton

plant plankton

69

Bottle-nose dolphins are among the most popular of animal entertainers. They are marine mammals, as whales are, but unlike whales, they are small enough to be kept in captivity. And because of their intelligence and willingness to cooperate, they can be trained to give very professional performances. Trainers must use variety in their instructions; with monotonous repetition, as in dog training, dolphins lose interest.

The sea cow, a creature which, like the whale, is a sea-dwelling mammal, may have given rise to the mermaid legend. Its head is shaped like that of the seal; its body is plump but somewhat fishlike. Its startling feature is a face that suggests an oversize, ugly human. It is believed that when early navigators saw sea cows raise their heads above water, they were struck by the animals' part-human, part-fishlike appearance; and as they did not have binoculars in order to see details in the distance clearly, they reported these creatures as glamorous mermaids!

Interesting Skeletons

Boys and girls can learn something about life on the floor of tropical seas by examining natural sponges – this is not true of the synthetic sponges. The sponge, when it is alive and growing at the bottom of the sea, looks more like a plant than an animal. There are many varieties of sponges, but not all of them can be used commercially because some skeletons are too thin or are scratchy or brittle. Sometimes the sponges destined for commercial use are obtained by divers or by workers who pull them from the ocean floor with tongs fastened to long poles.

Another sea animal that children may know from its skeleton is the coral. As is true of sponges, there are many varieties. Aside from the type used for making necklaces and ornaments, there is the reef-building coral, or stony coral. Reef-building corals grow in colonies and are responsible for the well-known coral isles of the Pacific Ocean, as well as the great coral reefs that are found near the Bahamas and off the coast of Australia. The Great Barrier Reef off Australia is more than a thousand miles long.

Any child's imagination is certain to be stimulated by the amazing way that the tiny, soft-bodied coral animal – known as a polyp – produces these gigantic structures. A newborn coral polyp is active at first and swims freely, but soon it fastens itself to a rock or to the sea floor. Using the chalklike carbonate of lime obtained from food and water, it forms a little platform under its body and a hard wall, called the skeleton, around itself. In most kinds of corals, any new polyps do not drift away, but remain attached to the parent and in turn produce new buds. As the older polyps die, young polyps build on top of their skeletons, and thus a structure grows until an island or reef is formed.

Seashore Life

If you could take your child on an exploring trip around a coral reef, you would find many fascinating forms of life, such as the giant plantlike sea anemones; and crabs and clams, effectively camouflaged by pieces of shell, coral, or sponge with which they cover their bodies. Such an expedition is out of the question for most of us; so it is fortunate that relatives of these tropical wonders can be seen much closer to home – in tide pools along the shore and on rocky coasts and sandy beaches. It is interesting to note the differences between the basic ways of life on these shores. On the sand, everything must be adapted to burrow for cover, then filter or hunt for food when the tide comes in. On the rocks, everything must hold fast in the surge and rush of the surf through crevices and channels.

Looking for these creatures and learning something of their way of life can be a delightful hobby. You will find that a magnifying glass is a valuable piece of equipment to help the youngster enjoy the discoveries to the fullest.

You may come across hydroids as you examine a tide pool. Like the giant sea anemones of the coral reefs, these tiny creatures resemble flowers. When they are magnified, the hydroids are revealed as animals. Like the coral they grow as polyps. Each individual is attached to a delicate stalk, and it has numerous threadlike tentacles that are equipped with stinging cells. Small creatures that come close to the hydroid are paralyzed and drawn into the opening that serves as a mouth. Many hydroids are transparent.

In tide pools you may also find sea anemones, much smaller than those of tropical seas yet larger than the hydroids. When undisturbed, they expand into flowerlike forms, but they can contract quickly into an unattractive jellylike mass. In this form they resemble jellyfish; actually the two animals are closely related.

Shellfish Are Not Really Fish

Children passing time on the seashore are likely to become aquainted with shellfish, for the empty shells litter the tide marks in colorful profusion. The mussels and clams that are exposed during low tide may cause youngsters to wonder how these animals can be fish when they are quite different from the common fish they are familiar with.

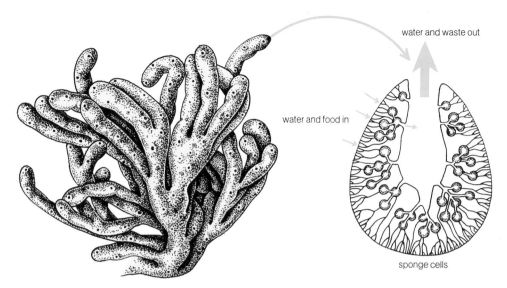

water and waste out

water and food in

sponge cells

Although a sponge looks like a strange, fleshy plant, it is in fact an animal—extremely primitive and simple. The diagram at left shows how one part of a sponge lives. Water is drawn into small holes on the surface of the sponge (seen in close-up in the photograph below) by the beating action of tiny hairs inside round holes in the animal's tissue. As water is pushed through, the sponge strains out tiny fragments of plant and animal food. The water is then pushed into a central chamber and back into the sea.

▷ Familiar household bath sponges are really the skeletons of a type of sponge which lives in warm seas. The living sponges are plucked from the seabed by divers and left in the sun until the living parts rot, leaving the soft structure behind. Bath sponges were used for washing and soaking as early as the days of ancient Greece.

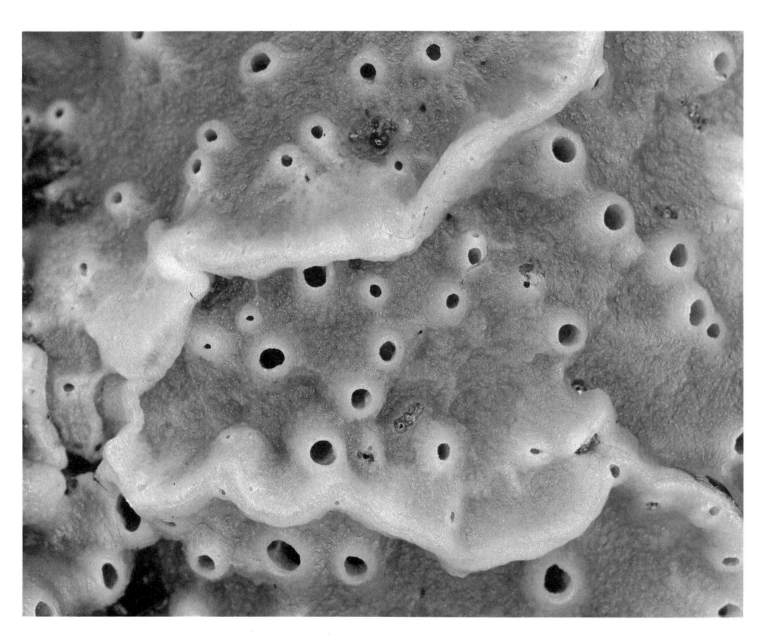

Actually the term *shellfish*, though constantly used, is incorrect. The proper term is *mollusk*. Every kind of mollusk – there are something like eighty thousand species – has a soft body enveloped in a mantle, which, in most cases, manufactures or secretes a hard shell. There are two siphons in the mantle; one of them brings water to the animal, the other carries the water away after it has passed through the gills.

The mollusk's shell is sometimes described as a skeleton. However, it is a skeleton without a backbone, and instead of being internal the skeleton is on the outside of the body.

One of the best-known mollusks, the clam, has a shell made up of three layers – a thin layer on the outside, a thick strong middle layer, and a smooth pearly lining. When a piece of sand or other foreign matter gets lodged within the shells, it becomes coated like the lining and in time may develop into a true pearl. We find mollusks not only in the sea but also in freshwater lakes and streams and on land as well. Some of them – the periwinkle, for example – have a single shell; others such as clams and oysters have two shells hinged along the back.

Although shellfish give the appearance of leading a peaceful existence, life is actually a constant struggle for them. They are devoured by a variety of animals, and they often vie with each other for living space. Oysters, as a rule, settle in fairly deep water, although sometimes a colony is located on a mud flat that is exposed to the air during low tide. In the case of the mud flat you may see an invasion take place. Mussels, which multiply with great rapidity, may move in and smother the oysters out of existence by sheer weight of numbers. One of the oyster's worst enemies is an innocent-looking snail with the sinister name of oyster drill. It plays havoc in oyster beds by boring holes through the oyster shells and feeding on the soft underlying flesh.

Crabs As Camouflage Experts

You must keep a sharp lookout if you want to catch a glimpse of crabs at the seashore. These creatures are expert at disguising themselves by putting seaweed or bits of sponge on their back. Some of them have a close friendship with those flowerlike, beautiful animals known as sea anemones. They 'plant' them on their shells for camouflage:

Corals, like sponges, are also animals. It is the skeletons of some coral types (bottom) that build the huge ocean reefs—over six thousand species of such stony corals have been discovered, mainly in the warm seas of the world. Reef-building coral polyps range in size from a pinhead to more than a foot in diameter, averaging around half an inch. Typically, they are cylindrical in shape, with a mouth opening at the top surrounded by tentacles armed with sting cells. These cells are deadly to the microscopic creatures that provide the polyps' food. A polyp also has cells that extract carbonate of lime from the water; this eventually forms the beautiful limestone reefs that can stretch for hundreds of miles.

the crab gains protection while the anemone obtains a regular food supply from the scraps created when the crab feeds. This ideal relationship has a patient beginning. The crab approaches an anemone, which is firmly anchored to its spot on the sea bed by a powerful sucker on its 'stalk.' The crab strokes the anemone with its claws for some time, until the creature lets out its long tentacles, and 'relaxes' enough for the crab to pluck it from the bottom, and plant it upon its shell. Here, with luck, it will stick for some time – or at least until the crab sheds its shell to grow, when the whole process must be repeated.

Other crabs hide completely in sand as they lie in wait for their prey. Many are very small. However, it should not be too difficult to discover the rock crab, which is common on most rocky shores. When fully grown it is a little over five inches wide and is commonly reddish purple in color. Like all crabs, the little creature has five pairs of legs. The first pair are adapted as pinching claws, and in some crabs the last two pairs, shaped like fins, serve effectively as swimming aids. It is amusing to watch crabs walk, for they move sideways instead of forward or backward. Shore crabs are rather slow in their movements; the swimming crabs are considerably more active.

If a crab accidentally loses a claw, it can grow a new one. During its lifetime it also replaces its shell, not because of a mishap but because its body eventually grows too big for the shell. When the original shell gets too snug, the animal pulls itself free; until its new covering hardens it is known as a soft-backed crab. Just before it sheds the old one, it is known as a peeler.

If you make a habit of observing activity among the seaweed in shallow waters, one day you may see a struggle between a lobster and a crab, although such encounters are rather infrequent. The crab – even a large one – has little chance against his opponent, since the claws of the lobster are extremely powerful. One of the claws is very broad and is used for crushing; the narrower one cuts food to bits. Its mouth can crush as well as bite. It also seems that the lobster has an advantage over the crab because its feelers, especially the second pair, are longer than the crab's. The lobster can investigate holes and crevices with its feelers and it is sensitive to danger as well as to potential prey.

Creatures with Spiny Skins

An expedition with a net, particularly in warm, shallow waters, can often reveal sea urchins, living balls or hearts of thin spines. Sometimes just the spineless test, or case, is found, of a dead one washed up with the tide. Although the living creature is often avoided, for the spines can be both sharp and poisonous, close inspection – with care – shows a fascinating animal. Its mouth, on the underside of the ball, consists of five bony plates of immense strength. The urchin moves by means of 'tube feet' that can be extended from all over its surface. Some of them pass food – tiny particles of animal matter – to the mouth. Some urchins also burrow, using the spines and sometimes the mouth to dig.

So powerful and persistent are their efforts that a few species can penetrate soft rock. Some steel piers, three-eighths of an inch thick, on the Californian coast, were found to have been weakened about twenty years after they had been constructed. They were riddled with holes made by the local burrowing urchin population. On other parts of the steel, the paint and the tough anticorrosion layers had been worn away, and the base steel polished to a good shine by the spines of thousands of urchins moving across it in their restless quest for encrusting food.

Shell Collections

Sea shells delight children who live inland as well as those who have the seashore close by. They may collect them in the same way that stamps and coins are collected – through purchase at stores, by order from catalogs, and through trading with correspondents the world over. Shells have a multiple appeal. Some, such as the giant conch shell, intensify the sounds they pick up in their spiral interior and thus bring to a child's ear the 'sound of the sea.'

Some shells have a special appeal because you can make art objects with them. One project that intrigues many young people is making book ends from shells. Begin with two triangular blocks of wood, each attached to a heavy wood base about six inches square. Then apply a coat of ready-mixed putty, nearly a quarter-inch thick, to the outer surfaces that are to be decorated. While the putty is still soft, press shells into it just far enough to be held firm. With good cutting tools you may cut the wood blocks into any of a variety of shapes. The shell groupings and designs are limitless.

◁ A rocky shore at low tide is the place to find lots of fun on holiday. A small net on the end of a long pole is ideal for lifting all kinds of animals out of rock pools and from underneath masses of seaweed. Many small creatures are left behind by the tide in rock pools, and must hide in cracks and crannies until the sea comes up again. Big banks of weed are always home to shrimps, crabs, small fish, snails, and other creatures. Look, too, for sea anemones.

△ Here are just two of the common creatures to be found on the seashore. On top, a shrimp moves cautiously out of a crack between the stones, ready to dart back if danger shows. The black sea urchin, below, is just as sharp and prickly as it looks, with its round shell covered in long, brittle spines. It is a good idea to wear rubber-soled shoes when moving around rocks where there are sea urchins and to look before taking the next step.

▽ The seashore is a wonderful place for exploring because of its varied, extraordinary animal life. At low tide acrobatic starfish may be seen gliding across the wet sand. Though its shell becomes rigid when a starfish dies, a living animal can squeeze through crevices no wider than one of its arms, can stand on the tips of its arms, and right itself if turned on its back. Most starfish have a five-armed body; some have more arms. This Caribbean species measures about a foot across its arms.

▽ ▽ Seaweeds furnish shelter for many creatures. The tough and hardy varieties can cling to rocky crevices even though constantly pounded by heavy surf.

▽ A hermit crab has no shell over its abdomen as most crabs do. However, it makes up for this lack of protection by moving into the empty shell of a mollusk. When it outgrows one shell, it looks about for a larger one and moves in.

◁ Sea urchins, commonly called sand dollars, are frequently cast up on beaches along seacoasts of the United States. Such specimens, however, usually consist only of the animals' limestone skeletons. Various species of urchins are found on beaches around the world. Although the animal has no arms as a starfish does, the spines on its back form a five-pointed star. The intact shell of a common sea urchin (bottom) is a prize discovery on a beach.

▷ Dense beds of mussels crowd the limpets on this rocky shore. Here, barnacles have also made their homes, not only on the bare rocks, but even encrusting the limpet shells. All creatures that live on rocky shores must be adapted to cling tight against the force of the surf. The limpets have powerful suckers, the barnacles a kind of cement, and the mussels tie themselves down with strong threads.

△ The delicate traces made on this rock are not the work of some seashore artist, but merely the result of a limpet's feeding excursion. As this mollusk moves slowly over the rock, it rasps away at the algae that live there with its hard, filelike tongue. After each outing, it returns to a favorite place on the rock, often so well-used that the outline of the limpet's shell is imprinted in the rock in a perfect fit.

◁ A sand collar snail can tuck itself tightly within its globular shell; but an observer may see a fleshy foot protrude and watch the animal travel along the sand as more of its body is exposed. From it a jellylike ribbon emerges which the snail pushes around the lower margin of its shell. This collar or necklace, giving the snail its name, is lined with a layer of tiny, transparent eggs.

Many residents of sandy beaches burrow to conceal themselves; there is even a burrowing starfish (top). The lugworm digs deep, but betrays its whereabouts by a small coil of sand paired with a depression (above). The coil consists of sand from which food has been digested; it is ejected at the tail end of a U-shaped burrow: the depression is at the head. A single hole may reveal the tube of a cockle (left).

The Beauty of Seashells

Shells can be found along the shore nearly everywhere in the world, from polar regions to the tropics. Even inland, far from the sea, fossil shells in the earth and rocks reveal to us that the land was once below seawater. Although some shells can be found in fresh water, the greatest variety, and the most beautiful colors, are found among the seashells.

When the fleshy snail-like animals that live inside shells die, or are eaten by predators, the shell either sinks to the bottom of the sea, or drifts with the tide until it is pushed up on the seashore. A little knowledge of which types of shell animals live on which type of coastline will help you to know where to collect the kind of shells you prefer.

Shells have been appreciated and used by people since prehistoric times. The 'Imperial purple' dye, which was used by the emperors of ancient Rome, was made from the murex shell. Pacific islanders used cowrie shells as money. Craftsmen and jewelers have made beautiful works of art out of the shimmering layer of 'mother-of-pearl' which is inside most shells. However, one need not have any experience to create many attractive items from shells. One simple, but effective, idea is to string small, brightly-colored shells like beads, to make a necklace. Carefully drill a hole through the shell, using a thin, hard-tipped hand drill, or an awl if the shell is fine. Cowrie shells are easy to string, by passing the cotton through the mouth of the shell and out the other side, and securing with a dab of glue. A single, large shell can be hung on a chain or a leather thong to make a pretty pendant.

If you have collected a lot of varied, small shells, you can use them to make an imaginative mosaic picture. Using a piece of stiff, colored card as your base, shuffle the shells around on the card until they form an attractive pattern. Alternatively, sketch in pencil the design you want to create, and select the shells to fit in the outline. When you are happy with the arrangement, pick up each shell alone and put a dab of glue on its base, and return it to the pattern. When the glue has dried, the shell picture can be framed.

Shells can also be stuck onto boxes – an old shoe box, or a cigar box, is ideal. When you have stuck all the shells onto the box, you can give it a bright sheen by spraying or painting it with varnish. Another idea is to make a lamp base by sticking shells to a bottle (square-shaped ones are best, as most shells have a flat base which cannot easily stick to a round surface) or a block of wood. Electrical shops sell special fittings to put in the mouth of a bottle, to hold the switch, light bulb and shade. When you turn on the lamp at night, the light will softly show up the lovely colors and forms of the shells.

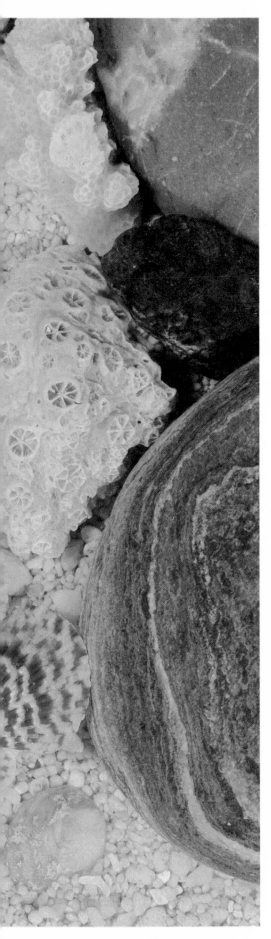

◁ The beaches of tropical islands are often a paradise for shell hunters. This beach in Jamaica is no exception, with its sparkling assortment of shells and pebbles.

▽ Underwater divers in warm seas and near coral reefs have a special opportunity to see large and beautiful shells—often with the living animal still inside. Here is a wavy volute shell, on the sea bottom off the coast of South Australia.

▽ The 'top' shells are one of the commonest types of shells, but there are many varieties of size and color, such as this painted top shell and purple top shell. They are so named because they are shaped like an old-fashioned spinning top.

▽▽ A simple but very effective design has been created in this shell picture by arranging all the shells in rows according to their shade of color.

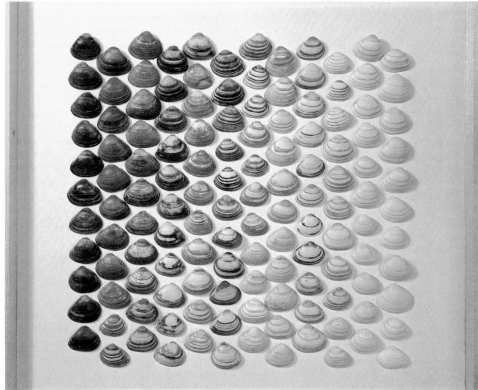

Fishes ~ from Sunnies to Sharks

How can fish breathe under water? Can they hear? How long do they live?

These are but a few of the questions that occur to children as they watch goldfish or tropical fish in an aquarium, for fish are interesting, thought-provoking creatures. Schools have recognized their appeal by making classroom projects of aquariums. Newspapers frequently print articles about the selection and care of tropical fish, and whole magazines are devoted to the subject. Large aquariums for the public are as popular as zoos with adults as well as youngsters.

Goldfish can be cared for by even a young child, and the beauty of their color and motion add immensely to the charm of any room. But beauty is by no means the only contribution of these creatures. As we watch them behind glass walls, we have an experience comparable to going into the sea, wearing a diving helmet: much of what we learn from the aquarium applies to fish that cannot be seen close up.

Children just learning to swim may be puzzled watching a fish, apparently motionless, remaining in one place in an aquarium. 'How does it just *stay there*?' they wonder. 'Why doesn't it sink or move up higher?'

The ability of some fish to stay motionless in one place is due to a unique organ known as the swim bladder. It is in the forward part of the body and is filled with gas – a mixture of oxygen and nitrogen. Since the gas is lighter than water, it balances the weight of the fish. Air can be pumped to or from it to allow for different pressures at different depths, in the same way as the great air tanks in a submarine. Most fish that have skeletons of true bone possess this organ, and they need very little fin movement to stay at a given depth. When they die, their bodies rise to the surface. The goldfish is one of the fish that possess the swim bladder, together with the other aquarium and sporting fishes that you are likely to encounter.

Sharks and some other kinds of fish have skeletons of gristle. They lack the swim bladder and consequently they can remain suspended in one position only by continuous effort. Some sharks, however, maintain a reservoir of lightweight oil in their livers, an aid to bouyancy that has caused them to be hunted commercially.

▽ *Points to look at and compare when trying to describe or identify a fish: this is a largemouth bass. For this analysis, the head is said to run from the snout to the rear of the gill cover; the tail is from the vent to the tip of the tail fin. The position of the mouth relative to the eye is also helpful. In an Atlantic salmon the mouth does not go past the eye; in a trout it does.*

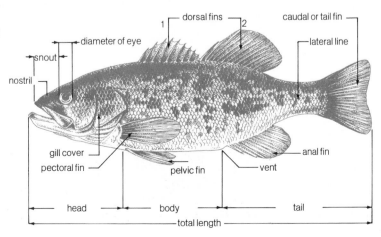

◁ The shape of a fish's body is related to the speed at which it moves and the type of water it inhabits. The pike (top) is an 'arrow' fish—slim, streamlined, with fins to the rear for short, fast sprints. The carp (center) has a high flat body, best suited for winding through the thick weeds of its lowland home in slow-moving rivers and lakes. The tuna (bottom) is shaped for speed and stamina, with a perfectly balanced, streamlined body and large control surfaces— the fins—for maneuverability. It lives and hunts in the sunlit layers of the open ocean.

▽ The beautiful veiltail goldfish is a striking contrast to the carp, which was its early ancestor. Olive-colored carp, discovered in China about a hundred years ago, had golden tones along their sides. By selective breeding, these bright pigments in the skin were increased until gold fish were achieved. Later, many other fancy varieties evolved.

How Fish Breathe

A fish has very small nostrils, which you can see if you look closely on either side of its snout. The nostrils lead to a small sac where the sense of smell is located but they have no connection whatever with breathing. When you see a goldfish constantly opening and closing its mouth, it is seeking air or oxygen. Fish need oxygen just as people do, but they need it in a different form. Most fish drown in the air just as a person will under water if submerged too long.

Instead of breathing through nostrils and lungs, a fish is equipped to breathe through its gills. You can see its gill covers – flat bony flaps – just behind its head, one on each side. When the fish opens its mouth, allowing water to flow in, the gill covers close against the body so that water will not enter from behind them. Then when the fish closes its mouth, the gill covers open, and the water is forced out through the gill slits. As the water passes through the slits, the oxygen in the water is absorbed by the tiny blood vessels making up the gills; at the same time these blood vessels give off carbon dioxide and other body wastes. The fresh oxygen is then circulated through the body.

How Fins Are Used

As you watch a goldfish swim, you may get the idea that its fins are an important element in its forward movement. This is correct, although nowadays scientists do not attach as much importance to the locomotion value of fins as they once did. Experiments have shown that a fish can navigate even without its fins.

There are seven fins on the common goldfish. Just behind its gill covers it has a pair called the pectorals. Farther back is another pair called the ventrals – if far forward, they are called the pelvics. On its back the fish has a dorsal fin, which it sometimes lifts and closes down like a fan. On the underside toward the tail is the anal fin. At the end of the tail is the caudal fin, often called the tail fin.

How the fins aid a fish's movement depends on their shape and location. The caudal, or tail, fin helps the fish propel itself as it presses its tail against the water, first to one side and then to the other. The shape of this fin seems to be related to swimming speed of the different species. The dorsal fin acts as a keel: it prevents rolling. The anal fin serves the same purpose and in some species it is also used to give the fish good up-and-down control.

Pectoral fins appear to serve chiefly as brakes for fish with bony skeletons – this is particularly true of perch – and these fins also have a slight balancing effect. In fish with other than bony skeletons the pectorals have a powerful balancing action but are of little use as brakes. Sharks, for example, which have a skeleton composed of gristle rather than bone, apparently are unable to make a sudden stop. As for the ventral fins, they contribute further to keeping the fish evenly balanced.

Varieties in Fins

The fins of the common goldfish are by no means standard equipment for all fish. Many fishes do not have ventrals. Some, like the cod, have three dorsal fins; others have two; others, one. Some have two anal fins; others, one.

Certain kinds of fish have specialized uses for one or more of their fins. The front ray of the first dorsal fin of the anglerfish is adapted as a rod and lure with which it attracts smaller creatures to eat. A number of fish have fins

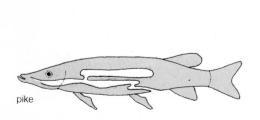

pike

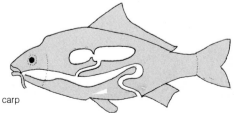

carp

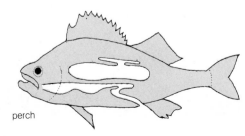

perch

▽ The purpose of the swim bladder is to maintain the fish at a chosen depth in the water without relation to the actual weight of its body. Like a submarine, fishes with hard bones such as pike, carp, and perch have special reservoirs of air that can be filled or emptied and adjusted to the pressure of water around them. The pike and carp reservoirs are connected to the gut cavities. The perch has no such connection and therefore can only make slow adjustments by allowing gas from the bladder in and out of its blood.

▽ Life underwater requires a different balance of senses than life on land. Because water contains more chemicals than air, the sense of smell is highly important. The conger eel uses its eyes to detect movement, but finds most of its prey (small fish and crabs) using nostrils that can detect the odor of food at considerable distances.

▽ ▽ The barbels of the carp are as sensitive to taste and touch as the human tongue. When the carp feeds, it throws up clouds of mud in the water and uses its nostrils, barbels, and lips to taste and feel what is good to eat.

▽ For a fish, the lateral dotted line on its skin (as shown) detects pressure waves that are beyond the perception of human hearing, touch, or sight.

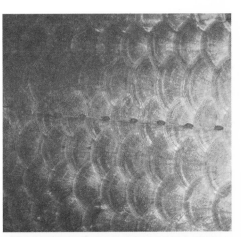

A fish's mastery of motion in the water is complete. It can dart forward with tremendous speed, starting from a com-

sinuous movement of the whole body, the movements of the fins, and the propulsion resulting from water being shot through the gill chambers. Most fish use all three.

When a child sees his goldfish cover the length of its aquarium with one quick swish of its body in what seems like no time at all, he may get the impression that fish always move with notable speed. It is true that many species are capable of extremely rapid bursts of speed, but over long distances they average a much slower rate. Salmon may swim at a rate of twenty-five miles an hour, whereas carp are not known to exceed seven and a half.

How the Goldfish Gets Its Color
Goldfish owe much of their attractiveness to their golden sheen. 'Is there *real* gold in a goldfish?' a youngster looking at the aquarium may ask. The goldfish scales do resemble this precious metal, but of course there is no trace of gold in their shiny covering. Color in fish is mainly the effect of pigments that are scattered in the surface layers of the skin and are visible through the scales.

The ancestors of goldfish were olive in color. They belonged to the carp family and lived in the rivers and lakes of China. Hundreds of years ago some specimens were found with golden tones on their sides, and selective breeding was begun with these. Gold predominated in some of their offspring, and breeding continued until fish completely golden in color were produced. About seventy-five years ago an American sailor brought goldfish to the United States from the Orient. They have had wide popularity ever since.

Today we see many fancy varieties, such as fantail, fringetail, telescope, and lionhead; the breeding of specially selected fish produces these highly ornamental creatures. The common goldfish characteristically has a long body,

◁ Most fish live in schools at some time of their lives, often when they are young. There are many advantages to this way of life. Many eyes seek food more efficiently and keep watch for enemies. Sharks and other hunters find it more difficult to attack a large group than to chase a single fish. Those fish that always live in schools tend to be marked with bright stripes or spots. Because of this, they can see each other clearly and stay in position. This is a school of grunts, so named for the curious croaking noises they make underwater.

△ Sea horses are among the strangest of all fishes, having a shape which looks more like a carousel horse than a normal fish. However, they are true fishes, with gills and tiny fins. With the long, flexible tail they have developed, they can cling to strands of weed and avoid being tossed by the tide. Sea horses are also unusual in that, after the female has laid her eggs, the male carries them in a pouch in his belly until they hatch.

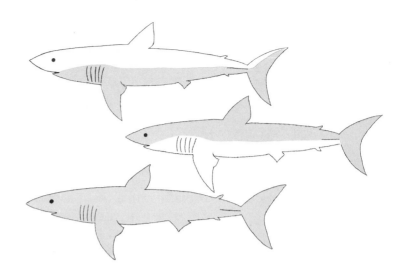

forked tail, and small head. It may be all gold, or it may be marked with black and silver. It is hardier than its ornamental relatives, and if it is transferred to a pond with ample food, it may grow to a length of twelve inches.

Fish Camouflage

The color of fish is often a definite camouflage, comparable to protective schemes on many birds and mammals. You may see a hint of protective coloration in a goldfish, as the orange tones of its back fade to pale lemon-yellow below. In general the color is darker on the backs of fish than on the undersides. As the darker color blends with the river or pond bottom, fish tend to be less noticeable from above. On the other hand, when fish feed near the surface, their light underparts blend with the sky, and therefore they are not so likely to be seen by enemies swimming below.

Perch, pike, and other species that live among weeds are protected by their vertical stripes. An extreme example of camouflage is the leaf fish of the Amazon River. It is the color of a dead leaf and has a projection from its lower lip that resembles a leaf stalk. Even its actions reinforce the illusion: in stalking its prey it drifts along like a dead leaf.

How Fish See and Hear

'Goldie winked at me. I saw him!' an exuberant youngster exclaimed one day during a close scrutiny of the aquarium.

He was disappointed when I pointed out that a fish has no eyelids and therefore cannot wink. However, fish do have eyeballs, and when one of these is flicked downward, you get the impression of a wink. The lack of eyelids also means that its eyes are always wide open, no matter whether the fish is awake or asleep (that is, when there is a suspension of all movement and consciousness).

'Can the fish hear us?' is another challenging expression from children who enjoy talking to their charges. It is doubtful that they can, but they do seem to be aware of hand clapping or the sound of tapping on the aquarium walls. The fish has no outside ear – it does not even have openings where you would expect to find ears. It does have other sense organs along the flanks and over the head, however, through which it can get some of the same impressions that other animals receive through their ears.

◁ *If a fish is the same color all over, light falling on it makes it bright on top and shadowed beneath, and thus easily seen by enemies (top). Most fish, therefore, are colored dark above, light below (center). When the light casts a shadow on their underside, the dark back—seen from above—blends with the water depths; and the light belly, seen from below, blends with the bright sky (bottom).*

▷ *The strange appearance of a flounder develops only as it grows. The diagram (far right) shows how a flounder larva has one eye on each side of its head, like most fishes. As it grows, one eye moves to the other side of its head and its mouth twists round, and the fish is ready for life on the sea floor.*

▽ *Fish camouflage: a flounder, below, is spotted to merge with the pebbles of the seabed. A perch (opposite, center) is striped to hide in lake reeds. An angler fish (opposite, below) looks like a weedy rock.*

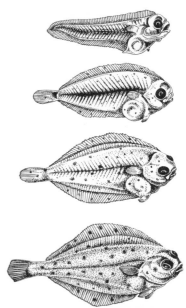

The archerfish has a unique method of hunting its food: it shoots aerial insects down with jets of water. Cruising slowly just below the surface, it waits until its prey alights on overhanging vegetation. The fish takes up position below, with its body as near to vertical as possible to reduce the bending of light at the surface that could spoil its aim (right). It then fires a stream of water drops to dislodge its meal. The fish's mouth is well-adapted for such marksmanship. Along its roof is a groove, and along the tongue a matching ridge. The fish takes a big mouthful of water and opens its gill covers wide. To shoot, it sharply closes its gills while bringing its tongue up to form a narrow water tube. For such a small fish (the picture below is about half natural size), the archerfish has a surprising range of fire. It can shoot fifteen feet, and is accurate up to six feet. It is not, however, always successful: often it shoots with such force that it knocks its intended meal far out of reach.

How Scales Grow

The scales of a fish suggest the shingles on a roof. Each scale grows separately from the skin, set at an angle; the result is an overlapping that forms a complete covering for the body. Naturalists sometimes call this scaly covering the outside skeleton.

Some fish, the catfish for one, do not have scales. Some kinds of scales – those of the freshwater eel, for example – are so tiny that they are hardly noticeable. A curious feature about some members of the tuna family is that they are only partly covered with scales.

As the fish grows, its scales grow too. You can tell the age of many of the bony fish by the marking on their scales; by examining the rings you can tell how old they are. Of course you will not want to do this with your goldfish pet; its scales should never be touched, let alone pulled out. A protective slime covers them, and if this is rubbed off by dry hands or in any other way, death may result.

'It Was That Big!'

Size is not so standardized among fish as it is among mammals. The goldfish is an outstanding case in point. In an aquarium it remains small; whereas, given the freedom of a pond, it increases its size by many times. Such factors as the temperature and acidity of the water and the type of food available determine the length and weight a fish can attain.

Most of the really big fish are found in the ocean – though the arapaimas that live in the rivers of Brazil attain a weight of four hundred pounds, and the European catfish, or wels, can reach over sixteen feet long and weigh over 600 pounds. Among the giants of the sea is a popular food staple, the tuna. These giants vary in size depending on the regions to which they are native, but a weight of a thousand pounds is about the maximum. Another big fish is the spectacular swordfish. Few sports are as adventurous as deep-sea fishing, and many a boy or girl, thrilled by pictures or films, looks forward to taking a marlin or swordfish with rod and reel.

Fish in Winter

'What happened to the fish when the water froze?' children may ask as they prepare to go skating over ice that was a rippling lake or stream only a few weeks previously. There is more than one answer to this question. Some fish – the common sucker, for example – burrow in the mud and may be frozen and thawed without being any the worse for the experience. Others remain active if the water under the ice is deep enough. As for carp and some other species, they move to deeper water at the beginning of winter.

Children accept the seasonal travels of birds rather casually because they can witness some phases of their migrations each year, but they are likely to be surprised to find that many fish migrate too. Even their parents often do not realize how widespread the migration habit is among fish. Except for the fish living in ponds, a great many may make migratory journeys in the course of their lives. Sometimes the individuals in a traveling school are counted by the million.

Aside from the journeys of fish to deeper waters for the winter, some species of freshwater fish travel many miles in search of food. There are also saltwater migrations by fish that swim away from their feeding grounds to deposit their eggs. A famous example is that of the North Sea herring, which migrate in the autumn to the coastal waters of Norway, Britain and France. They spawn there and then go northward again. When the young hatch, they swim to the surface to feed and gradually are swept north by the main currents until they reach the North Sea.

How Long Do Fish Live?

Many species of fish have a long lifespan, but in the natural state they are not likely to attain the full span. They have too many enemies, ever ready to take them as food. Some, such as the Pacific coast salmon, die after spawning. However, there are records of fish that live in ponds or in aquariums which show that catfish have lived to sixty years, halibut to thirty, and trout to eighteen. Carp live no more than fifty years, although there are many tales to the contrary.

The Little Fishes

An attractive resident of brooks and ponds is the tiny sunfish, or sunny – it is also known as tobacco box, pumpkinseed, and a variety of other names. The name pumpkinseed is a good description of its general form because, viewed from the side, it strongly suggests the seeds you find when

you carve a Halloween jack-o'-lantern. There are a number of species, the smallest being the pygmy, which is only about an inch long when adult. Although these fish occur naturally from southern Canada to southern regions of the United States, they have also flourished when taken to other areas, including Europe. The real drama in the life of the sunfish is the result of duels fought between rivals. If a male has competition when choosing a mate, he fights gamely to drive the rival away. If he is successful, he begins constructing a nest by briskly fanning the bottom of the stream with his tail. He works until he has a circular excavated area with a diameter about twice his own length. The female, won by right of conquest, then deposits eggs in the nest and takes leave of home and mate. The male, however, remains close by, defending the territory until the eggs have hatched.

Male mosquitofish grow to be little more than an inch long; the females may achieve a length of two inches or slightly more. These are the most widely distributed freshwater fish in the world. They enjoy great popularity because they favor mosquito larvae as a diet, and therefore help to keep down the numbers of these insect pests. There is a record of a mosquitofish in an aquarium that ate one hundred fifty mosquito larvae within ten hours.

Not all fish lay eggs. Some species, ranging from the great tiger shark to the tiny guppy, give birth to young that are in an advanced state of development. A guppy produces at least twenty-five, and perhaps as many as fifty, offspring at a time. But the parents eat many of their young, and only a small proportion survive.

The Truth About Sharks
Most people young and old enjoy frightening horror stories. Of course they want to be safely elsewhere when the horrors occur; but they find it exciting to read and talk about them. For this reason sharks receive an extraordinary amount of attention. An attack on a person by a shark is sure to be given more than its share of publicity, and horrifying details are piled up until we are apt to feel that sharks are the evilest of creatures.

'Are sharks really that vicious?' young people looking for facts are likely to ask. Before giving an affirmative answer,

△ In the first picture the pike has been waiting in ambush, camouflaged by its color, until a tiny stickleback comes close. In the second picture the pike has caught its prey and is beginning to adjust the dead stickleback to swallow it. In the third picture the stickleback is being swallowed headfirst so that the spikes and the fins do not choke the pike.

Although sharks are thought to be 'killers,' few deliberately hunt humans, as some books and films would have us believe. Even the great white shark (right), for example, can be approached—carefully—by an underwater photographer. (The specimen in the picture is quite small, though it may grow to 25 feet long.) If there is any blood in the water from man or fish, the story may be quite different. Sharks have an amazingly acute sense of smell, which can detect even a small drop of blood at a considerable distance. The smell of blood in the water can drive them into a kind of frenzy, and they may tear a wounded creature apart in a few minutes. If one of their own number is wounded, the others may turn on it too. The nurse shark (below), common along shallow, warm coastal waters of the Atlantic, is rarely a danger to humans, unless a swimmer carelessly touches one. Even then, the worst injury may be scrapes from the skin of the shark, which is covered with tiny, sharp scales.

it is important to point out that there are many kinds of sharks – about three hundred varieties. Some grow to only a foot in length, and some to a length of more than forty feet, the largest fish in the world. The biggest of them all, the whale shark, is not one to be feared. It is rare, it is slow-moving, and it is not known to eat anything larger than small fish, squid, and plankton.

The most dangerous of sharks is the great white shark, also called, with good reason, the man-eater. It is only half the size of a whale shark. It is lively, has great jaws and teeth, and it roams through all warm and temperate seas – it also enters colder waters. It is essentially a deep-sea animal, but it does prowl along coastal areas and occasionally enters the mouth of a river. Other kinds of sharks, such as the tiger and the hammerhead, are known to attack humans. It has been proved that vibrations in the water, as well as blood, attract these dangerous fish, which move speedily to snatch at any prey. Australia more than any other country has trouble with sharks. The United States is in second place for that dubious honor. Attacks have been reported in waters along both the east and west coasts.

The Popular Trout

Trout live in cool mountain streams or lakes, where they feed on a variety of insects that lay eggs on the water. They also greedily snatch the emerging insects as they hatch. These feeding habits make fly-fishing for trout an exciting sport for the fisherman as he lures his victim with imitations of its favorite foods. In small streams trout rarely exceed half a pound, but in larger rivers and lakes where food is abundant they reach a size from five to ten pounds, while those that feed on the abundant shrimps and small fishes in the sea often top twenty pounds.

The female trout seeks water with a gravelly bottom for her nest, where a brook flows into a larger stream. She shapes a depression from six to eight inches deep by lashing with her tail. Then she lays her eggs, hundreds of them. After the male has fertilized them, she moves a little way upstream and repeats the same process. Most of the discarded material is conveniently deposited over the first nest, protecting the eggs from underwater creatures in search of food. The mother trout makes several nests and lays eggs in all of them before she is finished.

In spite of the enormous quantities of eggs laid by all varieties of trout, these fish were in serious danger of extermination after motor highways began opening the wilderness to ever-increasing numbers of fishermen. Aside from being destroyed by their natural enemies, they were taken by many people who gave no thought to their size, the season of the year, or the decreased number of fish that might be left in a stream. The passage of effective conservation laws fortunately prevented the disappearance of trout from their native waters; regulations were instituted that limited the seasons for trout fishing, the number a person may catch in a day, and the size a fish must be before it can be taken.

The Hardy Eels

'Is that a fish? Looks like a snake to me!' With some reason children are dubious when one of these elongated creatures is displayed as part of a morning's catch. Despite its snake-like form, it is a true fish, having gills for breathing and fins for swimming.

The well-known figure of speech 'slippery as an eel' makes a good point of contrast between this fish and the snake. The skin of a snake is never slimy; that of an eel is always slimy, since quantities of tiny glands in the skin produce a sticky mucus. The eel's skin is thick and flexible, with the scales lodged in it rather than attached on the outside.

Eels live in all bodies of water, in mountain lakes and streams, in saltwater pools along the shore, and in stagnant ponds. Clean water or foul, it makes no difference to the welfare of these hardy fish. It might seem strange, therefore, that we do not see them more frequently. This is because eels are secretive creatures, and much of the time they lie buried in mud.

Like salmon, eels make astounding migratory journeys, but they reverse the procedure. Instead of leaving the ocean for fresh water, they travel from ponds and lakes down rivers to mate in the depths of the salty ocean. The two species of eel that spawn in the same area in the Atlantic – one European, the other American – travel in opposite directions. The young whose parents come from America take about a year to travel from their ocean breeding place to American rivers and lakes; the offspring of European eels take three years to swim to Europe.

The Salmon's Extraordinary Travels

Many children have heard about the travels of the salmon, for this fish has become a symbol of determination to reach a goal. Pacific salmon swim hundreds of miles to their spawning grounds in North American rivers; the Atlantic salmon go hundreds of miles to reach theirs in European as well as American rivers. How they find their way to the exact stream of their birth is still something of a mystery. At sea, they probably navigate by the sun and stars. When they reach the coast, they use their extraordinary sense of smell to find their home river.

If you had the opportunity to be at a waterfall where salmon were making their way upstream, you might see them putting their noses out of the swirling water as if sizing up the situation. They turn their heads against the falling water, twist their bodies like bows, and then straighten out again. They bring every muscle into play as they try to progress. Sometimes they succeed by practically climbing the cascade. At other times they top it with a single leap. No matter what their method, they never give up. If need be, they wait for days, even weeks, until a change in the volume of water provides a better opportunity to scale the barrier. Pacific salmon rarely survive spawning to return to the sea. Their usual fate is to die after breeding.

◁ Salmon let nothing stand in their way as they migrate from the sea to breed in the stream of their birth. Starting life as helpless little alevins (opposite), they soon grow, feed, and make their way to the sea after one to four years.

▽ A fisherman's family picnics on the banks of a Norwegian salmon river. Salmon can be difficult to catch, for they do not feed on their run upstream. Only habit, or perhaps irritation, makes them snap at the angler's lures. Although the youngster below is rightly proud of his catch, the largest salmon come much bigger—up to eighty pounds or more.

Fish That Are Different

The fish family has its share of fantastic creatures. In some
ways their qualities are more amazing than those of the
monsters of legend and myth. The climbing perch is the
commonest of these believe-it-or-not fish. It can survive out
of water for several days, and its pectoral fins, acting as
legs, are strong enough to support its body. This perch may
be said to walk rather than wriggle, and it has been found
on low tree trunks.

Perhaps more generally known than the walking fishes are
those that leave the water and glide above its surface. If you
travel in tropical waters, such as those around Bermuda or
the West Indies, you frequently see these gliders in action.
Most expert of the group, the flying fish travel through the
air about three feet above the water at forty miles an hour;
they may go as far as four hundred yards at a stretch. All
the flying fish—they glide rather than fly—live in the
ocean, with the exception of one little butterfly fish from
Africa, which inhabits fresh water.

The sea horse, despite its name, is a fish. It is strictly a
swimming fish, but its method of swimming is amusingly
different. Children delight in seeing a group of them in a
public aquarium as they move vertically through the water
with an appearance of great dignity – head upright, fins at
the back. An onlooker is bound to laugh when one of them
rolls its eyes; for a sea horse can look forward with one eye
and gaze backward with the other at the same time. These
features by no means exhaust the eccentricities of this odd
fish. Its eggs are incubated in a pouch that belongs to the
male, not to the female. The female sea horse transfers her
eggs to the male's pouch as soon as they are produced, and
there they stay until they hatch.

Another unusual fish you may encounter at the seashore is
the little electric stargazer, which spends much of its time
buried up to its eyes in sand. If you happen to step on one,
its hiding place is instantly revealed: its ability to give an
electric shock is its means of defense. There are other fish,
larger than the stargazer, that are also equipped with
'batteries.' One of these is the electric catfish of Africa.
Another is the electric eel of South America, which uses its
powers of shock not only as a defense but also as a weapon
for securing food and possibly as a detection device.

Many sea creatures have relationships with each other which benefit both animals – a process called symbiosis. Vivid clownfish (left) gain protection from predators by living among the sea anemone's stinging tentacles, to which they are immune; by doing so they attract other fish within range of the anemone, which catches and eats them. The cleanerfish, apparently attacking a goatfish (below), is really eating harmful parasites which thrive on the larger fish. A cleaner shrimp (bottom) is doing the same service for a sea bream and getting its dinner at the same time. Fish learn to recognize these cleaning animals; sometimes they even seem to line up and wait for their services.

The Colorful Courtship of the Stickleback

For much of the year the three-spined stickleback is a dull, green fish that one would hardly notice. It moves around in shoals, and although the spines on its back make it a spiky mouthful, it is happy to hide from pike and perch among the weeds of its home, in ponds and rivers. In the spring, however, great changes of color and behavior occur. The males leave the shoals one by one to stake out claims to their own areas of the riverbed. At the same time they become brilliant shades of red. Each one defends its territory against all intruders, particularly other sticklebacks.

Once he feels that his tiny little kingdom is secure, the male fish builds a nest by digging a groove in the riverbed and filling it with strands of waterweed, bound together by special sticky mucus. By poking his head through and wriggling he makes a tunnel through the middle. When the nest is complete his colors become still brighter and he looks for a mate. If a female that is silver in color and swollen with eggs passes in her shoal, the male approaches and begins a spectacular courtship dance.

Darting, zigzagging, and falling through the water, he tries to catch her eye. Sometimes he succeeds only in scaring all the shoal away, but if he is lucky the female will follow him to the nest. He shows that she should enter it by lying on his side, wriggling his body and nudging the entrance of the nest (see right, above). The male pushes and butts her impatiently until she lays the eggs. He then drives her out of the nest and fertilizes them. He may tempt two, sometimes three more females to repeat the process, driving them away too, after mating. He then guards the eggs, fanning a current of water over them with his fins to make sure that they get enough oxygen and to prevent dirt and infection killing them. When seven or eight days have passed the eggs hatch and the father escorts the loose, unruly group of tiny babies. He is an attentive father. If any of them stray too far, he takes them in his mouth, returns to the group and spits them back into place unharmed.

After a fortnight or so, the young become able to form their own shoal and the male loses interest in them. At the same time he changes back to his normal dull colors. He is far less ready for a fight, and rejoins another shy, retiring shoal of adult fish among the shady weeds and rocks.

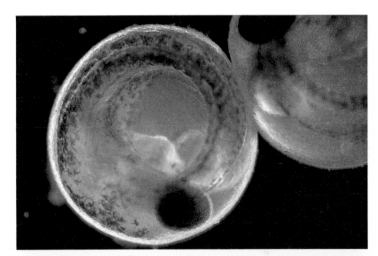

▽ A highly magnified picture of a developing stickleback egg shows the baby fish curled within and nearly ready to hatch. Quite soon after hatching (middle picture), the baby stickleback is almost ready to start feeding. By looking closely, one can see many starry black specks on its body. These are the cells with which the fish can change its color. They are shown through a microscope in the bottom picture. If the stickleback makes the cells smaller, it reduces the amount of black in its skin, allowing the red of another kind of cell to show through.

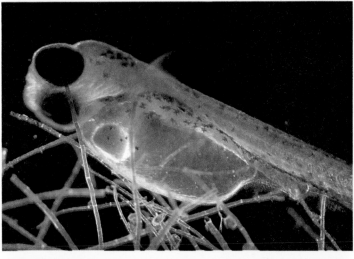

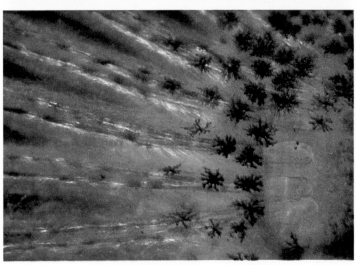

Bringing the River Home

A home aquarium may be a simple matter of keeping one or two goldfish or it may be a full-scale hobby involving a variety of fishes. Tropical and toy fishes are quite difficult to raise and keep, but the fishes that live in cold, fresh water (the goldfish is one of them) are easier. Furthermore, if you can set up a community of different types, all the drama of underwater life takes place within easy observation; there is probably no better way to acquaint the budding biologist with the facts of predation, life and death that occur in any animal environment. All of the fishes illustrated opposite can be caught with a net, small baited hook, or minnow trap in the waters of the countryside. The weeds can all be found wild. The tank illustrated is an ideal set-up, showing the possible range of species. Only with a very large tank and considerable experience could one keep all these species together.

There are two very good methods of catching tiny fish: the minnow trap and the drop-net. To make a minnow trap, take a wine bottle of the type with an indented, conical base. Carefully tap out the tip of the cone, then tie muslin over the neck. Attach two pieces of string so that the trap can be lowered on an even keel. Place the trap in a stream or pond. If there is a current the 'funnel' end should be downstream. In a surprisingly short time – particularly if baited with chopped worm and breadcrumbs – there will be minnows, sticklebacks and other species within the trap. A drop-net is simply a piece of netting or loose-woven cloth mounted on a hoop of wire, or an old bicycle wheel with the spokes removed. Two strings are laid across the diameter of the wheel at right angles to one another, and another string runs from where they cross, upwards. Baited at the center with a piece of fish, bread or other bait, it is lowered from a vantage point, such as a quay, into the water. It is then left awhile, then pulled up with a rapid, but even, pull. (This method also works well for seashore creatures of various kinds.)

The aquarium into which the catch will go should be as large as possible – a gallon of water per large fish is a good guideline. If a fish is subjected to a sudden change of temperature, it will die. Bring home the catch in a large supply of the water from which they were taken. Place each fish in a jar two-thirds full of this water, and float it on the surface of the aquarium water. After a few hours the temperature in the jar will be the same as that in the tank, and the fish can be rehoused.

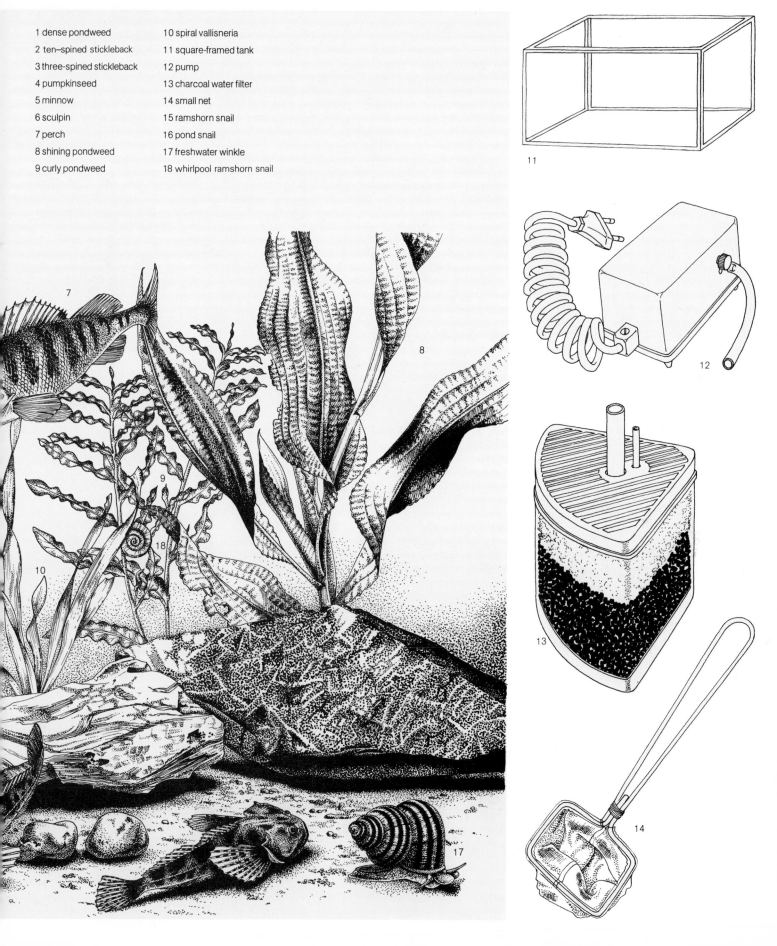

1 dense pondweed
2 ten–spined stickleback
3 three-spined stickleback
4 pumpkinseed
5 minnow
6 sculpin
7 perch
8 shining pondweed
9 curly pondweed
10 spiral vallisneria
11 square-framed tank
12 pump
13 charcoal water filter
14 small net
15 ramshorn snail
16 pond snail
17 freshwater winkle
18 whirlpool ramshorn snail

Snakes, Frogs, and Their Relatives

The chances are that snakes either fascinate you or arouse an intense dislike. Few people are neutral, and children are quick to adopt their parents' admiration or profound distaste for the crawling reptiles. However, some children are so fond of snakes that they will bring them home for pets regardless of how their families react to the creatures. One conscientious mother-said to me: 'How can I make myself like snakes? They revolt me, but my children are always bringing them home and have so much fun with them that I don't want to object.'

My suggestion was that she should not force herself to like snakes, but merely to try to understand them. Snakes are probably the victims of more erroneous beliefs than any other category of animals. Some popular misconceptions about snakes and the true facts about them:

1. False: All snakes are venomous. True: Most snakes are harmless.
2. False: A snake thrusts out its tongue as an act of hostility. True: A snake uses its tongue as a sensory organ to explore its surroundings.
3. False: Snakes have no fear of people and are continually on the lookout for victims. True: Most snakes do not display an aggressive disposition toward people; as soon as they sense a human, they creep away and hide if possible.
4. False: Snakes can sting as well as bite. True: No snake can inflict a sting.
5. False: Snakes have great hypnotic powers. True: Only the snake's unblinking stare, caused by its lack of movable eyelids, creates the impression that it is trying to hypnotize its victim.
6. False: Snakes spring from the ground to attack a victim. True: No snake jumps clear of the ground to strike.
7. False: Snakes are slimy. True: Snakes are completely covered with dry scales.
8. False: Snakes have yellow blood or no blood at all. True: The blood of a snake is red and practically the same as that of a mammal.

When you get to know the truth about snakes and understand why they behave as they do, you may find yourself regarding them with interest rather than horror. Indeed, once one has conquered a fear of snakes, an appreciation of their beauty is seldom far behind.

Reptiles Past and Present

Snakes are reptiles, a name scientists have given to a group of animals that also includes lizards, turtles, crocodiles and alligators. The name was derived from a Latin word that means 'creeping.' Millions of years ago reptiles were the most important animals on earth. Porpoiselike species lived in the ocean while batlike reptiles flew in the air. The land was dominated by reptiles, called dinosaurs. At first dinosaurs were no larger than rabbits; later species developed that were far bigger and heavier than the largest elephant of a later period. We do not know for certain the reasons why these creatures disappeared; changes in the earth's climate may have been part of the cause. Whatever the reasons, reptiles dwindled in species and in numbers, and warm-blooded mammals began to dominate the earth.

All reptiles are alike insofar as all are covered with scales or bony plates and are cold-blooded. (They derive their heat from external sources, whereas warm-blooded animals derive theirs from within their bodies.) Reptiles, however, vary greatly in the way they live and the places they inhabit. Many of them dwell only in regions where summer conditions prevail all year, but there are some snakes that adjust to a climate with extremes of heat and cold.

Although cold does not endanger a snake's life until the temperature reaches a few degrees below freezing, a noticeable drop in temperature is enough to cause sluggishness, and a sluggish snake does not have the energy to procure food. In cold climates hibernation in a well-sheltered rocky crevice or in the ground below the frost line is the best solution to the problem. Thus the snake is protected from a decrease in body temperature to a level that would cause death. The animal can survive hibernation without eating, provided it is in a healthy and well-fattened condition at the beginning of its long rest.

A Snake's Body

Many children, and many adults as well, think of a snake as a long tail attached to a head. This is far from true, there is a very efficient body between head and tail. It includes a stomach which is capable of amazing distension and digestive powers, a liver, kidneys and other organs. The snake's heart has only three chambers, whereas a mammal's heart has four.

Who would want this snake for a pet? Many people would, for it becomes sociable when well treated, and enjoys being picked up because of the warmth of its owner's hands. And it is not venomous! It is a species found throughout Europe, commonly known as a grass snake, although it has other local names. It is closely related to American water snakes—not, however, to the dangerous water moccasin.

If you scrutinize a snake's underside, you will see that the tail has a definite starting point. A distinctly enlarged scale sometimes divided into two overlapping parts covers the orifice through which wastes pass. This marks the beginning of the tail. The length of the tail differs according to the species.

There is another way of distinguishing the tail from the body in most snakes: on the undersurface of the body the scales are large, each of them extending across the whole body; whereas the scales on the underside of the tail are arranged in two columns. A zoologist dissecting a snake observes a still more obvious division of tail and body; the long series of ribs terminates where the ribless tail begins.

There are two reasons for the snake's fixed gaze: it has no movable eyelids; and its eyeballs are capable of only slight motion. This results in its stony stare and the false belief that snakes hypnotize their prey.

Although snakes have no ears, they might be said to have a sense of hearing since sounds are transmitted to them through ground vibrations. Tests have been made with cobras to illustrate this point. After the snakes' eyes were bound with adhesive tape, someone walked towards the animals. Immediately, they reared and faced the direction from which the footsteps were approaching. By contrast, the sounds made by blowing a bugle brought no response.

This inability to hear sounds transmitted through the air tends to disprove the snake charmer's claim that music charms serpents into dancing. The truth seems to be that the snakes merely follow the continuous movement of the musician's limbs as he plays his reed instrument, swaying rhythmically back and forth.

How Snakes Shed Their Skin

In the course of his summer wanderings, your child may be thrilled by the discovery of the discarded skin of a snake. If he visits a zoo, he may see how this molting takes place. The snake loses its lustrous appearance before shedding; its bright colors are dimmed. Even the eyes become milky. This continues for a week or two; then the snake's normal coloration returns and it is ready to molt. It finds a rough hard object and rubs its nose and chin against it until its skin breaks. Once the head is freed, the snake wriggles its body until the whole skin peels off, inside out.

Molting is necessary because the skin to which a snake's scales are attached cannot grow. After the skin has stretched as much as possible while the snake is growing, it must be discarded. A new layer of skin forms beneath the old one before molting takes place. There is no regular interval for shedding; it depends to a great extent on the age and vitality of the reptile. Young snakes shed more frequently than adults and individuals that are healthy more often than those that are not.

How Snakes Move

If you discover a snake on hard-packed soil, you will notice that it moves very slowly. Off this smooth surface – in grass or on rough ground – it will whisk out of sight with surprising swiftness.

By observing a captive snake, you will see the reason for this change in pace. When it is placed on a large piece of glass, the snake will slip and slide ineffectively, but if it is transferred to loose sand, it is immediately able to move forward. It progresses with sideways movements, keeping the full length of its body against the ground. You will observe that the creature leaves in its wake a series of slightly curved piles of sand; these are pivots the reptile has raised in pushing its body forward. A snake on rough grass will travel with even greater ease because each blade of grass serves as a pivot.

To produce this undulating movement – apparently its usual method of traveling – the snake depends largely on its muscles and its ribs which, in effect, are footless legs. The ribs are attached to the backbone as well as to the muscles and the slightly overlapping scales on the underpart.

When the muscles are moved forward, the scales are also carried forward. When the muscles are pulled back, the lower edges of the scales are pressed down. The scales catch against the roughness of the surface over which the snake is moving, and thus aid in pushing it forward. The snake does not move all muscles along its body at the same time; instead, it brings them forward gradually, and the scales move in waves using the rough spots for leverage.

These are just a few of the amazing animals that inhabited the earth between 150 and 70 million years ago. The pterodactyl (top left) was a huge flying reptile. Tyrannosaurus (top right) weighed about eight tons; it was a ferocious meat-eater, but the huge diplodocus (center) probably ate only plants. The tuatara (below), a smaller reptile, lived in prehistoric times and is still flourishing.

Pterodactyl

Tyrannosaurus

Diplodocus

Tuatara

109

The Private Life of Reptiles

Much of people's horror of snakes stems from a fear of the unknown, of creatures so different that they seem dangerous. It is perfectly true that some species are best avoided, but it is also true that in the majority of cases the snake itself will flee first to avoid contact. Indeed, it is a lucky explorer who manages to witness the events depicted on this page. Snakes and lizards live in a world where warmth and food are the first considerations, but evading many enemies—including man—is the second.

Snakes begin life as eggs. The eggs of some species hatch within the mother's body; others are laid and guarded; some are simply left in a warm place. The snakes that lay eggs usually choose such places as leaf litter, rotten tree stumps and logs, or warm farmyard manure heaps to incubate them. Those that guard are remarkably faithful to the clutch of eggs, leaving it only to visit a moist place to drink or cool off. One snake is recorded to have stayed with her eggs for three months. Some species, such as cobras, even make attempts to guard the young before they scatter. At hatching time, the baby snake uses a sharp 'egg tooth' at the tip of its snout to cut through the leathery shell of the egg and make its first, usually timid, entrance to the world.

As the snake grows, it sheds its skin at intervals. Sometimes it manages to do this in one unbroken piece, and a complete skin, perfect right down to the scales over the eyes, is a treasured find for any young naturalist. Just before the molt, the snake ceases feeding, its eyes become dull, and its temper gets very short. Usually finding some thorny or rough surface to help pull the old skin away, the snake relieves itself of what is obviously an uncomfortable covering and appears with its colors beautifully fresh and a healthy appetite. How many times a snake sheds its skin depends on many factors, not least the temperature: the hotter it is, the more often snakes molt.

Snakes defend themselves in some ways that do not involve poison: the majority of them do not even possess it. The hognose snake, for instance, pretends to be dangerous by spreading a cobralike hood—a very effective bluff from a totally harmless snake. If this fails, it rolls over to play dead, showing its stomach and remaining perfectly still —with occasional cautious peeps—until it is sure that the danger has passed.

◁ *Shedding the skin makes snakes notoriously ill-tempered. This African cobra has nearly finished ridding itself of its old and irritating covering, but is quick to rear in threat at the slightest intrusion.*

◁ ▽ *A harmless grass snake curls over its eggs to guard them. Only in very rare circumstances can a snake be said to brood eggs; since it is cold-blooded, it could lend them no warmth.*

▽ *As a last-resort defense measure, some harmless snakes play dead in the hope that the enemy will not be interested in a lifeless prey. This grass snake, however, has one more trick: it can exude a foul smelling liquid when handled roughly.*

▽ ▽ *The gila monster of Arizona and its cousin, the beaded lizard, are the world's only venomous lizards and are very rare.*

Wherever there are large numbers of snakes in Asia, snake charmers entertain the local villagers by handling large and sometimes dangerous snakes. The traditional music player who 'dances' with them is scarce, but street entertainers like this Nepali with his king cobra are quite commonplace. They are often cruel to their charges, forcing them to perform in the heat of the day when they would rather be resting under a cool rock.

There is another movement method that snakes occasionally employ: a snake will curve its body into an S form, using the tail as a curved anchor, and then straighten out again, pushing forward a little in the process.

Some desert snakes have developed a specialized method called sidewinding, which is practically indescribable; the body is apparently thrown into great loops and seems to be flowing sideways. Using these movements, a snake does not waste energy building pivots, yet it does not slip backward during its extraordinary progress.

The trails that snakes leave in sand or dust are just as revealing as mammal footprints. Not only do experts identify the type of snake by its trail, they can also tell the approximate rate of speed at which it was moving when the trail was made.

How Snakes Breed
It is often said that some snakes lay eggs while others bear living young; yet in fact all species reproduce by means of eggs. The so-called live-bearing female retains the eggs in her oviduct until the embryo is fully developed. When the offspring are released from her body, they are covered by a thin membrane, which soon bursts. About one-fourth of the known species of snakes give birth in this manner.

When a female of a species that does not develop the embryo in the oviduct is ready to deposit her eggs, she finds a sunny sandbank or rotting log in which to make a burrow. She lays her eggs there. The number, size and shape of the eggs depend on the species. Usually they are elliptical with flattened ends. When first laid, the eggs are covered with a moist and sticky skin, which gradually becomes tough and leathery. After they have been deposited they absorb water and therefore continue to expand until they have increased about one-third in size.

Projecting from the middle of the upper jaw of the fully developed embryo is an egg-tooth with which it slits the tough egg skin when it is ready to emerge. If you were able to rub your finger over its nose, you could feel this egg-tooth, which remains until the baby is about a week old. The young snake emerges from the egg; it is a perfectly formed snake.

How Snakes Kill
The horror that snakes arouse in many people may very well be evoked by snakes' methods of killing. A tiger's prey is just as dead as a snake's prey; yet constriction and poison somehow seem more sinister means of inflicting death than the mammals's fang and claw.

Snakes get their food in three different ways. In one method, which is the most primitive, the reptile seizes its prey by throwing its coils about the prey without constriction and then it swallows the victim alive. Constriction is a second method, suffocating the victim until its heart and lungs can no longer function properly. At one time it was believed that constrictors crushed the bones of their prey; we now know that this theory is erroneous. In fact, the snake merely tightens its coils each time the victim breathes out, effectively robbing it of air.

Poison is the third method of killing. There are several types of poisonous snakes. Those known as vipers and pit vipers, including adders, rattlesnakes, copperheads, water moccasins, bushmasters, and the tropical fer-de-lance, have the most effective poison apparatus. The fangs of these snakes are in the upper jaw, anchored in the bone; they can be moved forward for a strike. They are hinged at their bases, so when not in use, the fangs are folded back against the roof of the mouth.

As a child, you may have been told that the mere pressure of a snake's fangs against a solid substance brought forth the venom. It is not that simple. The snake has its poison supply in two sacs, one in either cheek. Each sac is connected to the fangs by a duct that runs under the eye and over the bone to which the fangs are attached. When the viper strikes, muscles that surround the poison sacs contract and force the venom through the ducts into the fangs, from which it flows to the wound the snake has inflicted.

Hearty Eaters
The ability of snakes to swallow objects larger than themselves is one of their most spectacular traits. The larger snakes, such as pythons or boas, sometimes devour a goat or small deer whole. Such a feat would be impossible without a number of special body features with which nature has provided them.

A Meal in a Mouthful

Cold-blooded animals such as snakes do not make their own body heat, but rely on warmth from the outside to keep their bodies at survival temperature. Most snakes move quite slowly and spend much of their time motionless, especially in colder weather. This lack of energy means that a snake cannot afford to be constantly on the hunt for food, so when it does eat, its meal is often remarkably large in proportion to its own body size. Its method of eating is uniquely adapted to deal with its huge but infrequent meals.

Most snakes kill their prey either by venom, using the sharp fangs in their mouths to inject the poison into the prey, or by constriction, winding their muscular coils tighter and tighter round the body of the prey until it has suffocated. Both types of snake, however, have the same method of swallowing their dead prey. Every snake has an extra hinge-bone at the back of each lower jaw, so that it can open its mouth at the back as well as the front, thus making an enormous gape. As well as this vertical extension, the two halves of the lower jaw in front can be stretched apart without breaking, since they are held together by flexible ligaments. As a result, the mouth expands to several times the body diameter.

The word 'swallowing' as we understand it does not really describe the way a snake takes in its meal; rather, it gradually pushes its extended jaws around the prey. Because its teeth point backward, they slide smoothly over the prey's body, but lock firmly against it if pushed in the other direction. Slowly but surely, the snake pushes one jaw forward a little, locks its teeth into the meal, and then pushes the other jaw a bit further. Once the prey has passed through the jaws, the snake's stomach expands to receive a meal which may take days or even weeks to digest. The stomach becomes so distended that it is sometimes possible to identify a snake's recent meal by the shape of its waistline!

This unique method of eating is demonstrated by the boomslang snake, shown here enjoying a favorite meal of chameleon. The boomslang (its name means 'tree snake' in Afrikaans) is one of the most dangerous of poisonous snakes. Its venom, delivered through its rear teeth, acts both on the blood and the nervous system of the prey and is fatal in even tiny quantities.

◁ △ This African boomslang snake has just killed a chameleon. Carefully the snake 'tastes' its prey by flickering its sensitive tongue near the chameleon, making sure that it is dead and can be eaten.

◁ ◁ The boomslang opens its mouth wide and takes a firm grip on the head of the prey. The snake does not chew its food, but uses its backward-pointing teeth as levers to push the food gradually into its mouth.

△ By now the chameleon is half way down the throat of the snake, stretching its jaws and skin to double their normal size. When the food is eaten, the boomslang will sleep for a few days while its stomach digests the giant meal it has just taken in.

◁ A common garter snake pulls its prey, a small dace, from the water onto a soft, slippery layer of floating algae. Like many other land snakes, it can swim very well.

A good example of these special features is the jaw. An extra bone hinges the upper jaw to the lower, allowing them to be spread far apart. Also, the lower jawbones are held together only by elastic ligaments, and they can separate at the chin to further increase the size of the mouth. The teeth point backward and thus present no obstacle to objects taken into the mouth. Even the snake's sides are adapted to the task. They have great elasticity and can stretch to many times their normal dimensions.

Despite all these special features, you might still expect a snake to choke to death swallowing anything large enough to force its jawbones wide apart. The snake overcomes this possibility by extending a portion of its windpipe forward, even a few inches beyond its open mouth if necessary. By this means it can breath during the slow process of forcing down a meal that seems far too big for its size. Some species of snakes can live on three or four big meals a year; others may eat a moderate meal every week or ten days.

Vipers and Pit-Vipers

A parent is likely to be asked more questions about venomous snakes than about those that do not harm or kill victims with poison. In the Old World the most common viper is the European viper, known also as the adder. Members of the species may grow to a length of almost thirty inches, but even a full bite from one of them is not likely to be fatal to a person. However, a small dose injected into a lizard or a mouse will probably kill the small mammal in a few minutes. What distinguishes the pit viper from a true viper is a small pit in its face. It is a special sense organ which enables the snake to detect warm-blooded prey.

Rattles – How They Grow and Are Used

Rattlesnakes arouse a child's curiosity for several reasons. How does the tip of the tail turn into a rattle? Why do some snakes have rattles? How is the rattle used? The rattle is made up of a series of horny sections on the end of the spinal column. They are loosely interlocked, and when the snake vibrates its tail, they click against each other. Many other kinds of snakes also vibrate their tails, and if they are lying among dead leaves, the rustling sounds somewhat resemble a rattle. However, the rattlesnake's vibration is distinctive. It is a half-metallic, half-insectlike sound, comparable to the dull buzz of the bumblebee.

At birth a rattler has a bulbous swelling at the tip of its tail. When the snake molts, the tail end of its old skin cannot be pulled over this enlargement; thus it remains, forming the beginning of a rattle. As successive molts take place, the tip of the skin that cannot be shed forms an additional segment or ring. The rings form around a bone known as the shaker, made up of the last seven or eight vertebrae, which fuse together soon after the snake is born.

The old theory that a ring is added each year has been disproved. Sometimes several molts take place in a year and rings are added; it is also possible for the snake to molt without a new ring being created. This irregularity, as well as the fact that rings are often broken from the end, makes it impossible to determine a snake's age by the number of rings. If a rattle in unbroken, however, you may approximate the age by allowing one year for every two rings.

Many snakes have the habit of vibrating the tip of the tail when they are excited, but the rattler is the only snake equipped with a noisemaker. We do not entirely understand the purpose of the rattle. The common belief that this reptile always rattles before striking is no longer credited. Apparently it does use its rattle, as a rule, to try to frighten away enemies dangerous to its own safety. As for the theory of warning prospective prey, some observers believe that this snake sounds its rattle to startle birds, rabbits, or other potential victims into momentary inactivity, thus gaining time for a strike. Other people claim that it never rattles before attacking. There are many reports of rattlers that never rattled at any time and habitually struck both food and potential enemy without warning.

There are no less than fifteen species of rattlesnakes in the United States, and they live in many localities. The diamondback of the Southeast frequents neighborhoods where water is plentiful; the timber rattlesnake lives in woodland mountain regions; the prairie rattlesnake haunts the Great Plains of the West.

The Good-Natured Boa

Among the most spectacular of snakes is the boa constrictor, a large reptile of South America that can reach a length of eighteen feet. It is quite hardy in captivity, and many specimens are good-natured and easily fed with birds and

◁ Vipers and pit vipers have the most highly developed venom apparatus in snakes; their fangs are much enlarged and are folded back in the mouth when not in use. They are erected only when a strike is made. Pit vipers have additional equipment in a small pit on the face; this is a special sense organ with which they can detect warm-blooded prey. Rattlesnakes (pit vipers) are considered the highest form of snakes' evolution.

▽ Best known of the vipers is the common European viper, also called the adder. Found not only in Europe, it ranges also across northern Asia. Its venom is effective for obtaining its normal food of mice and other small animals, but is not deadly to a healthy adult person. The snake is variable in coloration, sometimes being entirely black but more usually dark gray with zigzag markings along the back and tail. An entirely harmless reptile called the grass snake is frequently mistaken for the common adder, even though the grass snake has a conspicuous yellow collar.

117

▷ *Although cobras are deadly snakes, mongooses have no fear of them. Here a family group tease a cobra, tempting it to strike, and leap aside at the last moment (as in the bottom picture), trying to ambush it from below a bank. In the end, worn out by constant efforts to slay its agile enemies, the cobra slowed down and was easily killed and eaten.*

small mammals. Although some South American Indians dread the boa and believe it to be poisonous, it is not. It kills its prey by constriction. As a rule the boa seems eager to keep away from humans, but it will occasionally appear in a native village, apparently attracted by domestic fowl. Still greater in size than the boa constrictor is a water boa known as the anaconda, native to the river valleys of northern South America. Reliable records show that this species sometimes attains a length of twenty-eight feet. The anaconda is the largest snake in the New World.

Pythons and Cobras

Among the most fearsome-looking reptiles are pythons, native to Asia and Africa. There are giants among them; a twenty-five-foot Indian python may weigh more than two hundred pounds; the reticulated python, not quite so thick in body, may be nearly thirty feet long. The large pythons eat a variety of animals, but they have a preference for fairly large mammals.

Snake charmers frequently use relatively small specimens of the rock python in their acts, since these snakes become very docile in captivity. Nevertheless, there is always some danger. If the snake accidentally throws a complete coil about the body of the performer, it will begin to constrict and throw new coils. If the snake charmer does not quickly straighten out the reptile, he is in real danger of strangulation. Anyone who closely watches a snake charmer with a python or a boa will observe that every movement of his hands and arms is to prevent the snake from forming a coil.

A child who has been reading colorful stories about the Orient in which cobras are presented as sinister creatures may be disappointed if he sees this snake in a zoo. When it is not excited, it looks quite commonplace. Alarmed or angry, it presents a far different picture, weaving its raised head back and forth with its hood erect. The hood is actually only the skin of the neck stretched taut. The cobra has a series of ribs on the sides of the vertebrae of the neck, and when it becomes excited, it uses powerful muscles to draw these ribs forward, thus stretching its skin and forcing the scales wide apart.

Seen from the back when its hood is spread, the Indian Cobra gives the impression of having eyes on top of its head.

Actually what the observer sees are merely markings; the eyes are at the sides of the head, which are not readily visible when the hood is open. It is a mistake to think that cobras can be identified merely by the erection of a hood; other snakes – such as the harmless hognose snake – possess the same ability.

While people most frequently think of India as the home of cobras, these snakes are also found in Africa. The king cobra, which may grow to a length of eighteen feet, is the largest venomous snake known. It is very aggressive and its poison is deadly. The common Indian cobra rarely attains a length of more than six feet.

The Harmless Snakes

Most types of snakes in the world today are entirely harmless as concerns people, or their poison is not potent enough to create serious danger for a person. They secure prey in various ways. For example, racers and whipsnakes, which abound around the world, pin a small mammal to the ground with part of the body, at same time moving their jaws toward the creature's head, ready for a big gulp. Some nonvenomous snakes, such as the garter snakes of North America, depend mainly on earthworms for food, although they also eat other small animals that come their way. Garter snakes rarely grow longer than thirty inches. Their main body color may be olive, brown, or black. There is usually a stripe of yellow, green, or whitish hue down the center of the back. Along each side is a similar stripe, subdued in tone, which sometimes is broken up into spots. The underside is greenish white or yellow. You are most likely to come upon garter snakes in summer along the banks and edges of streams. In the fall they gather on rocky ledges or stony hillsides, where each one will find a crevice or make a burrow, which may extend more than a yard underground, and will sleep through the cold weather.

Hognose snakes are completely without venom, yet they can act in a way that makes them appear very frightening. When one is startled it swells its body, flattens its neck in the manner of a cobra, and hisses viciously. This dramatic act has earned it such names as spreading adder and blowing viper. Its appropriate popular name of hognose is the result of a hard trowel-shaped shield over its nose with which it can root out toads in loose soil.

The giant tortoises of the Galápagos Islands in the Pacific may reach over two feet high and weigh two or three hundred pounds. They were first discovered by pirates, who soon found that these gentle giants were a fine source of meat for long voyages. Later on, whaling and sealing ships would stop at the islands and take thousands of tortoises on board. At the same time, human visitors to the island brought such animals as dogs and rats, which ate the tortoise eggs and young; imported goats and donkeys ate the tortoises' plant food. As a result, these huge but harmless creatures are now in danger of becoming extinct.

Sea turtles usually are thought of as bulky giants, weighing hundreds of pounds. Though there are some that fit this description, other species are considerably smaller. The smallest of all is the ridley. Those of the Atlantic Ocean on the average grow shells no longer than about twenty-four inches; there is a larger form in the Pacific. Although the ridley and other turtles produce large numbers of eggs, many of the young do not survive; they are eaten by gulls and crabs. Females move inland to lay their eggs so the young, when hatched, may travel some distance to reach water. The young explorer here is planning to help some babies by moving them to the ocean's edge.

The Remarkable King Snakes

King snakes are often called cannibals because they are noted for attacking and eating other snakes. They eat even venomous species, suffering no ill effects from the victim's poison taken into their system. Many battles between a king snake and a rattler have been described by observers and the 'king' snake is usually the winner. This snake (there are fourteen species of king snakes found throughout the United States) is closely related to the smooth snake of Europe (found from Scandinavia to Greece and on the British Isles). The smooth snakes rarely are longer than two feet; king snakes may attain six. The smooth snake also has a taste for reptiles: it is usually found over old growths of heather, the home of its favorite prey, the sand lizard.

Also related to king snakes is the so-called milk snake, a reptile that is the subject of a fantastic nature myth, which tells of the milk snake actually milking cows. Not only is this feat physically impossible, but also no milk snake in captivity was ever persuaded to drink milk. The snake's presence in barns is explained by its liking for mice and rats. Thus instead of a menace the milk snake is an ally of the farmer, hunting some of his worst pests.

Care and Caution

Children who go fishing are likely to encounter a water snake. This dingy brown reptile haunts dams, wharves, rocks, and bushes near water. Because of its protective colors, it may escape notice until it moves suddenly. In certain areas of the United States, particularly from southern Virginia to Florida, one must be extremely cautious about snakes that appear to be water snakes; the deadly water moccasins, which superficially resemble harmless water snakes, live in those regions.

The inside of a water moccasin's mouth is whitish in color. Unlike many snakes, which attempt a hurried retreat when disturbed, this species aggressively tries to fight off an intruder in its territory.

Even the common European water snake and the brown snake of the United States inflate their bodies, flatten their heads, and strike out viciously when frightened. However, a bite from either variety is only mildly painful; their venom is not potent.

Unlike tortoises, the hind feet of water
turtles are webbed between the toes to help
them swim. They can stay underwater for
several minutes before they must surface for
air (below). Most turtles are quite small, but
the diamondback terrapin of the southern
states may reach eight inches in length
and was once considered very good to eat.

Tortoises and turtles are popular pets and are certainly among the easiest reptiles to keep in the home. A tortoise can be kept in a hut or cage in the garden, but should be watched when it is allowed out for a walk (top) as it may move faster than expected and may get lost in the bushes. Turtles such as the red-eared terrapin (center) spend much of their natural life in fresh water, so in captivity they must be kept in a tank containing water in which to swim (bottom) as well as rocks and plants.

A child who wishes to collect snakes should be well coached in safety rules. Of prime importance is a knowledge of the character of the snakes in your locality. If there are poisonous species among them, it is essential to distinguish them from the harmless ones. Collecting poisonous species should be left to the experts.

If you accidentally come upon a snake, do not be frightened; bear in mind that the snake is doubtless just as eager to get away as you are. Remember that snakes do not have powers of hypnotism. This has been proved many times by experiments in which birds, guinea pigs and other animals were placed in cages with a snake; these small animals acted entirely unconcerned about their reptile companion. If you think of a snake as simply another animal it will be easy to move away quietly and calmly if you wish.

Anyone actively interested in snake collecting ought to be thoroughly familiar with first aid for a poisonous snake bite; a snake-bite kit is a necessity on field trips if there are poisonous species in the vicinity.

Turtles

Of all reptile pets, turtles are probably the most popular. Your child is quite apt to bring one home from camp or from an outing to ponds or fields. They are also easily obtained in pet or novelty stores. Unfortunately thousands of turtles are entrusted to the care of people who understand little about their way of life.

If your child has a turtle, you and he will certainly want to know more about it. And even if you don't have a turtle pet, you will agree that they are fascinating animals, to watch and study. Turtles are the oldest type of living reptiles; they are traced back many millions of years – they are even older than the dinosaurs.

At times a turtle may give the impression of an inanimate piece of armor. When it is uncertain of its surroundings, it cautiously keeps every part of its body under its hard shell. Once it feels safe, however, it will project its snakelike head from the front of its shell and poke out its pointed tail from the rear and its two wide legs at each side. Then you will notice that even the soft body is covered with rough coarse skin and often with many scales.

The chameleon uses its long, sticky-tipped tongue to catch insects for food. After careful stalking (top left), it makes one try for a grasshopper–and misses. At the next attempt, it is more successful (top right) and is retrieving the catch. The closeup on the bottom shows the lizard with its meal and also highlights its colors.

You will appreciate the effectiveness of this protective covering when you realize that turtles have survived countless centuries with no means of fighting off innumerable larger animals. Their success is strictly due to such defensive equipment.

The upper shell (the carapace) varies in shape, depending on the species of turtle. This shell is attached to the turtle's backbone. In a few species it is quite flat, in others it is rounded. The lower shell (the plastron) also varies in shape and size; it is attached to the breastbone. The size and color of a turtle's body also varies greatly from one species to another. Oddities include the tail of the snapping turtle, which bears a saw-toothed armor of plates, and the front and rear 'trapdoors' of the box turtle, which can be pulled against the carapace to enclose the body completely. A child may wonder how a creature so completely encased manages to breath. The turtle's shoulder and hip bones do most of the work in contracting and expanding the lungs. The constant pulsation observable on the throat is caused by air being swallowed.

Like snakes, turtles lack movable eyelids. However, turtles have a protective membrane, which comes up from the lower edge to cover the eye. Some species have nostrils no larger than pinholes; thus their poor sense of smell is not surprising. Others, better equipped, have a keen sense of smell. A turtle has no real teeth, but its mouth has sawlike edges. It does not chew food but simply tears it to pieces.

The mud turtle and the musk turtle are water dwellers; the only time they come to shore is to deposit their eggs. They find their food in muddy bottoms of ponds and streams and eat only underwater. The musk turtle, which has two broad yellow stripes on either side of its head, gives off a strong odor when it is handled. The head of the mud turtle is ornamented with greenish yellow spots.

In damp woods you may find a wood tortoise. Its upper shell is made up of many plates ornamented with concentric ridges. With the exception of the top, the head and the limbs, the color of all the fleshy parts is brick red. It thrives in captivity and will soon learn to accept food from your fingers. Tender vegetables, berries, insects and chopped meat make up an acceptable diet.

Another turtle that you can tame with satisfactory results is the spotted turtle, found in many ponds and marshy streams. Its black upper shell is decorated with numerous spots. The spotted turtle enjoys perching on a log for long stretches of time, but it feeds underwater. Another turtle– often called the painted terrapin – is recognized by the red mottled border of its shell. This is a good aquarium pet, but it is much too aggressive to be kept with other creatures.

Alligators and Crocodiles
These giant reptiles are usually seen only in zoos or on reptile farms. People who enjoy a sense of danger may watch them in safety, at the same time recalling the gruesome stories about their behavior in the wilds. Certainly much has been related about man-eating crocodiles to give them a frightening reputation and to some extent the reputation is well deserved. A very large crocodile in search of food along a riverbank may grab an antelope or deer, pull it beneath the water's surface and then twist and roll the body while tearing it to pieces. Although a person in a similar position could suffer the same fate, crocodiles are not sinister monsters that deliberately prey on people.

Crocodiles and alligators change their diet during their growing years. When very young they consume insects and shellfish. Later they depend largely on fish. As adults, their prey includes not only mammals but also birds, they even prey on young crocodiles and alligators.

A question commonly asked by children is 'How can you tell the difference between an alligator and a crocodile?' A close look will decidedly reveal a definite difference in the shape of the snout. The alligator's snout is wide and more rounded than that of the crocodile. There is also a difference in the teeth. In the case of the crocodile, the fourth tooth on either side of its lower jaw fits into notches on the outside of the upper jaw so that even when its mouth is closed, the fangs show. The effect gives the crocodile a more fierce and belligerent appearance than the alligator. Nor are these looks deceiving, for generally alligators are timid and try to escape an encounter with human beings, whereas crocodiles are sullen and ferocious by turns. At a zoo a keeper will step among alligators while cleaning their pool, but he does not take these chances with the crocodiles.

Both alligators and crocodiles spend much of their time in water. Their nostrils, located on top of little bumps at the end of the snout, take in air as the animals float just under the surface of the water. They can even feed underwater by shutting off the food tube from the tube that guides the air to the lungs.

Unlike most reptiles, alligators and crocodiles are able to make noises through their mouths. The young produce a curious grunting sound, while the bellowing of the old bulls may be heard a mile away.

Chameleons and Other Lizards

If you take a casual look at a lizard, it will remind you of a snake. Outwardly there is not much difference between them, except that most lizards have legs while snakes do not. Nevertheless a legless lizard is still a lizard, not a snake. One observable difference between the two is in the structure of the lower jawbone. In all snakes the lower jaw is made up of two bones joined at the chin by a more or less flexible ligament. The lizard also has a lower jawbone on either side, but these are attached firmly at the center of the chin, limiting the size of prey it can tackle. There is another visible difference. Lizards generally have movable eyelids, something which no snake possesses.

At a fair or circus boys and girls frequently buy a little lizard for a souvenir, which they are told is a chameleon. There is a type of lizard often called the American chameleon, which, like a true chameleon, has the ability to change color frequently; it is this American lizard that is usually peddled at amusement places.

Chameleons do, to a great extent, harmonize with the foliage on which they rest, but several factors may be involved. Light and temperature can be important influences in color change. So can excitement and fright. Not only does the tone of the body change, but also strange patterns come and go on the skin. How does this happen? To put it briefly: beneath the reptile's skin are a number of tiny branched cells containing pigment of various colors. Whenever the chameleon contracts or expands these branches, the position of the pigments is changed. Those that travel to the surface of the skin are partly responsible for the various colors the animal takes on.

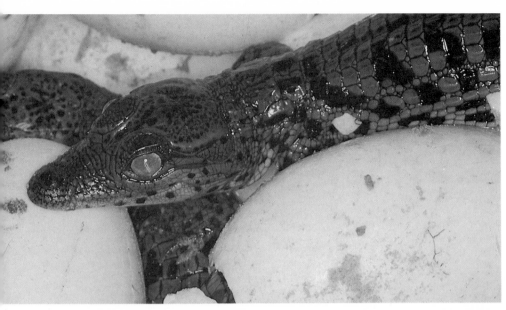

Crocodiles and alligators are extremely similar. The most noticeable difference is that when an alligator closes its mouth, its upper teeth fit outside its lower ones; the teeth of the crocodile are usually visible, especially the two large teeth at the corners of its lower jaw (as in the Nile crocodile, far left). Alligators and crocodiles hatch out of eggs (left), and at first they feed on insects and small animals near the waterside. As they grow larger they will eat almost any animals found in or near their riverside homes, such as fish, snakes, frogs, and rats. Some types of crocodiles and alligators grow very large, such as the Mississippi alligator (below) which has a maximum recorded length of over 14 feet. Large specimens are rare nowadays, however, as these animals have been widely killed for the sake of their hides.

Frogs occur in many surprising shapes, sizes, and colors, from the big burly bullfrogs through the delicately camouflaged edible frogs (opposite, top) to the tiny and acrobatic tree frogs (opposite, bottom), which perform apparently impossible gymnastics among the trees and twigs. There can be few, however, that match the bright colors of the tiny frogs below, which come from the tropical rain forests of South America.

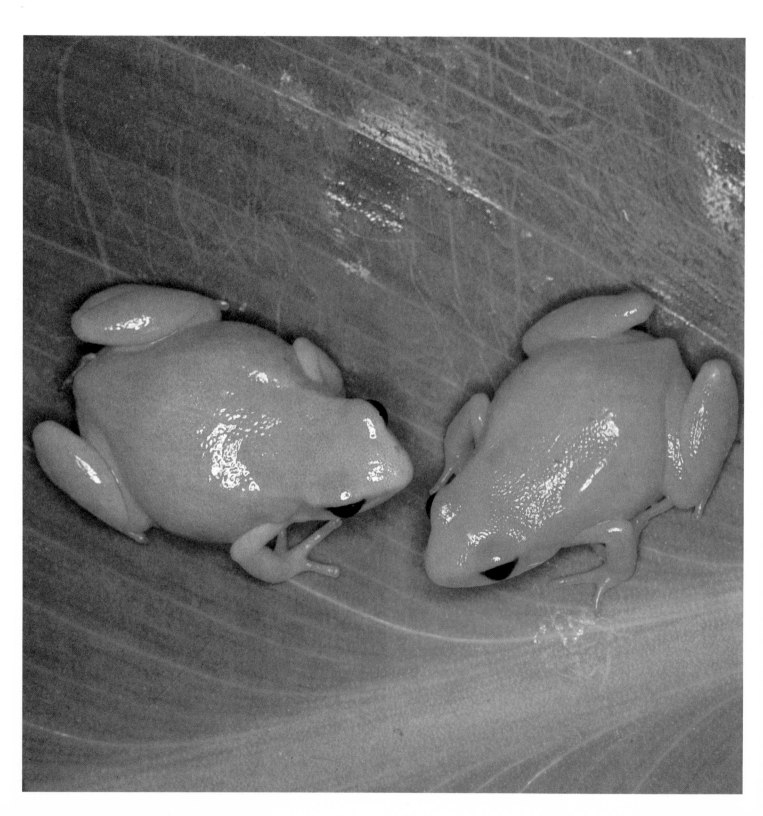

The true chameleon has a versatility that can be positively startling. It can roll one eye upward while the other rolls down, or turn one eye forward and the other backward. Its tongue is a kind of secret weapon that shoots out of its mouth to a distance of seven or eight inches. On its sticky tip the chameleon snares insects, which appeared to be well out of harm's way.

Amphibians Lead a Double Life

Most creatures of the earth are at home either in water or on land; they are not dependent on both realms. But this is not true of amphibians, who lead a double life. In some respects amphibians are like fish; they lay their eggs in water. In other ways they are like reptiles: the adults live on dry land. They are considered a connecting link between fish and reptiles. Frogs, toads, newts and salamanders are the best known of the amphibians. Salamanders are often mistaken for reptiles because they closely resemble lizards. However, a salamander is distinguished by smooth skin that is often damp; a lizard is covered with scales. The skin of certain salamanders is quite rough and dry, but it is never covered with scales. Salamanders do not have claws; lizards do. Sometimes salamanders are called newts, and some of these are named for individual features. An example is the spectacled newt of Italy, with markings around its eyes that suggest spectacles.

We find a greater variety, however, among frogs and toads. Toads vary in size from giants such as an African species more than nine and a half inches long – which can eat several mice at a single meal – to a dwarf species of South America only an inch in length. Frogs in North America vary from the great bullfrog, which often measures as much as eight inches, to a tree frog commonly known as the peeper, whose length is no more than an inch.

From Egg to Tadpole

Frog eggs are laid in a transparent protective jelly, the shape of the jelly mass being one of the clues to the species. The eggs of the leopard frog, for example, are in masses in the form of a flat-ended sphere; those of the wood frog are in rounded masses.

In the earliest stages of an egg's development a single cell gradually divides into many cells: this development can be followed only with the aid of a magnifying glass. When the embryo begins to lengthen, then it can be easily seen with the naked eye. After five or six days the embryo has the form of a tadpole, although it is still inside the jelly mass. About the ninth day the tadpole breaks loose from its protective covering.

At first the tadpole is shapeless, and the only way to determine head from tail is to observe the direction in which it swims – the head naturally goes first. But soon the head grows larger. Instead of a mouth the tadpole has a 'V'-shaped raised sucker by which it attaches itself to water weeds. Later this gives way to a small round mouth which has horny jaws. As the tadpole grows, the mouth becomes wider and larger.

By observing a tadpole, you will see little tassel-like gills that grow on either side of the throat. Blood passing through the gills is purified through contact with the oxygen in the water. Later the feathery gills disappear; a membrane grows down over them and they function inside the body rather than outside. Water taken in through the nostrils passes through an opening in the throat, over the gills and out through a little opening, or breathing pore, at the left side of the body. This breathing pore may easily be seen in larger tadpoles.

A tadpole's flat tail, bordered by a fin, is a valuable swimming aid. But in a matter of weeks the first sign of legs foreshadows the decline of the tail's usefulness. The hind legs appear first; they are mere bumps but soon push out completely with five webbed toes. Meanwhile the front legs show just in back of the head, the left leg pushing out through the breathing pore. The front feet have only four toes apiece and are not webbed; they are used for balancing, whereas the back feet serve for thrusting forward. While these changes are taking place, the tail is being slowly absorbed by the body.

Young frogs do not always wait for the completion of their adult form before venturing onto land. In late spring or early summer you may see one hopping about still showing its stumpy little tail. From then on the frog is primarily a land animal, although the members of most species stay near water.

Toads – Fiction and Fact

Although most children delight in catching frogs, many hesitate to touch a toad. They have heard the popular myth that a toad is sure to produce warts on a hand that touches it. While this much-maligned amphibian does have warts on its back, it has no power to transfer them. The so-called warts are really glands that secrete a disagreeable-tasting substance when the toad is seized by a hungry enemy. These protective features are successful in some cases, but many toads become victims of some species of snakes as well as some other animals.

Unlike the slippery, slimy frog, the toad has a perfectly dry skin. It is cold to the touch because toads, like all amphibians, are cold-blooded. Though the toad sheds its skin periodically, it is promptly swallowed by the toad itself. A toad's skin is very absorbent. When the animal is thirsty, it does not drink through its mouth; it stretches out in shallow water and absorbs moisture through its skin. If pools are not available and if the atmosphere is dry, the toad will die in a short period of time. The toad's breathing technique is also curious. You may notice a steady pulsation in the throat, which is the result of its swallowing air. Lacking ribs, it cannot inflate its chest to draw air into its lungs, so it pumps regularly with its throat.

Protective coloration in toads and frogs is specialized to blend with the surroundings. A toad also has another way of becoming inconspicuous. Instead of squatting where it can easily be seen, it kicks backward into soft ground, scooping until its body is covered with earth. At the approach of an enemy the toad quickly jerks its head back letting earth tumble over its head as well. A threatened toad may also flatten out its body and when actually trapped, it will play dead.

Toads are rarely out in the open during the daytime; therefore a child's best chance to observe their habits is to keep one as a pet. They go abroad mostly at night, hunting for slugs, worms, and insects in cool damp places. In suburban areas you may discover one under a porch or dug in under a sidewalk. In the fall they burrow deep into the ground to hibernate. When they awaken in the spring, they make their way to a pond to breed and lay their eggs. The same pond is used year after year.

◁ A walk along a woodland path or country road shortly after a spring rain offers a good opportunity to see some of the little amphibians called salamanders. Often they are mistakenly thought to be lizards, which they resemble. However, a salamander's skin is never scale-covered as is the skin of a lizard, and it has no claws. In addition to small salamanders of subdued coloring, there are spectacular species, like this European fire salamander.

Many salamanders can exude an irritating secretion from glands on their head. The fire salamander has this ability; although its secretion can produce considerable discomfort, the effect is far from fatal. Nevertheless, for centuries its reputation as a deadly poisonous animal has been wide-spread. Alpine newts of Europe and America (above) are also colorful and have a mild poison to use defensively.

Exotic Zoo Animals

▷ Orangutans are in dire need of protection to prevent their becoming extinct. Not only are their homelands in the forests of Borneo and Sumatra being taken over by lumber industries, but illegal capture of young ones continues; usually a collector shoots a mother orang so her baby may be more easily taken. Here a mother and young are thriving in a zoo.

▽ African mountain gorillas, too, are being protected in zoos, but this baby did not have a capable mother and was cared for in a nursery until it could fend for itself.
▽ ▽ Apes need activity, as with these special gym bars.

Visiting a zoo can be exciting and educational for the whole family, but it must be the *right kind* of zoo. The qualification is important because unfortunately there are still some zoos where large animals are confined to small areas, with no opportunity for exercise, and little attention is given to the well-being of the creatures exhibited. In recent years zoo conditions have been changing for the better, and now some of the great zoos of the world are helping to save a number of endangered species from extinction as well as providing their animals with good care. They also provide adequate space, often closely reproducing the natural habitat of each species.

The pioneer in this enlightened method of exhibiting wild animals was Carl Hagenbeck, who opened his own zoo in Hamburg, Germany, in 1907. The first visitors to the zoo were amazed to discover that the usual cages and bars were missing; the animals gave the appearance of living in freedom. Hagenbeck also proved for the first time that many animals from tropical climates could enjoy the outdoors in European winters, and he showed how the captives could be handled with love and understanding rather than with harsh treatment. Hagenbeck's innovations soon began to influence other zoos, and new concepts for exhibition were accepted.

All too often a zoo cannot make improvements because of lack of funds and limited space. However, enlightened directors and curators of modern zoos no longer aim to have the greatest possible variety of animals. Instead, the goals are to provide homes for creatures in danger of becoming extinct, to present them to the public in attractive settings, and to stimulate an interest in the conservation of wildlife.

All children do not have the same zoo favorites, but there are some animals that are outstandingly popular with almost everyone. Among these are the sea lions with their graceful diving, their awkward waddling, their hoarse yawps and deadpan horseplay; the acrobatic monkeys; the huge elephants with their fantastic trunks; the tigers and leopards with their sleek grace.

Apes – Great and Small
Monkeys and apes offer, besides amusement, endless opportunity for observation. The anatomical differences

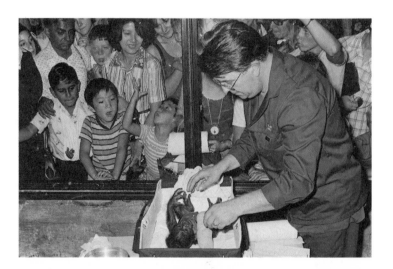

between the two groups are not easily discernible, but one noticeable difference is in the arm movements: apes have long, free-swinging arms, which can reach out in any direction, whereas a monkey's limbs move mostly forward and back, as when walking and running. The relative proportions of the body also differ. An ape's body is short, wide and shallow – a monkey's tends to be long, narrow and deep.

The four classes of apes vary in size from the giant gorilla to the gibbon – smallest of all – with chimpanzees and orangutans in between. Gibbons are by far the most active and most monkeylike in their behavior. In their natural habitat they spend most of their time among tree branches.

Gorillas gradually have been winning the admiration and respect they deserve. For many years they were looked upon as monsters – the villains of many adventure stories. But since scientists, beginning with George Schaller in 1959, actually lived among gorillas in the African forests, we can see them in a different light. Actually, they are shy and gentle, acting otherwise only when forced into unnatural surroundings with no space in which to make use of their natural energies. Enlightened zoos now try to provide them with roomy enclosures and branches and other objects with which to work and play. Some zoos even provide television for the gorilla's entertainment.

Chimpanzees are widely known as show-business characters, but at a zoo you are not as likely to see them in the role of trained performers. Nevertheless they are fascinating to watch simply being themselves. They have been rated as the most intelligent of the apes.

The Lively Monkeys
Monkeys are likely to be seen to better advantage than apes at most zoos because they are not as inhibited in captivity and consequently behave naturally in family groups. You may see rhesus monkeys chasing each other and hear them chattering and sometimes screaming. You may watch a woolly spider monkey with its feet attached to one branch and its prehensile tail holding on to another, swinging gently back and forth.

The presence of a prehensile tail is a distinguishing feature among monkeys. The prehensile tail, which can be used as an extra hand for grasping and holding, is not found on any of the Old World species. With a few exceptions, New World monkeys do have prehensile tails. Some species of monkeys have no tails at all.

As you learn more about monkeys and apes, you will find it rewarding to look for some prosimians, or the so-called half monkeys. This kind of animal developed some time before true monkeys began to inhabit the earth. A number of zoos have excellent exhibits of lemurs, which are among the most attractive and interesting of the half monkeys.

Elephants – Largest of Land Mammals
Elephants at the zoo are particularly fascinating because often we are allowed to feed them and thus see in action the amazing trunk, which serves them as arm, hand, and fingers. The size and muscular strength of an elephant's trunk make it possible for it to carry heavy objects.

The fingerlike tabs that project from the end of the trunk enable it to pick up an object as small as a peanut and swing it through a great arc into his mouth. At the end of an African elephant's trunk there are two tabs of about equal length. An Indian elephant has only one tab. Elephants of Africa and India can also be distinguished by size. As a rule the African species grow considerably larger than the Indian species, and their ears are much larger.

In the jungles of West Africa, however, there are elephants that are an exception to this rule. Since they average considerably less in size than most African elephants, they are described as pygmies or dwarfs.

Indian elephants are far more common in zoos and circuses than the African species; Indian elephants are obtained more easily and can be trained more rapidly. For thousands of years the natives of eastern India have been skilled in the training of elephants, and this skill has been handed down from father to son. An important factor in their success lies in the use of the human voice: the trainer first wins his charge's trust by softly chanting what is known as elephant song, after which he bribes the beast with its favorite foods. Wild elephants eat leaves and grass, but they relish sweet fruits and other dainties. In the zoo they are fed mostly on hay and grain.

An artist's portrayal of a mountain gorilla emphasizes its long tremendously powerful arms and awesome face. When gorillas were first encountered in Africa by Europeans, they were thought to be as ferocious as they looked and were regarded with terror. Recent studies have changed this impression. Gorillas are known to lead peaceful lives; such acts as chest-beating are largely a show to intimidate enemies.

HELMUT DILLER.

The Fourlegged Tank

Besides drilling some elephants for circus performances, the natives of India train others for use in hunting and for carrying heavy materials. In ancient times elephants played an impressive role in warfare as forerunners of the modern giant tank. The most famous instance of their military use was during the Second Punic War in the third century B.C., in Hannibal's victory over the Romans after he had brought these huge creatures through a pass over the Alps. Eventually elephants were given up for military purposes because they were easily terrified by the noise and violence of battle and in their panic trampled both friend and foe.

Elephants have always aroused a great deal of interest, and many curious beliefs have grown up about them. One of these is that elephants are afraid of mice. There seems to be no scientific evidence for this notion. Another fallacious idea is that elephants live a century or more. The lifespan of these giant mammals is about the same as that of human beings: from sixty to eighty years.

River Horses and Rhinos

Next in size to the elephant is the grotesque African hippopotamus, which may achieve a weight of four tons or more. It is perhaps this creature's very ugliness that makes it appealing to children. The hippo spends a great deal of time in water, which must always be provided in its enclosure at a zoo. The name hippopotamus comes from the Greek and means 'river horse.' In the wild state it seeks out the calm waters of a tropical river, browsing on water plants as it swims or floats. When frightened, it escapes by sinking to the river bottom where it can walk easily and quickly. Ten minutes is about the longest period of time it can stay under water; when it comes to the surface, it usually spouts a cloud of spray from its nostrils.

A mother hippo often rides her baby on her back in the water, and the young clings there even when they go below the surface. Once your child realizes the extent to which hippos are water animals, he may see the advantage of their peculiarly placed eyes, ears, and nose. All these features are at about the same level on top of the animal's huge flat head. Thus they need keep only a small part of the head above water periodically in order to see, hear, and breathe while all the rest of the body is submerged.

Like the elephant, the rhinoceros is native to both Africa and India. You can tell the African black rhino by its two horns; the large Indian rhino has only one horn. Rhinos spend much of their time sleeping and browsing on twigs.

They have remarkably keen senses of smell and hearing, and they are quickly alert to danger. They may charge an enemy with surprising agility or do a right-about-face and gallop away. Their poor eyesight makes their actions especially unpredictable.

The name rhinoceros is based on the Greek word for horn. It is surprising to realize that the horn, which is important as a weapon, is not composed of bone. Rather it is made of a substance that grows out of the skin, as toenails do. It contains a tough protein called keratin.

Giraffes – Walking Skyscrapers

A giraffe is fascinating because of its long neck. A youngster who already knows something about anatomy may wonder whether this ungainly animal has more than the normal number of vertebrae from head to shoulders. Actually it has the usual seven vertebrae in its neck – they are simply longer than those of other mammals.

The long neck makes it possible for the giraffe to feed on the leaves of trees. It can manage to reach its head down to a pool for drinking water without becoming dizzy, but it depends for most of its liquid nourishment on the moisture on leaves. The giraffe can cover ground speedily with its long legs and has been known to go more than thirty miles an hour for short sprints.

Camels – Avid Water Drinkers

At some zoos children need not content themselves with looking at a camel; they may ride on the animal as well. Thus they can come to know something of the sensation of a desert traveler as he progresses over the sands on camelback. Of course the youngsters do not have a chance to appreciate how this useful animal weathers a sandstorm in its natural surroundings. The camel can close its nostrils against the flying sand; in addition, its double row of eyelashes offers excellent protection for its eyes. A one-humped dromedary in good condition can travel nearly a hundred miles a day.

Modern zoos have two great objectives: conservation and education. The fashion of capturing exotic animals and keeping them in cages merely for display as curiosities is outdated. Today there is a crucial need to preserve many species from becoming extinct. Elephants present both special joys and particular problems to zoological parks. However, they can be trained, and they actually seem to enjoy life in settings quite different from their natural homelands. Yet feeding such giants is not easy; an adult may eat hundreds of pounds of forage daily. At the London Zoological Park the great pachyderms are given splendid care and considerable space in which to move around. Young observers who cannot see over the wall are able to watch the animals through low-level viewing slits (left).

▽ As in the wild, zoo elephants enjoy bath-time and this, incidentally, provides a good show for zoo visitors.

▽ The African rhinoceros, one of the largest animals on earth, looks like a living dinosaur. In the heat of the day it likes to take a dust bath in the dry earth to help it to cool off and to get rid of irritating parasites on its thick skin.

▷ White egrets perch on a rhino's back and hunt food in the grass around its feet. They have learned that as the immense beast trundles through the grass, many insects, lizards, and other tasty morsels are frightened out of cover and easily caught.

▽ An angry hippopotamus charges into the water towards the photographer. This animal can be a dangerous enemy, as it may be 14 feet long and weigh as much as four tons. It also has long, slashing tusks, which it may use on enemies with deadly effect.

△ During most of the day, hippos like to laze around in water, which keeps them cool and helps to support their weight. They can swim underwater with surprising grace. Their heads are shaped so that they can keep just eyes, nose, and ears above water.

The Arabian camel is well adapted to survive in some of the hottest and driest regions of the world. Its single hump stores not water but fat to give it the energy to keep moving. Its body uses water sparingly, so it can travel for several days without a drink. It has always been a servant of desert tribes and is famous for its bad temper.

Although fossil remains tell us that the camel originated in North America, they no longer exist on that continent. In prehistoric times they migrated to Asia and developed into two types, the Bactrian camel with two humps (below) and the Arabian camel, which has one hump (opposite). The Bactrian camel of central Asia lives in cold, dry areas and has a thick coat. It has been used for many centuries as a beast of burden and thinks nothing of carrying two children at once at a zoo (bottom of page).

The accomplishment for which camels are most noted – the ability to do without water – seems improbable if you see them drinking. When water is available, a camel will drink six or seven gallons a day. Although records show that some animals have survived for several weeks without water, a camel bearing a heavy load usually cannot go without liquid for more than three days. At such times the camel draws upon moisture stored in its body tissues and actually drinks from the inside.

The two-humped Bactrian camel grows a heavier coat than the dromedary, the one-humped species of Africa. The Bactrian camel is native to Central Asia, where people often depend on their camels not only for transportation but also for food. They drink the milk and eat the meat. Camel hair is used for clothing. In the spring a camel looks disreputable as its winter coat peels off in ragged patches. Flabby humps are a sign of poor physical condition, as the hump provides a storehouse of reserve nourishment which the animal draws upon when food is scarce.

The Big Cats

Tigers and lions have a strong appeal for children because of a child's natural affection for cats. A small cub appears as gentle and playful as a kitten, and even an adult – particularly a tiger – suggests an overgrown tabby.

Lions and tigers are the two biggest members of the cat family. Some kinds of tiger grow considerably larger than others. The Bengal tiger, one of the best known, may be twelve feet long and weigh more than five hundred pounds. The Siberian tiger, which is even larger, also has longer, heavier hair, to protect it during the cold winter in the northern forests of its home.

A mother tiger has two to four babies in a litter. In a zoo tiger babies are sometimes raised by human foster parents, who feed them milk from nursing bottles. In captivity they sleep, purr, play, and chase their tails like domestic kittens. In the natural state young tigers start killing small game by the time they are seven months old. They stay with their family about two years.

The usual diet of a tiger is wild game, such as deer, but many prey on sheep, cattle, and other domestic animals.

Well-fed tigers in a zoo are usually peaceable and contented but because of their restless nature they do a great deal of pacing back and forth.

Lions are more tranquil. In a natural state they like to rest quietly in shady places by day. At night they are on the alert, seeking such game as zebra and antelope. The clichés 'king of beasts' and 'brave as a lion' help keep alive the idea that lions are the most daring and courageous of all animals. Although they look the part, they do not really live up to it. While a tiger is often self-confident enough to take on a more powerful foe – a water buffalo, for example – a lion rarely tries to overpower any animal that is large enough to be a match for it.

◁◁ *The puma or mountain lion is the largest of American wildcats.*

◁◁▽ *The leopard is an agile climber, and its spots help to camouflage it in a tree.*

◁ ▽ *A lion takes a midday nap in a shady tree, where he can escape the flies.*

◁ *A lioness looks elegant on a bare branch.*

▽ *The tiger's stripes blend with long grass.*

The walrus, grotesque in appearance yet strangely appealing, is not seen at many zoos. It is a very expensive animal to support, and its needs include a really large swimming pool. With good care it can flourish in climates far different from that of its natural habitat—the ice floes of the Arctic Ocean and its rocky coasts. In that region the natural enemies of walrus are killer whales and polar bears. While bears do not have the daring to attack an adult, one will sometimes try to steal a youngster. However, it meets strong opposition from the mother, who slashes out savagely with her tusks. Both male and female walrus have tusks, but those of the bulls are heavier. An adult walrus weighs two thousand or more pounds.

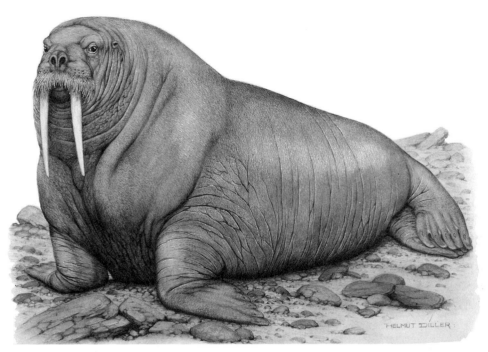

Polar bears are the swimmers of the bear family, and they do very well in propelling themselves through icy Arctic waters. However, they do not have the speed or agility of seals—a favorite food— and they must trap them by stalking them on ice floes. Until American and European hunters began hunting the white giants on a grand scale, they were fairly secure as a species, but now they are endangered. Zoos are helping to increase their numbers. This baby at the London Zoo, tipping the scale at fourteen pounds, is off to a good start in life. The National Zoo in Washington, D.C., has a 171,000-gallon swimming pool for its polar bears, where visitors can view the bears swimming underwater as well as above.

Natives of the Frozen North

All kinds of bears, especially when young, are appealing to zoo visitors, but perhaps the most intriguing of all are the polar bears – those great white giants of the frozen north where their normal life is spent in frigid water and on ice floes. In spite of their heavy fur they do not suffer in warm climates. What they do require is a pool of water – the larger the pool the better – in which they can dive and swim to cool off when they wish.

Walrus, neighbors of the polar bears in the far north, are seldom seen in zoos. They are not easily obtained, and feeding them is extremely expensive. They are like sea lions in some ways, but they belong to a different family of the animal kingdom.

The Giant Panda

Also extremely rare at zoos are the giant pandas— probably the greatest 'star' animal attractions of all time. Their capture and exhibition first took place in China more than three thousand years ago. A few of them were kept for the pleasure of China's rulers during the Chou dynasty. It was not until 1869 that the western world knew of them, through the explorations of the pioneer French zoologist and missionary Père David. He penetrated their wild and rugged home in the cold, misty valleys of the mountain provinces of Yunnan and Szechwan, where south- west China rises to the Tibetan plateau. Since that time, few zoos have been fortunate enough to be able to exhibit them. In 1977, of the western zoos, only Washington (with two), Paris (with one) and London (with two) keep some giant pandas. The greatest potential for breeding in captiv- ity seems to be in London. In 1974, the People's Republic of China donated a female, *Chia-Chia,* and a male, *Ching-Ching,* to the London Zoo. Both were about 15 months old. They have settled down happily, and will soon approach the age at which they can be expected to breed. If they do, the zoo will prosper, for it would be difficult to think of an exhibit more attractive than pandas with cubs.

There is still some discussion among scientists as to whether the giant pandas should be grouped as a family with the raccoons or the bears. Some people believe that they and the lesser pandas (also known as cat-bears) comprise a family by themselves. They are certainly peculiar. Their

anatomy – not least the teeth – suggests that they are meat eaters. Both species, however, eat far more plants than animals, although the giant panda has a taste for small birds, rodents, and fish flipped with a bearlike flick of the arm from streams.

The vegetarian habits of the cat-bear were brought home to the keepers of one famous zoo in the nineteenth century. The first one to be brought back from Nepal was in a sorry state of underfeeding. The keepers deduced from its shape and teeth that it was a meat eater, and offered it every kind of flesh, to no avail. It did, however, mop up some peas with enthusiasm. It was then turned loose in the garden of the zoo's director, to see which plants it preferred; it started with some windfall apples, went on to some leaves and young shoots, and made a dessert of the director's prized rose bushes.

Oddities from Australia

As you enjoy looking at the unique animals native to Australia, an interesting point may be discussed. Why is this relatively small continent the homeland of so many of those seemingly peculiar mammals – the marsupials? The female of the marsupial has a pouch over her abdomen in which newborn undeveloped babies spend their first weeks or months. The kangaroo is the best known of this group. Besides the kangaroo there are many other marsupials, and yet, except for the American opossum, all of them are native to Australia and certain islands of the South Pacific.

A study of this question leads to a consideration of the great changes that have taken place on our planet. It involves a discussion of continental drift and how some great masses have split apart and others joined together and the effect this has had on animal life. These are weighty matters, yet children enjoy thinking about them, especially because exciting discoveries are still being made that are helping to answer age-old mysteries concerning the earth.

Children have always been intrigued by the kangaroo and its built-in babycarriage. Usually a kangaroo mother has only one baby at a time, and the baby stays in the nursery pouch for five or six months. After that, it pokes its head out and often hops out to explore on its own. When it gets tired or hungry, it quickly dives back.

Living in a remote forested area in China, the giant panda is so rare and also so attractive that it was chosen as the symbol of the World Wildlife Fund, which is dedicated to the conservation of wild animals.

HELMUT DILLER

The kangaroo can jump over a five-foot fence with ease; it may even leap more than twice that height. In Australia the animal has been trained to be a skillful boxer. It is a vegetarian, and it lives for about ten or fifteen years. Smaller types of kangaroos are known as wallabies.

The charm of the koala is somewhat the same as that of the giant panda – it looks like the work of a toy designer. In fact, some people believe that the koala inspired the popular teddy bear. As with the giant panda, koalas are rarely seen in zoos, but this is largely because of a feeding problem. They thrive only on the leaves of a certain species of eucalyptus tree, one that is not easily grown outside of Australia. At one time the koala came dangerously close to extinction, but splendid conservation measures saved it. Like the kangaroo, the koala is a marsupial. A newborn baby is less than an inch long, and it stays in the mother's pouch for about two months. After emerging, the baby clings to the fur on the mother's back, riding there until it becomes quite a heavy load.

Popular Zoo Birds

In good modern zoos birds have freedom that exhibitors years ago would not have thought possible. Small birds may have accommodations that make possible the same life-styles they would enjoy in their natural habitats. Efforts are being made to give even large flying birds, such as the condor, room enough to glide, if not actually fly.

The largest birds on earth today are not fliers. These are the earthbound ostriches, whose small wings could hardly get their heavy bodies airborne; a large specimen weighs about three hundred pounds. Despite its inability to fly, an ostrich can move very fast when necessary. On its extremely powerful legs it can run at speeds of thirty to forty miles an hour. In keeping with its size, the ostrich lays huge eggs – about eighteen times larger than chickens' eggs. A family of ostriches is composed of a cock and several hens. All of the hens lay their eggs in one large depression, which has been scooped out of the sandy earth. One of them covers the eggs during the day, but the cock takes over during the night. Your child may well inquire about the 'stupidity' of an ostrich. The bird has such a reputation because of the widespread notion that it sticks its head in the sand when it senses danger. This is completely false, however. Probably

Koalas are rarely seen at a zoo because of problems in feeding them. They thrive only on eucalyptus leaves—and they must be the right species of eucalyptus. If a koala is moved from one eucalyptus grove to another in its native Australian habitat, the animal's digestive system is so specialized the transfer may prove fatal. Though koalas are probably the most appealing of pouched animals, kangaroos have countless admirers. Unlike koalas, they are easily fed in captivity. As with all marsupials, kangaroos and koalas give birth to incredibly small babies, which immediately crawl to the mother's pouch, remaining there to be suckled for a number of months.

In many zoos penguins practically become land birds because they are not provided with enough water to behave as they do in their natural environment. Nevertheless many species are thriving at those zoological gardens that have sizable pools and buildings with air conditioning to give them comfortable temperatures. Living a natural life, penguins spend most of their time in water; to them, land serves as a base for breeding, raising their chicks, and molting. Pictured here are: king penguins on a beach of South Georgia (below), a chinstrap penguin feeding her chick in Antarctica (below, bottom), and jackass penguins from South Africa. The swimming birds show how their wings serve as flippers.

it is based on the fact that when a young ostrich is alarmed, it flops to the ground and extends its long neck flat.

At a number of zoos you are likely to see peacocks strolling freely among the visitors. You might not recognize the female as a peacock, for she is drab in comparison with her mate and she has no train. The male is handsome even when not displaying, but when you see him open his train, you will be witnessing one of the truly beautiful sights of the bird world. The train is not a true tail; it is made up of stiff blackish feathers, which are entirely concealed but which furnish support when those long brilliant feathers of the train are opened up like a fan. Although a male peacock displays in this fashion primarily to impress the female of the species, one sometimes performs when only admiring humans are watching.

Of the birds that amuse as well as interest children, none surpass the penguins. There are at least sixteen species, from the giant emperor of the Antarctic to the little blue penguin of New Zealand and Australia, which is about the size of a small duck. Their black and white 'dress' gives them the appearance of wearing formal attire, and their upright posture adds to an illusion of dignity. Even the heavybodied emperor penguin can leap several feet out of water into the air to land on its breast on an ice floe, where it toboggans for a short distance, then pulls itself upright.

You may see at a zoo a grotesque-looking bird which is labeled on the sign of its enclosure as a stork, although it looks quite different from storks described in stories and fables. A closer look at the sign may reveal that you are looking at a jabiru stork. This is one of the twenty or more different kinds of stork. It stands between four and five feet in height and is striking in appearance because its white plumage forms a strong contrast to its bare head and neck, which are black. Its homeland is South America. To Africa belongs the shoebill stork, with its bill as prominent as its name suggests. You may also find at zoos the marabou stork of Africa and India, as well as black storks, handsome birds with red legs and a red beak of Europe, Africa and Asia. The so-called good luck bird, the stork associated in fables with delivering children, is white. It is native to Denmark, Germany, Holland, and Turkey.

Popular Pets and Their Origins

Perhaps your family does not consider your pet as a suitable subject for nature study. However, domestic animals, including those that have been adopted into the human realm, have traits inherited from their remote ancestors, and it is often useful, as well as interesting, to understand the backgrounds and potential of those that share our homes, as well as their origins.

Cats, more than dogs, retain a close relationship to their wild relatives. A number of elegant pedigree breeds have been produced, but if one of these cats mates with a common shorthair and their offspring mate with ordinary cats, all trace of breeding disappears.

A trait that makes the cat a suitable house pet is one that it shares with its wild relative, the lion: both enjoy taking it easy. Living free on the African plains, the lion must hunt prey when hungry, but as soon as its appetite is satisfied, it lies quietly, sleeping or resting, for long hours at a time.

Cats as Hunters

If you look in the mouth of a cat, you see the equipment of a real denizen of the jungle. There are two sharp canines in each jaw. The molars are sharp-edged wedges, perfectly adapted for cutting meat.

Pet cats are often expected to have split personalities – to be alert hunters ready to pounce on rodent pests and at the same time to be creatures tolerant of birds, tame or wild. If properly trained when young, some cats will refrain from molesting birds. The most successful training method seems to be that of association – creating situations where the cat can observe its mistress or master being friendly with birds. Punishment as a means of curing cats of birdhunting is usually quite unsuccessful.

Cats as Mothers

It is rare that a mother cat will shirk the responsibility of caring for her kittens. As a rule, she shows her solicitude, even before her babies are born by looking for a dark secluded spot – just as in the primitive state a cat sought a dark cave for giving birth. Though kittens are active almost immediately after birth, they do not begin to open their eyes for about five days. Within ten days the eyes are fully opened.

Meanwhile the mother nurses the kittens and industriously washes them from nose to tail with her rough tongue. She allows them to romp and play boisterously even to the extent of frolicking around her; if they go too far, she may box their ears soundly. When they are older, she gives them lessons in hunting, if circumstances permit, showing all the tricks she knows for catching mice and other prey. She will even instruct them in the skill needed for backing down a tree trunk, an important accomplishment for a cat. Instinct prompts a cat to climb, but many cats that have no coaching may reach the top of a tree and then find that they are too terrified to descend. Cats usually bear up to eight kittens, occasionally up to thirteen.

The Mysteries of the Cat

Watching a cat, your youngster may find many things to wonder about. How can it be resting, curled in a tight ball, then a second later spring straight into the air, arching its back – all in one quick move? How can it turn its head around so far that it can lick almost any part of its body?

The explanation lies in the remarkable anatomy of the cat. Its skeleton is made up of more bones than that of a human. The human skeleton has two hundred and six, whereas that of a cat has about two hundred and thirty, not counting the bones in the ears and certain other small bones. Also, these bones are distributed differently; the cat has more of some kinds of vertebrae while a human being has more of other kinds. In comparison with a human shoulder joint, that of a cat is free and open.

Another mystery is the delightful purring sound the cat makes when it is extremely happy. Where does this come from? It can be felt all along the cat's sides as well as around the throat. This is a puzzle a number of scientists have tried to unravel without being entirely successful. They have noted that cats have two kinds of vocal chords, with one kind for calls, the other specialized for purring.

In complete contrast, a cat registers fright or defiance by arching its back, with its body hair standing on end. How can that soft sleek coat suddenly become a mass of bristling hair? Each of the hairs grows out of a tiny sac buried in the skin. Muscles are attached to the sac, and

The personalities of cats vary so widely it is
difficult to give an opinion or judgment
about the cat as a pet. For example, a Manx
usually is brave, lively, and affectionate;
Persians are likely to be more shy and
nervous. But all breeds, even those with
very mixed ancestry, share certain traits:
they have a tremendous sense of curiosity;
they greatly enjoy rest and relaxation; they
are independent, yet respond to loving care.

when a cat is alarmed, the muscles react automatically, pushing against the sac and causing the hair to stand out.

Seeing, Hearing, and Feeling

Since ancient times the ability of cats to see well in the dark has given them a touch of the macabre. Because of their remarkable sight, people came to associate them with the nighttime activities of witches and hobgoblins. As a result a child is likely to be interested in how cats' eyes function. In darkness the pupils dilate, allowing any light that is present to enter onto the retina of the eye. There is also an iridescent layer of cells on the retina that catches even the slightest speck of light, and this brightens the images focused on the retina. It is this layer which makes cats' eyes shine in the dark.

Like dogs, cats have moist noses, and their senses of smell and hearing are keen. The hairs in their ears, far from being obstructions, are sensitive aids in picking up sounds. Cats can detect vibrations beyond the range of the human ear. They are often critical of musical performances, removing themselves as far as possible from objectionable sounds such as shrill music.

The hairs on a cat's face – its whiskers – are valuable as feelers. They are set in four lines above and at the sides of the mouth and are connected to sensitive nerves. Feelers are useful to hunters, especially a wild cat which is a night hunter in its natural habitat. The hairs give back information about the underbrush or other terrain through which the animal is moving.

The Origins of Pet Cats

Although the cat family can be traced back millions of years to prehistoric times, there is much about the ancestry of domestic pets that remains puzzling, for conflicting theories have been advanced regarding their origin. The striped tabby pattern is a strong indication that the forebear of present-day pets was either the European wildcat or the African wildcat, since both species have a striped pattern. Which of the two was the original ancestor is a question that has been much debated. General opinion favors the African, or Kaffir, cat, which was tamed by the ancient Egyptians and probably was used in protecting stored grain from rats.

As trade developed between Africa and Europe, tame cats were taken along in ships to Italian and other European ports. In their new surroundings these tabbies often bred with native wildcats, and before long an interesting variety of tame cats and semi-wild cats had developed.

The popularity of cat pets increased, and people of various countries began to take pride in producing unusual breeds. Perhaps the most outstanding example of this took place in Siam (now Thailand), where a special breed was developed and jealously guarded by that country. However, a breeding pair eventually were taken to England in 1884, and from there Siamese cats were bought by enthusiasts in other countries, reaching the U.S.A. some ten years later.

The Siamese breed is distinguished by its form. The hind legs are longer than the front legs, which gives the body a slight tilt, and the head is long and wedge-shaped with a flat forehead. The cats are also distinguished by their peculiar coloration; there are three distinctive types – seal point Siamese, blue point, and chocolate.

The Manx is another special breed. It is usually distinguished by its lack of tail – although a kitten with a tail sometimes appears in a litter of purebred Manx. With or without a tail the Manx is noted for being lively, affectionate and brave. The ancestors of the modern Manx were native to the Isle of Man in the Irish Sea.

Persian, or long-haired cats are generally believed to have originated somewhere in eastern Asia. Today almost all domestic longhairs are properly called Persian, although for years another longhair, the Angora, was ranked as a special breed. This type originally came from the Orient; traders brought them from Angora, in Turkey, to American shores. As considerable interbreeding with Persians took place and the Angora characteristics receded, Persian became the accepted name for all.

Variety among long-haired cats for the most part lies in the color of their coats. There are at least twenty distinctive varieties, from tortoiseshell – with bright patches of orange, black, and cream – to pure white. Typically the body and legs are compact and short. Generally the voice is soft and well-modulated.

Dogs and Wolves

For many years there was a widespread belief that the wolf was the dog's ancestor, but we now know that this theory is only partially correct. Dogs and wolves may have had a common ancestor fifteen million years ago, and scientists believe that the earliest breeds of dogs probably developed from this animal. Research in Bronze Age villages seems to suggest four basic breeds: a huskylike one, a sheepdog, a hound, and a terrierlike house dog.

We can clearly trace some of the modern dog's outstanding traits to its wild ancestors. When a dog gives chase, he usually barks – a throwback to the wild pack that barked or bayed to keep together while hunting. Similarly the modern dog's habit of turning around a number of times before lying down is a characteristic he owes to his distant ancestors – it was the way they made themselves a comfortable place for lying down in brush, grass, or reeds. Sometimes when a dog is gazing at the moon or when he hears music, he will emit a series of mournful howls. This too may be a reversion to the past – to the time when the pack was called together from all over the countryside, perhaps to hunt together by moonlight.

The friendly association of human beings and dogs goes back through countless ages. A conjecture exploring this association may be the following. In the course of their hunting excursions the early cave dwellers found litters of puppies and brought them back to their primitive homes. The puppies grew up tame because they were fed and sheltered by people; in return they began to defend the cave from enemies. It was their home, the humans were their masters. Certainly primitive man could not have failed to appreciate a dog's keen senses of smell and sight, and he would have quickly recognized the animal's usefulness on hunting trips in uncovering game.

As centuries passed, men gradually changed their ways of living. A crude cave was no longer a good home, and hunting was no longer the only means of supplying food for the family. Yet the desire to keep a dog in the household did not change. All over the world they had become established as friends and helpers and were bred for many special purposes. They proved to have a remarkable ability to adapt to a variety of conditions.

◁ *Most dogs can be trained to do many tricks, provided you are patient and gentle. Repeat the command in a light tone of voice, as you show the dog what you want it to do: for example, gently press it down as you ask it to 'sit.' Do not be impatient if it does not obey immediately. When the pet does it right, reward it with enthusiastic approval. Soon the dog will love to do such things as begging (left) and fetching a stick, even from water (below).*

▽ ▽ *Many pet dogs can do a useful job of something that comes naturally to them – like guarding a home. Large breeds, such as the Great Dane (left), German shepherd (middle), and boxer (right), are usually very gentle with children, but their size alone is often enough to scare off any unwelcome visitors. Dogs have keen hearing, and even while they are asleep at night they will wake in an instant if there is a strange noise in the house and raise an alarm by barking.*

◁ ◁ *Most of the great explorations of polar regions would have been impossible without the use of husky dogs. Teams of them are trained to drag heavy sleds for many miles, often in bad weather and over thick snow or ice.*

◁ *A closeup of a husky shows the thick coat of long close hair, which keeps it warm in temperatures far below zero. When the husky sleeps in the snow, it curls up and puts its furry tail over its nose; no part of its body is exposed to the bitter cold.*

▽ *Another pack of well-trained working dogs provides a* **complete contrast to the huskies** *of the north. Here in the English countryside in winter a pack of foxhounds sets off at the beginning of a day's hunting. The hounds are trained to respond to the sound of the huntsman's horn. Using their keen sense of smell, they will track a fox over all kinds of ground.*

How Breeds Are Established

The ancient Greeks bred dogs small enough to sit comfortably in a woman's lap – presumably to keep the owner's stomach warm. In England quite a different kind of dog was desired. Almost a thousand years ago a breed was developed there with a retreating nose, an undershot jaw and menacing teeth. It became known as the bulldog, because its special purpose was fighting bulls – a ferocious sport that enjoyed great popularity for hundreds of years. The peculiar formation of the bulldog's snout enabled it to breathe easily while biting and gripping a bull.

The Scottish terrier with its shaggy eyebrows evolved from breeders' efforts to provide small dogs with protection against dirt as they were digging into fox holes. What appears to be merely a matter of style today had a practical purpose at the time of the origin of a breed. Poodles, used as retrievers, had wool left on the chest to protect them against cold while their flanks were shaved to streamline them for swimming. The cropping of ears became the fashion in the eighteenth century to protect the floppy ears of hunting dogs from being torn in the underbrush.

In general as animals have been domesticated, certain changes resulted in their bone structure. With dogs this was particularly true in regard to head and face, the front of the face becoming shorter than that in wild dogs and wolves. There are exceptions, however; with collies, for example, breeders have concentrated on lengthening the face. On the other hand, no domestic dog has jaws longer (in proportion to the body) than the jaws of a wolf.

How Dogs Sniff, See, and Hear

Dogs depend on their sense of smell much more than on the other senses. The soft, damp skin that covers the dog's nose carries all scents to the wide nostrils, which can be lifted in any direction. The upper sides are slitted. This enables the nostrils to quiver, making them even more sensitive to odors. The inside of the nose and air passages that lead back to the throat are lined with millions of special scent cells.

A dog will frequently rely on its nose where another creature would use its eyes. If it loses something – a bone or a toy – it does not look for it; it sniffs until the object is located. A foxhound stays on the trail of a fox for many miles, guided by a scent that may be several hours old. This ability has been put to good use in several breeds. An outstanding example is the bloodhound, which does an extraordinary job of tracking down lost or straying people when all other means have failed.

We speak of a dog's eyes as 'beautifully soft' or 'soulful' rather than 'keen.' The fact is, though, that dogs are usually sharp-sighted, despite their reliance on their sense of smell. Dogs even see fairly well in the dark, though they seem to be inferior to cats in this respect. There is an interesting contrast in breeds between the hunting dog, which stays on a trail guided solely by scent, and the greyhound, swiftest of all large dogs, which hunts by sight. In most breeds the eyes are a rich brown – though puppies usually have blue eyes – and the pupil, as with human eyes, is round.

There is a considerable range of difference in the shape and appearance of the outer ears of dogs, which might lead to the conclusion that there is a great deal of variation in the hearing ability of the various breeds. Actually most breeds of dogs possess an acute sense of hearing. Whether the animal has long or short earflaps, the action of pricking up his ears is typical of an alert dog. As the hound lifts his long ears they form tubes, thereby bringing sound more effectively to the inner ear.

Choosing a Dog Pet

Parents who are dog enthusiasts are often disconcerted to find that their children fear these animals. Experiments tend to prove a child's timidity with animals is often the result of a previously unpleasant encounter or of his association of the animal with a frightening experience. At the same time I cannot help also advancing a very simple theory – that the generally unpredictable actions of dogs and their sudden movements are enough to make some youngsters wary and hence distrustful of them. There is also the matter of size; to a toddler even a spaniel must appear as large as a lion does to an adult.

With so many breeds to choose from, the wise parent will give careful consideration to the type that is best suited for the household. In fairness to yourself, your child and the pet, you should select an animal that you can care for without overtaxing your time, purse, or living space.

Horses to Ride Upon

Even in our machine age, an interest in horses remains high among young girls and boys, particularly since movies and television bring ranch life dramatically to city dwellers. Although supporting a horse is both expensive and time-consuming, it is not necessary to live on a ranch to have a personal acquaintance with horses. There are numerous farms where we may see different breeds, and horse shows are held throughout the country. In some cities there are the magnificent steeds of mounted police, as well as riding horses in parks.

The child who feeds a horse discovers it is wise to offer lumps of sugar in an open palm rather than grasped in the fingertips. The large incisor teeth might easily nip the fingers along with the sugar, with no such intention on the part of the horse. It is by the incisors that an experienced horseman can estimate the age of a horse. As the teeth develop, growth rings are formed in them annually, with an effect somewhat like that of growth rings in a tree trunk. As the teeth wear with age, these rings become clearly visible. The time-honored warning not to look a gift horse in the mouth is based on the fact that the animal's age is revealed by the state of its teeth.

The Horse's Wild Relatives

A well-groomed horse is sleek, glossy and thoroughly civilized in appearance, but an animal that has been running in the pasture all winter long presents an entirely different picture. Like wild horses, which grow a thick covering of hair during cold weather, it has a shaggy coat. This hair is shed in the springtime.

Wild horses still exist in limited numbers. These include the tarpans of Mongolia and Central Asia, which, though smaller than domesticated horses, are strong and stocky.

There are still some semi-wild horses on western prairies of the United States – descendants from horses brought to Mexico by Hernando Cortez and to Florida by Hernando de Soto. A number of these imports from Spain strayed from their masters and roamed far and wide over the new continent. Eventually members of the two groups met and mated, mixing colors, sizes and other characteristics, and before long thousands of unbridled horses added a colorful note to the American scene. Comparatively few survive in the wild state today. Of the remnants, many are captured by ranch owners, branded, and then released.

The African zebras, members of the horse family, have resisted all attempts to be domesticated. By contrast Shetland ponies, which still run wild on Shetland and other islands about a hundred miles north of Scotland, are valuable pack animals and trustworthy pets.

Where Horses Came From

The distribution of horses in the modern world follows a long history of wanderings and migrations. Millions of years ago the horse family began in North America with an animal known as the dawn-horse, the original ancestor. This was a creature about the size of a fox, with several toes on each foot. Over a long period of time gradual changes took place, notably in the lengthening of the legs and the steady enlargement and greater specialization of the middle toe. At the same time the other toes, becoming smaller and smaller, gradually vanished and were finally replaced by the enormously enlarged middle toe, which developed into the hoof as we know it today.

Even before the Ice Age some of the ancestral horses had been leaving North America for other continents, for in the distant past, land bridges existed that connected continents. The true horse of the Ice Age also migrated. Although the horses that reached Asia, Europe and Africa flourished, the original North American family died out, and there were no horses in North America until Spanish explorers reintroduced them in the sixteenth century.

Thoroughbreds

Even when many horses still lived in the wild state, men in various countries were breeding the animals for specialized uses. Eventually from their efforts such breeds evolved as the German coach horse, the Belgian saddle horse and the American saddle horse. Especially notable breeds were developed in England, among them the thoroughbred, which became so famous as a horse of high quality that people began to use the word incorrectly, using *thoroughbred* when they meant *purebred*. (A purebred animal is one that has a recorded ancestry and represents but one breed.) A fine horse usually has ears pointed forward.

Horses make challenging pets because of the responsibilities required of their owners; besides being fed properly, they need grooming and proper exercise. This mare and her foal are examples of handsome, healthy pets. Ponies delight many youngsters, as do donkeys giving rides at a zoo.

▽ The elevation of laboratory specimens to pet status has happened a number of times with rodents. White rats are old favorites.

▽ ▽ Guinea pigs were valued by the Inca Indians, and Spanish explorers took them back to Europe.

▷ Hamsters were brought to the United States about 1938; soon after, they were accepted as pets.

Thoroughbreds excel in running, and the finest racehorses are of this breed. All thoroughbreds today are descended from three horses taken to England more than two hundred years ago – two of them Arabian steeds, the remaining one from southern Turkey.

Originally Arabian horses were creatures of the desert and needed little food and water. So great was the dependence of the Arabs hundreds of years ago on their horses that they bred the animals with great care, raised them virtually as members of the family and trained them like children. The result after several generations was one of the most remarkable triumphs of domestication – a truly great breed, outstanding in appearance, intelligence and performance. Not the least value of the Arabian horse lies in its contribution to new breeds, including the thoroughbred.

Ponies

Small children are likely to be more easily attracted to a pony rather than to a horse. Its size seems especially suitable for children. The smallness of its size, however, does not mean that a pony is necessarily easier to care for and handle than a horse. If it is kept in a stable and fed grain, a pony is apt to develop inflammation in the feet due to the rich food and inactivity. Also stimulated by a diet of grain, it may kick and bite. Yet if it is turned out into green pastures, it may eat too much in relation to the exercise it is given and again develop an inflammation. A well-trained pony can be a joy to own, but it is not especially easy to give proper care to one.

Guinea Pigs and Other Rodent Pets

Guinea pigs are among the oldest of rodent pets, and their popularity has not diminished through the years. There are a number of reasons for this. They enjoy the company of people, are playful and can find sufficient exercise indoors simply by running about on their short legs without climbing or jumping on furniture. They are hardy, practically odorless and easily fed.

Today there are various breeds you may choose from at pet shops, from the Abyssinian with short rough hair that grows in swirls to the Angora with hair so long it sweeps the floor. The English guinea pig, with smooth short hair, is among the most popular. These appealing rodents were discovered in South America by invading Spaniards. Although the Inca Indians used them as food, they also had great respect for them; the mummified body of a pet would often be placed in the tomb with its owner.

A guinea pig is usually quiet but may make soft grunting sounds, as when pleased at being fed. This apparently suggested the gruntings of pigs to the Spaniards, which accounts for the second part of its name. When Spaniards sailed back to Europe taking along some little 'pigs' they had discovered they frequently made a stop at Guinea on the western coast of Africa. In time 'guinea' was added to the animal's name. Now they are also known as cavies, but guinea pig remains an ever-popular name.

Hamsters and Gerbils

From the oldest of rodent pets your child might like to turn to the newest. These include gerbils and hamsters, both of which first became known as laboratory animals. When their intriguing behavior became appreciated, they soon were sold in pet shops and brought into the home.

The hamster, first brought to the United States from Syria in 1938, has a broad pixielike face, shiny black eyes and often a reddish-gold coat. It retains some of the habits of its wild ancestors such as hoarding food until ready to eat. First the food is packed into cheek pouches and then carried to a hiding place. Usually this is retrieved during the night. Besides the golden hamster, there are others native to Europe, Asia, and South Africa. The European – the largest – is a great pest because of the damage it does to crops.

Gerbils were imported into the United States from Asia in 1954; ten years later they were being eagerly adopted as pets. Their bodies are more streamlined than those of hamsters. Their hind legs are elongated while those of hamsters are not. The gerbil has a long fur-covered tail with a tuft at its end; the hamster has a very short tail. Gerbils are lively, filled with curiosity, and they take pleasure in playing with toys.

Gerbils leading a normal life in the wilds are active during the day, getting their rest at night. Pet gerbils are more likely to follow such a procedure than the nocturnal hamsters; yet some do not.

A youngster who is enthusiastic about either hamsters or gerbils perhaps should be warned of a disturbing happening that could take place: a mother gerbil sometimes eats one or more of her babies. Studies have been made to determine why this happens, but only theories have resulted without a conclusive explanation. One suggests that the mother's diet before giving birth was inadequate, especially in minerals. Or there may be too many babies in a litter for her to nurse. Or perhaps there has been too much disturbance in the nursery, including handling. Depending on your child, it might be better not to mention this possibility, but simply to keep watch on the newborns and explain it if it should happen.

Tame Mice and Rats

In spite of their being in the same family as the dreaded pests of our society, mice and rats have enjoyed widespread popularity as pets for many years. The tame varieties, however, are specially bred for pets. They are intelligent, scrupulously clean – they constantly groom themselves – and extremely playful. Some time ago these pet rodents were usually white mice, or white rats, but gradually breeders produced a variety of colored coats such as silver, pink, and orange or a combination of tones. Of the many varieties that have been bred there are some with long wavy hair, some with curly tails, and others with no tail at all.

The development of more than a hundred different kinds within a fairly short time was made possible by the reproductive ability of these rodents. They begin to mate when only two or three months old and they produce one litter after another. As a pet owner, you can regulate the number of offspring by keeping males and females in separate cages.

Rabbits and Hares

These popular animals cannot be grouped with rodent pets because they are not rodents. Many people refer to them in that way, mistaken perhaps, because of the chisel-like front teeth, which are obvious in rodents. However, there are a number of structural differences in the two groups. Watch a guinea pig scamper and then watch a rabbit hop, and you will see one of the obvious differences.

Once your child is aware that rabbits and hares are not rodents, the next question may be 'What's the difference between a hare and a rabbit?' Here is confusion indeed because of the popular names that have been given them. For example, the so-called Belgian hare is really a rabbit, and the snowshoe rabbit is really a hare. With housepets the difference between them is not important. In their natural habitats, however, there are obvious differences in their life-styles: with true hares the young are born covered with fur and their eyes open. Newborn rabbits are naked and sightless. Rabbits make their nests in underground burrows, whereas hares nest on the earth's surface.

Nearly all domesticated breeds are attractive and gentle and may be recommended as pets. Especially popular are albinos, Dutch, Himalayan, English and New Zealand varieties of rabbits.

Birds in the Home

Nature exploring under your own roof is a really stimulating experience when you adopt bird pets. That is when you will notice these feathered creatures sleeping soundly on a perch, never in danger of falling off. Or you will see one turn its head almost completely around. How are these things possible? An answer to the first question: although a bird may relax, its feet never do, and as it sleeps, its head tilts backward so that the body is in perfect balance. At the same time the threadlike tendons in the feet pull the toes so that they turn inward, securely anchoring the bird. To the second question: the neck is superflexible because it includes fourteen vertebrae – twice as many as in the neck of a giraffe, or any other mammal.

Parrots long ago became famed as pets through adventure stories. Pirates seemed to enjoy their companionship! Today these amazing birds are rarely found in homes because caring for them – cleaning the cage and providing proper food – is a considerable chore. However, smaller members of the family, the parakeets, have wide popularity.

Parakeets were discovered – great flocks of them – in Australia more than a hundred years ago; the native people called them *budgerigars*, their word for nice bird – although it has never been truly established whether the Australian people were referring to its taste or its appearance! (From it comes the name budgie, now also commonly used.) A number of these birds were taken to Europe and America, and they flourished in captivity.

◁ Pets should be domestic rather than wild animals. A wild animal may be taken if it is found injured or orphaned when too young to care for itself, as happened with this fox.

▽ Ravens are intelligent, affectionate birds, often talkative, and very loyal.

▽▽ A young owl may require rescue after falling from its nest.

There is a great fascination about animal pets that can imitate the sounds of human speech. The parrot family and the starling family (which includes the mynah bird) do this particularly well. They also mimic such sounds as the songs of other birds and the barking of dogs. Shown here are three of the most popular pets from the parrot family: the sulphur-crested cockatoo (top), the green Amazonian parrot (traditionally the pirate's bird), and the Australian budgerigar (opposite).

There are other species of parakeet sometimes seen in cages. Other members of the parrot family that make delightful pets are the lovebirds and the cockatiels. Cage birds need to excercise and stretch their wings. If you let your bird out to fly around at the same time every day, it will soon learn to return to its cage when tired.

At one time canaries surpassed all other caged birds as pets. They became big business for breeders, and breeding them became a popular hobby. The two types recognized today are the roller (known for long trills and a variety of soft low notes) and the chopper (whose song is strong and loud with staccato notes).

If you buy a young parakeet, your family will undoubtedly look forward to teaching it to talk; however, when buying a canary, you should choose one that already can sing. Although a canary's general singing ability is inherited, a breeder usually has a tutor bird give the young ones a good start in vocal expression. Pet male canaries are more inclined to sing well than the females – a carry-over from the wild bird state. It is believed that canaries, as well as some other birds, can store air in sacs connected with the lungs, and this reserve can be used to sustain prolonged singing.

A family living in country or town may enjoy having pigeons, birds that have been domesticated for thousands of years. There are more than two hundred varieties, and it is believed that all are descendants of the rock pigeon, native to Europe, Central Asia and China. People interested in these birds rarely are satisfied with one. They want at least a pair, or perhaps a whole flock.

Country living gives opportunity for a wonderful variety of pets. Sometimes a wild mammal, bird or reptile that has been injured or has been orphaned when young may be adopted. But in such cases advice is usually needed about its care and a child should realize from the start that the animal will be only a temporary pet. Most creatures taken from the wilds are better off there and should be released as soon as they are self-sufficient. The crow family make an entertaining exception to this rule. From the humble jay to the large crows and mighty ravens, they are the most intelligent of birds, and can be taught a wide range of words, sounds and tricks.

The Misunderstood Spider

Does your child have an aversion to spiders that amounts to real fear? Do spiders inspire in you nothing but distaste and dislike? If this is the case, your family is somewhat typical as concerns spiders; spiders are certainly not the most popular of animals. Yet, as is true of snakes, much of the hostility would disappear if people learned the real facts about them rather than believed half-truths and outright superstitions.

Let's consider first the good that spiders do. These little creatures each year consume millions of insects that are destructive to grain crops, such as locusts and grass-hoppers. They also eat insects that feed on green leaves, such as beetles and caterpillars. They prey also on mosqui-toes and other flies. This aid in controlling insect pests has gone on for centuries, long before man-made pesticides were developed. Even now when chemicals are being used in great quantities to save crops and vegetation, spiders should be valued, since pesticides frequently are harmful to the environment. Spiders carry on their insect control with-out creating ecological problems.

People are inclined to think of the classic encounter of the spider and the fly, 'Will you walk into my parlor?, said the spider to the fly,' as a confrontation between two kinds of insects. This, of course, is not the case because a spider is not an insect. Your young nature explorer can check this out (with a picture if a live specimen is not easily available) by counting the legs. A spider has eight legs, which is two more than any adult insect has. Another distinction is that a spider has only two major body divisions: the head and thorax merged into one unit, and the soft rounded abdomen. An insect has three divisions. Still another difference is that a spider, unlike an insect, has no antennae.

Spiders may be found almost everywhere, from under–ground caves to mountain peaks. They live near, and even in, water as well as in arid regions. They flourish indoors and outdoors. In fields they make their homes on tall plants and low shrubs. In forests they ascend trees and find shelter under dry leaves and fallen logs. Many prefer dark, shadowy locations.

Nearly thirty thousand species of spider have been de-scribed, and their numbers are incredible. Both in England and the United States there have been spider counts that revealed more than two million individuals living in a single acre of grassy meadowlands. It is no wonder that these creatures can effectively keep down the insect popula-tion of an area.

Spider Venom

It is the possibility of being poisoned by a spider's bite that has caused an aversion to spiders in many people; they feel that spiders are sinister creatures that lurk in shadows, waiting to make a surprise attack. Actually, most species of spiders are timid and try to avoid people. They bite only when hurt or threatened; usually they will walk harmlessly on a person's skin. Although the bite of some species can produce painful results, those normally encountered by people are not capable of biting through the human skin. The front jaws with which they seize and kill small prey are not strong enough.

The size of a spider, however, is not an indication of the seriousness of its bite. There are large wolf spiders whose bite may cause no great problem. On the other hand, the venom of a black widow can result in severe reactions, and a black widow is only half an inch long. If treated effi-ciently, even the victim of a black widow's bite (especially a person in good health) should recover in a fairly short time.

The Tarantula Legend

We find a certain confusion in the name of the fearsome-looking spiders that in America are generally called taran-tulas. In Europe they may be called bird spiders. The name of the tarantula is said to have originated in medieval times, derived from the name of the city of Taranto, Italy, where a certain type of hairy spider was common. At the same time there was a popular frenzied folk dance which government authorities disapproved of and forbade. Appar-ently in an effort to be allowed to continue their frantic dances, some of the citizens claimed that they had been bitten by the spiders and that the only way to recover from the effects of the poison was to dance with feverish excite-ment. As a result, the dance became known as the taran-tella; the spider as the tarantula. In recent years this spider has been studied in Italy, and it was found that no serious ill effects developed from its bite. It may properly be called a wolf spider, and it is closely related to many species found

Although many people find spiders
unpleasant or frightening, they should know
that spiders serve a very useful function
by eating many harmful or destructive
insects. In many countries it is considered
unlucky to kill a spider, and numerous
folk legends have grown up around these
tiny creatures.

in the Americas. Their genus name is *Lycosa*, taken from the Greek word for wolf. Wolf spiders do not spin webs in which to trap their prey. In a wolflike way they pursue their victims on the ground. However, they do produce silk, using it to make linings for their burrows.

The Orb Weavers

The spiders most famous for their spinning – and deservedly so – are the orb weavers. Besides the orb, there are three other general types of web: the irregular mesh (commonly found indoors, to the displeasure of tidy housekeepers), the funnel web (constructed just outside the spider's retreat), and the sheet web (about two inches square, woven on a horizontal plane among grass roots, or suspended from one stem to another). All of these are marvels of construction. But it is the orb that inspires artists to reproduce its beauty, writers to describe it poetically, and engineers to study its creation with deep respect. It may be likened to the original suspension bridge.

How does a spider begin construction? First comes the bridge on which the whole web will hang. The spinner produces a thread and lets it float through the air until it catches on an object and sticks; then she pulls the thread tight and fastens its end with a disk of small threads. Or she may first fasten the end of the silk to an elevated spot on a plant stem or fence and then carefully move down one side of the area to be covered by the web. When she climbs up again, it is to a point that will be the other side of the bridge. Using either plan, the spider is constantly letting out her silken thread. With this fastened so that the bridge line is established, the spider pulls it tight and strengthens it with additional thread.

Now the spider drops to a lower level to anchor a line to an object such as a twig or blade of grass. This action is repeated twice so that three foundation lines are set, forming a triangle or some other style of framework. Within these lines the trap is placed first by dropping a line across the framework, then pulling it tight and walking halfway across it. The halfway mark will be the center of the orb trap, and the little spinner begins to attach to the frame lines resembling the spokes of a wheel. Spiral lines are then added over the spokes, which will hold them in place while the finishing work is done.

All the silk used so far is dry. Now the spider begins to produce sticky silk, usually putting some in corners; moving in a spiral, she then attaches it to the spokes until she reaches the center of the web. There she begins to bite out the dry lines of the scaffolding and either eats them or kicks them away from the trap. Some orb weavers put on finishing touches, such as a white zigzag band across the web or below its hub. Usually this whole exquisite weaving job is accomplished in no more than an hour.

A child may wonder why the female spider is the one that usually does the weaving. Do not the males also spin and weave? When very young, they do. But after a male molts for the last time and achieves adult size, he no longer spins. Often he stays on or near the web of his mate.

Females as Killers and Egg Layers

A popular notion is that male spiders are always killed by their mates after the mating act is completed. Yet this is far from true. In a few species this often happens (for example, among black widows), but in most species the male and female separate peacefully. In some cases they share the same web, or a retreat, for a considerable time. Males usually do not live as long as females. The females of certain species may live for three years or more; more often they die shortly after laying their eggs. At least they do not survive the winter.

Female spiders produce silk for important reasons besides building snares. Silk is used to protect their eggs. A running-type spider weaves a sheet on which to lay her eggs, then wraps the sheet around them. Other spiders make nests on stones, covering them with a waterproof silken coat. Some may use folded leaves or crevices as nests.

The garden spider, which is exceedingly expert at orb weaving, also constructs the most proficient egg sacs. If we could watch one of these little weavers preparing her nursery on an autumn day, we would see her fasten yellowish silk threads to a structure until a simple roof was formed. Then she would add to this a thick mass of fluffy silk and against that a layer of dark brown silk. Working upside down, she deposits eggs against this silk roof until they hang together like a small yellow ball. Quickly she spins more silk to form a strong thin cover over them and joins it to the brown silk.

▽ The name 'tarantula' is enough to inspire fear in anyone who dislikes spiders. The red-legged species below looks fearsome enough to demonstrate why, although the long-standing reputation of such spiders for deadly venom has been largely discounted by modern scientists.

◁ The tarantulas of Europe are only distantly related to those of the New World, but it is from Europe that the name comes. A certain dance was banned by the authorities of the Italian town of Taranto, but the people continued to perform it, claiming that it cured the effects of a local spider's bite.

More silk is spun, and using her hind legs as a comb, she pulls and pats it into a soft blanket around the eggs. The final work is to make another covering of silk, spun very close and smooth – one which when hardened will look much like parchment. This amazing achievement of egg laying and the construction of the sac, which is about the size of a hickory nut, has taken only a few hours, but these have been hours of steady activity.

Hundreds of baby spiders hatch within the sac during early winter, but they remain within its protective walls until spring. Weather is a deciding factor in how long they stay crowded in their little home. It has long been a theory that many of the spiderlings turn cannibal during this waiting period, the stronger ones devouring the weaker. However, the theory has never really been proved.

Flying Spiders

Occasionally you may have had the disconcerting experience of having a very tiny spider fly in your face. Particularly in the spring and autumn great numbers of these eight-legged creatures sail through the air. It may seem that they are actually flying; however, if you look closely, you will see that the spiderling is attached to a long thread – yet another use for silk. Aided by the thread, it makes use of rising air currents to float from its hatching place to new territory, well apart from its numerous and hungry brothers and sisters.

To begin its journey, the young spider climbs up a tall blade of grass or a large plant. Then it spins a silken thread and sends it out on the air. When the thread is long enough, the friction of air currents buoys it upward, and the spider, letting go its hold on the blade of grass, is off on a journey to an unknown destination. Usually the flight is ended when the spider bumps against an elevated object, but sometimes it decides its own fate by pulling in the streamer until all buoyancy is lost. Flying spiders have even been discovered in mid-ocean and a whole community of spiders constitute the world's highest animals; they feed on tiny fleas, over 20,000 feet high in the Himalayas.

Flying or ballooning is not the habit of only a few kinds of spiders. Most species use this means of getting from one place to another.

The Wonderful Silk Factories

Nature exploring in the realm of spiders is certain sooner or later to prompt the question, 'Where does all the silk come from? Surely it cannot be stored in those little bodies!'

The answer involves a description of special glands within the abdomen. There are at least seven different types of glands. In some species an individual may have as many as six of them; others have fewer.

In the abdomen there are also several spinnerets, usually as many as six of them. Flexible as fingers, these organs can be extended or compressed, and in general they can be used like human hands, combining single strands to create thicker ones and coating dry strands with a sticky substance. When it is first produced the silk is in liquid form.

Because of spiders' fame as silk producers, children may wonder why spider silk has never been used by people in the way silk produced by silk worms has been. For one reason the varying thicknesses of its strands is a disadvantage. For another it does not stand up well in the weaving process, and it lacks the luster of the silk produced by silk worms.

Still, primitive people have found a number of uses for spider silk. For example, fish nets and waterproof coverings for themselves. Spider silk has also proved useful in the manufacture of sophisticated instruments: engineer's levels and rifles' precision sighting marks are made possible by its incredibly fine fibers.

Spiders in Water

The wonders of spider activity are not confined to those spiders that live in fields and meadows. There is a European water spider that constructs its home underwater. Actually the spider makes more than one; there is a summer home and a second one to be used in winter.

This little brown water spider – a mere half inch in length – manages to bring its oxygen supply under water by going to the surface, raising its abdomen, and trapping an air bubble underneath. If it remains quietly in one place, after it has dived back down, this air bubble may suffice for several hours. If it swims and works energetically, the stored oxygen supply gives out more quickly.

Poets may liken a spider's orb web to a piece
of lace, but an engineer is apt to speak of it
as a marvel of construction, built with the
techniques used in building suspension
bridges. Such webs are usually three or four
feet in diameter, but they can be much
larger. As a rule, one is made in an hour.

The technique of building a web follows a definite sequence. To begin with, the spider makes a bridge line by spinning a thread of silk from one point across to another—she does this either by fixing the line at one side and walking round or by letting a line of silk blow in the wind until it connects on the other side. Then she spins the other lines that will form the outer shape of the web. Starting from the upper bridge threads, she then constructs the radii, or 'spokes of the wheel,' dropping down a line from the top to the bottom, moving a little way along and spinning another line back to the top, passing through the same center point each time until the outline is filled. Going back to the middle of the web, she spins a spiral thread round and round the web to the outer edge, to strengthen it. Finally, she makes a spiral back from the outer edge into the center point, laying this time a different type of silk which is covered with a very sticky glue. At the same time she takes up and destroys the strengthening spiral. When the web is complete, the spider usually hides in a small hole or under a leaf until an insect flies into the web and is caught on the sticky spiral threads. Alerted by its jerks the spider runs out and spins a tight jacket of silk round her prey. If the insect manages to break free from the web, the spider repairs the tear, usually waiting until evening.

garden spider

179

The warm-weather home is built fairly close to the surface of the pond or stream. It begins as a small, closely woven platform of silk, suspended from plants. Once this platform is completed, the weaver goes to the surface and again traps a large air bubble. It then dives quickly under the little platform and releases the oxygen so that it rises against the silk, causing the platform to puff out. The procedure is repeated until the silk is formed into a tiny diving bell, open at the bottom. Further supports are then added to make the bell secure, and additional weaving is done.

The male water spider may construct a similar home near that of his mate and then join the two homes with a tunnel of silk. Or he may share his mate's home.

With the approach of winter the water spiders find a new building spot for shelter deeper in their watery surroundings, perhaps next to a mollusk shell. A solid closed sac is constructed, and the spider remains in it until the water warms up in the spring. A supply of air has been stowed away, and because the spider is completely inactive, this lasts for months.

There are other spiders near or on water that you might be inclined to call water spiders, but they are quite different from the European species and more properly are known as fisher spiders. The typical fishers are twice as large, and they not only prey on aquatic insects but also sometimes catch small fish. They can easily walk on water and go under its surface for rather long periods. However, they do not live underwater as the European water spiders do. In England there is a so-called raft spider that constructs a raft from silk and a few dead leaves. It can rest comfortably on this little perch, watching for prey as it floats along.

The Many-Legged Creatures

Spiders are not the only eight-legged creatures in the animal kingdom. One kind that looks like a spider at first glance is really the harvestman or daddy longlegs. Its legs are remarkably long; if our legs were as long in proportion to our body as those of the daddy longlegs are to his, our head would be about forty feet above the ground. It lives in woods, long grass and low vegetation, but is usually encountered when turning over stones or pots in a garden, for it moves mainly by night.

The daddy longlegs differs from spiders in that it does not have a waist – that is, no constriction between the front part of the body and the abdomen. Its abdomen is segmented whereas that of the spider is not. It does not spin silk, and it lays its eggs under stones and in crevices without giving them further protection. It has the power of regrowing a leg if one is broken off.

The several pairs of legs are of varying lengths. The first pair is usually the shortest. The second pair of legs are spread wide apart and kept in rapid motion; the sensitive tips of this pair of legs serve as feelers and relay information about the nature of the animal's surroundings. If one of these creatures passes over something that suggests food, it stops running to investigate further with the little feelers (palpi) under its head.

A mere six or eight legs are nothing when compared with certain other small creatures, which have many more. Probably the best known is the centipede – the hundred-legs. There are so many legends and stories concerning centipedes that it is difficult to sort out the simple facts. Does one really have those hundred legs their name indicates? It depends on the species. Certain species (the kind you may find indoors, perhaps in a cellar or bathroom) may have only thirty. Others, found outdoors, may have more than a hundred. Are they venomous? To varying extents. Some of their feet have poison-bearing claws, and if one were to walk across your bare skin, it could cause irritation and raise welts. Large centipedes found in the tropics – some of them reaching over a foot long – can cause more serious harm. There have been records of even adults dying after being bitten by one of them. A centipede also carries poison in the first segment of its flattened body.

Like centipedes, millipedes have two main parts to their structure: head and body. The millipede has two pairs of walking legs to each body segment, whereas the centipede has one pair to a segment. Their size and number of legs vary according to species, but all species of millipedes have so many legs that they are frequently called thousand-leggers. We usually find millipedes in damp places, although they may appear almost anywhere in a garden. They feed on vegetable matter, and they do not bite. If disturbed, they roll up into a spiral.

◁ The daddy longlegs is easily mistaken for a spider, for it too has eight legs. It differs from a spider, however, in several ways. The spider has eight eyes in a cluster on the head; the daddy longlegs has only two, set curiously back to back on the body. Spiders have sharply divided sections of body; the 'daddy' has only a small division that marks the head. Unlike spiders, daddy longlegs never spin webs. To add to the curiosities of this strange creature, it appears to be indifferent to the loss of a limb, an event that occurs quite easily. Daddy longlegs eat small insects, mites, and spiders and in turn are eaten by centipedes and large spiders. This one is carrying a load of tiny mites on its legs.

▽ Another creature that inspires the same sort of feelings as the spider is the crane fly. It is a familiar sight in warm weather, blundering around walls and windows. Less obvious is its larva, the leatherjacket, that plagues farmers of root crops by eating stems and roots of valuable food plants.

The Kingdom of the Insects

Is It an Insect or a Bug?

Who doesn't enjoy a puzzle? Most young people do, especially when it gives them a chance to exhibit knowledge. By asking, 'Is there any difference between an insect and a bug?', a youngster has the opportunity to stump most people, and then give a simple answer: 'All bugs are insects, but all insects are not bugs.'

Bugs form only one relatively small part of the large animal class Insecta. They are distinguished by the form of the wings, a broad thorax, and rather small head. The mouth parts are distinctive also; they are suitable for piercing and sucking. Included in this class are stinkbugs, squash bugs, and cinch bugs, all of which feed on plants and are harmful to vegetation. There is a bug, called the damsel bug, which feeds on these and other harmful insects.

To describe an insect, it may be said that it is an animal with six jointed legs, a body made up of three main sections, and a shell-like covering over the body with no internal skeleton. Mention of a specialized mouth is unnecessary. Anyone interested in this aspect of identification can easily find out about the different types of mouths that serve insects. Beetles and grasshoppers bite and chew, bees lap, butterflies siphon, flies sponge.

The endless variety of insects in the world can be appreciated when we learn that there are at least 680,000 species. By contrast the total number of species of all other kinds of animals (including mammals, birds, and fish) is less than a third that number.

This enormous group does not mean monotony for anyone of a studious nature, for the life histories and activities of insects, as well as their appearances, vary drastically. Some, such as certain wasps, are skillful engineers and manufacturers. Bees and ants live in complex societies that rival those of mankind. The doodlebug always walks backward. The queen of a tropical species of termite may produce ten million offspring in her lifetime. Some wasps keep their food fresh over a period of time, just as successfully as we keep ours in a refrigerator, by injecting into their victims a fluid that paralyzes without producing death, and then storing the bodies until needed for food. Many insects thrive in cities, undiscouraged by miles of concrete.

How Insects Move

Insects have no internal bone structure to help them move as our bones help us; but movement, even for those without wings, is possible because each end of a muscle is attached to the hard outer covering that serves as an external skeleton. A muscle, for example, that moves a leg forward has one end attached to the hard covering of the leg and the other end attached to the covering of the thorax in front of the leg. When this muscle contracts, it pulls the two attachments closer together, and the leg moves forward.

It might seem impossible for a creature encased in a rigid covering to bend. However, the insect has joints in places where the body wall is flexible, and it therefore moves somewhat in the manner of an ancient warrior in his suit of heavy armor.

How Insects Develop

A crawling caterpillar that changes into a winged butterfly indeed seems one of nature's greatest wonders. However, this is not the only fascinating pattern of growth among insects. Butterflies and similar insects are said to undergo a complete metamorphosis (this term comes from the Greek word that means 'change of form'). The first form is the egg; the next the larva (often an active, feeding creature such as a caterpillar). Then comes the pupal stage, a period of relatively quiet resting and rearrangement of body shape. Finally the pupa develops into the adult. The larva of a butterfly is commonly called a caterpillar; the pupa is known as the chrysalis. The larva of a fly is called a maggot; that of a bee or beetle is a grub.

Another type of insect growth is called an incomplete metamorphosis because the insects do not usually go through a striking change in form during their growth after the egg stage. They do, however, gradually change their proportions. The young of this group are known as nymphs; both in appearance and in choice of food they are like the adults in most respects. The grasshopper is a well-known member of this group.

In the case of some water-dwelling nymphs, such as a young dragonfly, there is a very noticeable change when the gilled nymph becomes an adult, but the metamorphosis is still considered incomplete.

Insect study is a pastime with a million rewards. There are hundreds of thousands of insect types, all with minute details that range from the grotesque to the beautiful. This desert locust, for instance, caught at the moment of takeoff, shows off its incredibly powerful back legs, the detailed geometry of the head, and a delicate tracery of surprisingly strong wings.

The silverfish illustrates yet another type of growth. The general body form does not change noticeably from the time it leaves the egg until it is fully grown. All insects shed their coverings a number of times while they are growing.

Seeing, Hearing, and Feeling

You may have seen a photograph that depicts a strange-looking object which suggests a mosaic of diamonds but actually is the compound eye of an insect greatly magnified. The curiously intricate pattern is made up of many tiny eyes set close together, somewhat like the cells of a honeycomb. An adult insect has one of these compound eyes on each side of its head.

The six-sided areas into which each compound eye is divided are known as facets. The compound eyes of ants and other insects that live on the ground have only a few facets, and their vision is not sharp. The eyes of dragonflies and other keen-eyed species may have thousands of facets. There are also many species with three simple eyes situated between the compound eyes. These are so tiny, however, that you will need a magnifying lens to find them. Insects can perceive mass and motion and light, and to a certain extent they can distinguish colors. Bees, for instance, see little of what we perceive with our own eyes. They are, however, able to see beyond our spectrum, and many of the colors of plants are visible to them but concealed from the human eye.

The hearing equipment of certain insects is not in the usual places on the body. The grasshopper has an oval membrane sensitive to sound located on the side of the first abdominal segment. Crickets, ants, and katydids have hearing organs on their front legs, and the male mosquito hears through its antennae.

Antennae, or feelers, of insects vary in shape and degree of complexity according to species. The segments that make up the antennae vary both in number and in form. A grasshopper's antennae may have more than twenty segments, whereas the common housefly has only three stubby segments. An insect uses its antennae to investigate its surroundings, and in many species they are related in some degree to a sense of smell. They are attached to the head in front of or between the eyes.

◁ The fabulous feelers of this American moon moth are covered in sense organs, which allow it to find a mate by smell. The male cockchafer (bottom) has fan-shaped feelers. This one is just taking off, displaying the delicate wings which are kept hidden under the glossy wing cases when the insect is on the ground.

▽ Thousands of minute individual eyes make up the two massive compound eyes, which nearly obscure the head of this horsefly.

▽▽ The monstrous mandibles of the greater stag beetle look just like the antlers of a stag and give this insect its name.

Breathing Without Lungs

Insects do not breathe the way that humans and other mammals breathe. If you examine almost any insect closely, you will discover a series of tiny openings along the sides of the body. These are spiracles, or breathing holes, through which air passes into the body. They lead into a system of thin-walled tubes, which distribute air throughout the body. As the insect's blood comes into contact with these tubes, it becomes purified just as your blood does when it bathes the air tubes of your lungs. In the case of grasshoppers and a number of other insects, some of the spiracles are used exclusively for inhaling, others only for exhaling.

Each of the three main segments of an insect's body – head, thorax, and abdomen – has smaller divisions. The thorax is made up of three segments, each bearing a pair of legs. The front legs are attached to the first segment while the front wings, if there are any, and the middle legs are attached to the second segment. The hind wings, if present, and hind legs are attached to the third segment.

Once an insect has acquired wings it is fully grown; when you see little flies and big flies you know they belong to different species.

The legs of all insects are jointed and made up of about ten segments, though the number and size vary with different species. In many species the last segment of the legs bears one or two claws.

Glamorous Butterflies

Lovely winged butterflies are an especially artistic gift of nature. Many children who are generally oblivious to outdoor beauty are captivated by the sight of a butterfly perched on a bright flower. If the color interests them, they may be curious about the varied hues and patterns that decorate wings. Looking at the wings of a butterfly under a microscope, they will see that these are covered with dust-like scales that overlap like the shingles on a house. These scales are responsible for the pattern and brilliant coloring of the butterfly.

A common species that children can easily learn to identify is the monarch, or milkweed, butterfly. Monarchs are noted for their migrations. They gather in large flocks in late summer and then move southward. The habits of the mourning cloak – a brownish and yellow butterfly, ornamented with blue spots – are in marked contrast to those of the monarch. The mourning cloak sleeps in hollow trees or crannies during cold weather and is one of the few insects that hibernate in the adult stage.

Despite their ethereal appearance, you may discover that butterflies are not averse to down-to-earth fighting. The male of many species will try to drive away others that encroach on territory they consider their own. Duels often take place, with the contenders darting and dashing at each other, sometimes buffeting their wings to shreds. The red admiral and the buckeye are particularly noted as enthusiastic scrappers.

How Moths Differ from Butterflies

Children are more likely to become acquainted with the caterpillars of moths than with the moths themselves, since these winged insects (with few exceptions) sleep by day and fly only at dusk or after dark. As butterflies are abroad during the day, this night-time activity is a factor in distinguishing moths from butterflies.

There are several other guides which, as a rule, aid in distinguishing a moth from a butterfly. When at rest, butterflies hold their wings vertically above their bodies; moths extend theirs almost straight out from their bodies. A moth's body is thicker and more wedge-shaped, and its antennae are feathery or finely tapered. A butterfly's antennae, though smooth, end in knobs or thickenings.

The development of a moth is much like that of a butterfly, except that the caterpillars of certain moths weave a covering about themselves, a covering which is usually called a cocoon. Most species of moth caterpillars, however, dispense with a cocoon. For example, when caterpillars of the sphinx moth, commonly known as tomato worms, are fully grown, they burrow in the earth and become pupae. If you are digging around the base of a tree in the late fall, you may discover these caterpillars.

In contrast there are caterpillars of moths such as the cecropia, promethea, polyphemus, and luna which are sometimes called American silkworms because they pro-

The development of the swallowtail butterfly is one of the wonders of the insect world that can be watched indoors. The eggs may be found on the leaves of carrots, parsnips, or parsley (left), each looking like a tiny drop of honey. They hatch after ten days, and the first act of the spiny little caterpillars is to eat the egg shells and to continue on to the leaf on which they were born. As a caterpillar grows, it sheds its skin from time to time and becomes the striking two-inch 'carrot worm,' brightly patterned in green, black, and yellow (center, left). The colors warn of its defense technique, which is to poke out evil-smelling orange horns from its head. After feeding for some time, the caterpillar spins a button of silk against a solid support and fastens itself to it. It then sheds again to reveal a green pupa (center, right). The butterfly within begins to take shape. After some weeks, the magnificent adult emerges (below), dries its crumpled, damp wings, and after half an hour it is ready for its maiden flight.

duce strong lustrous silk for their cocoons. Processing this silk never became a commercial success because these insects proved to be too difficult to breed in large numbers.

Hibernating Caterpillars
You may often discover woolly bear caterpillars along a roadside in the bright fall sunshine. If you pick one up, you will notice its defensive resource of rolling itself into a ball. It also uses this trick to make itself less attractive to a hungry bird. There are many kinds of woolly bears, all of which develop into moths.

The caterpillar of the tiger moth is black at the ends with a middle band of brown. According to popular belief it is possible to forecast the weather by the size of the band on many woolly bears. If the brown band is wide at the beginning of fall – that is, if it measures at least half the body length – a mild winter may be expected. If most have narrow bands, the coming winter will be severe.

After sleeping through the winter, the woolly bear rouses in the spring, eats a little grass, then starts to spin a cocoon, weaving into it the hairs from its own coat. The finished cocoon looks as if made of felt. About the end of May the adult moth emerges.

Beetles – Mysterious and Valuable
Probably the easiest of all insects for people to become acquainted with are the beetles. Not only can they be found in innumerable outdoor places, they also turn up, unbidden and unwanted, in country homes and city apartments. There are twenty-three thousand species in North America alone.

There is an amazing degree of variation among them. They vary in size from minute specimens to some tropical species that are larger than a mouse. Varied as the members of this group of insects are, nearly all the adults are easy to identify by the hard veinless forewings that meet in a straight line over the abdomen and form a sturdy shield for the insect's hind wings and body. In flight these forewings provide elevation for the beetle while propulsion is accomplished by the hind wings. Some of the giant tropical beetles have huge upper jaws. Most of the smaller species also have well-developed mouth parts.

Fireflies and Ladybugs
The firefly is an insect that always intrigues children as it creates bright spots of light in the darkness of a summer evening. In spite of its popular name, this is not a fly but a beetle, one that is valuable to humans because its larvae feed on slugs and snails which often cause extensive damage to cultivated plants.

What is the secret of this beetle's light, which flashes so rhythmically as it flies? There are segments in the abdomen where two chemicals are produced in the tissues. One gives off light as it is activated by the other. In order for this to occur, oxygen is needed. In the tissues are tiny thin tubes, and air, containing oxygen, enters the tissues through these tubes. The light that results has no heat; it is known as cold light and is of great interest to scientists. The male of this family has several light-up segments; the female has fewer, perhaps only one. In some species of beetles only the males can fly, but the eggs, larvae, and flightless females produce light. These are commonly called glowworms.

Another beetle dear to the hearts of children is the ladybug, which is no more a bug than the firefly is a fly. The old nursery rhyme that admonishes this insect to fly away home to its children and its burning house often creates a personal interest in the little beetle. These small, hemispherically shaped insects are also favorites of fruit-growers, but not for sentimental reasons. The ladybug preys on great numbers of destructive pests such as soft-scale mealy bugs on citrus trees.

If you are exploring the countryside in the fall, you may come on a great assemblage of ladybugs. They congregate in large numbers before going into hibernation for the winter under rocks and forest litter or in hollow trees.

Ground Beetles, Water Beetles, and Bombardiers
If you turn over a stone, log or board lying on the ground, especially damp ground, you are likely to discover a beetle hideout. The ground beetle family has many members, and most of them remain under cover during the day. Usually a ground beetle is plain black or brown, and its long slender body is carried rapidly over the ground on thin legs. Ground beetles feed mostly at night, looking for food under rocks, among refuse, or in the soil.

You may find the tiger beetle along the shores of streams, lakes, or the ocean, although it may also be seen on woodland trails. About half an inch long and often brilliantly colored with metallic greens and purples, it is particularly handsome. It too is a swift runner, quick to take flight, and is not easily trapped.

The bombardiers are among the strangest of all beetles. At the first sign of danger these creatures eject a drop of liquid, which quickly changes to a tiny cloud of evil-smelling vapor. The source of the liquid is a gland at the abdomen, and four or five discharges can be made before the liquid 'bomb' supply is exhausted. This unpleasant counterattack often discourages a bird or other aggressor at least long enough for the beetle to scurry to safety. Many ground beetles have this ability, but one species makes its discharge with a distinct popping sound. This is the true bombardier. It has a yellowish head and a bluish body.

Ants – Colonists, Workers, and Warriors

Ants, like beetles, are almost easier to find than to elude. You see them on lawns, roadways, city pavements as well as in gardens, forests, and pastures. These extraordinary insects vary in size and color from the big black carpenter ants to the little brown species, well known both in Europe and North America. In Europe its popular name is simply the dark-brown ant. In America a subspecies, because it has been studied chiefly in cornfields, is widely known as the cornfield ant.

Like all members of the ant family, the cornfield ant lives in colonies. Each is made up of three principal types: the queen (that is, a fertile female); the short-lived males, which die soon after the mating flight; and the infertile females. The infertile female ants, the great majority of a colony, are the ordinary hardworking citizens of the ant world. They are divided into workers, soldiers, or other specialized castes. The workers have larger heads, and their front legs are slightly thicker than in the other adults of this species.

When people come upon a mound of earth which is obviously populated with ants, they are often tempted to dig into it simply to see what an ant colony is like. However, in order to examine a nest successfully, one must dig down with great skill; otherwise it will be ruined.

The nests of cornfield ants vary greatly in size. The mound of a long established colony covers a much larger area than that of a new one. As a rule the underground rooms are only a few inches below the earth's surface, but if there has been a long dry spell or if the nest is located in sandy soil, the rooms are deeper – soil that is very dry becomes too crumbly for excavation.

In the winter the rooms are occupied only by inactive adults and larvae. In midsummer they are bulging with tiny eggs, larvae, pupae, workers (infertile females), and a queen. The larvae are white maggotlike creatures; the pupae are enclosed in whitish cocoons about an eighth of an inch in length. Often mistakenly labeled ant eggs, the pupae are collected in large numbers and sold as fish and bird food.

Ant Organization

If you were to discover an ant nest on a fine afternoon in August or early September, you might find the occupants swarming excitedly about the entrance. You would also notice that many of them have wings. Every few minutes a winged ant takes to the air. Some of these winged ants are males; some females. Mating takes place in the air, high above the ground.

When a female returns to the earth, she breaks off the wings and then burrows a few inches into the ground. Or she may find an opening beneath a log or stone. Here she forms a small cell. She may immediately start to lay her eggs, or she may wait until the following spring to do this. As time passes she eats some of the eggs and continues to lay more. Eventually the eggs that have escaped being eaten hatch and develop into larvae, which are then fed with the saliva of worker ants. After the larvae have passed through the pupal stage, they emerge as adult ants. Now there are workers to get busy finding food for the female which is now the queen and is enlarging her nest.

During the first year the new queen's colony increases to about twenty-five adult workers. Their duty is to search for food. They feed her and any new larvae, and they also help the larvae to spin their cocoons. In time they assist the new adults that are making their escape from these cocoons. **Their mandibles and forelegs are excellent tools, which** they use to dig out new tunnels and rooms. As they dig and

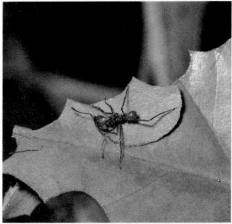

△ This leaf-cutting ant is busy in the final stages of biting out a piece of leaf. It then carries the piece back to its nest, holding it over its head, thus earning the name of parasol ant. Once in the nest the leaf fragment is chewed up and used as fertilizer for the fungus which the ants grow underground as food for their whole colony. Although many of them live in tropical rain forests, there are also leaf cutters in America.

△△ These wood ants have come across a dead small white butterfly. The butterfly is too heavy for a single ant to carry, so a cooperative effort is needed to drag it back to the nest.

◁ The massive swelling on this tree trunk is one sort of ants' nest. Some build their nests as tall mounds, while others dig underground. In all of them there is a complex system of tunnels and rooms.

bring soil up to the surface of the ground, the anthill grows larger. When the weather changes and the soil becomes cold, they close the entrance to the nest and rest quietly below ground until the following spring.

Savage Ant Warriors

Not all ants are as settled in their ways as the cornfield ant. There are some that do not bother to build homes at all. They are constantly on the move, wandering from place to place in search of food. Among these nomads are the driver ants of Africa and tropical America. They march in close formation in columns an inch or two wide – sometimes the columns are a mile long.

Many species of ants are savage fighters. Sometimes battles are fought by two colonies of the same species, but more often it is a struggle of one species against another. The fighting may occur between two large groups or even between two individual ants. Watch a lively group of ants on the ground, you may see two struggling over a bit of food. Or you may watch without ever discovering the cause of the conflict.

Since members of different colonies look exactly alike, you may wonder how ants in such a struggle know friend from foe. You may see individuals meet and move peacefully along, or at other times individuals may immediately start fighting. It seems possible that an ant's antennae help it to distinguish its own partners from the opposition; when two individuals meet, the antennae of each automatically touch the head of the other. There is also a theory that ants have a characteristic odor, which varies with each colony and thereby helps distinguish the members of various colonies.

Some Unpopular Insects

A young nature collector who can add an abandoned hornet's nest to his home exhibits is rightly proud. It is a real showpiece and an impressive example of the skills of certain insects. Nevertheless, because of its dreaded sting, the wasp itself is rarely admired.

The bald-faced hornet is one of several wasps that manufacture paper by chewing bits of wood to a pulp and then use it to construct a nest. Some wasps like the hornet suspend their nest from a branch of a tree or bush; others attach their nest to eaves or barn roofs; and yet others locate them in cavities in the ground or in tree trunks.

Wasps, when they are busy with their home construction, fly off in search of weathered wood, such as wood fibers in an old post or building, or a piece of dead tree trunk. From any one of these sources a wasp builder bites and tears the fiber with its mandibles, taking enough to form a pellet about an eighth of an inch across the middle. It tucks this pellet under its chin and chews until the wood is turned into a mass of doughy pulp.

The wasp then returns to its nest, and landing astride an unfinished layer of paper it has been making, it presses down the new ball of pulp, biting it to fasten it in place. It walks slowly backward, unraveling the ball and fastening it to the layer of paper below. When the new pulp is laid out, the wasp then runs forward and backs up once again, biting the pulp all along the way. Then it flies off to collect more fiber while the pulp is drying.

It is usually safe to watch bald-faced hornets (or yellow jackets, which also are papermakers) at work so long as you do not disturb them. But if you poke at their nest or meddle with their activities, you will quickly discover the significance of the phrase 'mad as a hornet.'

Paper nests are not the only kind built by wasps. Your observant youngster may come across cartridge-shaped cells made of mud attached to the walls of garages, barns, or other buildings. Such cells are constructed by mud-daubers. At first there is only one cell, about an inch long. Soon another is added to it, and before long there may be a half dozen more. If on a hot summer day you catch sight of these wasps collecting little balls of mud at the side of a puddle of water, you know that the insect masons are in the midst of home-building.

Wood-Eating Termites

Most children know something about the notorious termites and the damage they do to wood, but few get to see them. These insects live in the seclusion of tunnels, and the first intimation of their presence in a house may come when a wooden step gives way, or the foundations show signs of crumbling. Termites have been known to eat through window frames and demolish tabletops. The one time you are likely to see termites in daylight is during the marriage flight of a colony. On such an occasion swarms of winged male and female termites may emerge from the walls, porch supports, or wood foundations of a house and fly upward.

Although termites are often called white ants, they belong to an entirely different order of insects. It is easy to distinguish them by their shape; termites are broad where thorax and abdomen join. They do not have the indentation, or waist, that all ants have. Worker and soldier termites are almost colorless and are blind. The winged females and males, the future queens and kings of the new colonies, do have vision. Actually termites are more closely related to roaches than to ants.

Nearly any child can tell you that termites eat wood. But few people are aware of a strange alliance that makes it possible for them to live on this substance. Each termite harbors in its body numerous tiny one-celled animals. These minute creatures break down the cellulose content of the wood so that the termite can digest it. (This is one of the more remarkable examples of symbiosis – that is the living together of two totally different living things in which both may benefit from the relationship.) If a termite were placed in a temperature high enough to kill these parasites, the termite would continue to eat wood for a while but would derive no nourishment from it and would eventually die of starvation.

How Bees Behave

What probably impresses children above all else about bees is their stinging ability. 'Can only females sting? Is it true that a bee dies after it stings you?' I have heard youngsters eagerly wait for answers to these questions while the topic of producing honey never came up.

Tormenting humans is hardly the primary use of the bees' stingers. The first queen bee to hatch in a colony immediately rips open other queen cells, and unless restrained by worker bees, stings the other queens to death. This does away with all potential rivals. Queens have the ability to sting again and again, but they use their stings only on other queens. It is the worker bee that may sting a person, and it commits suicide by doing so. Stinging brings

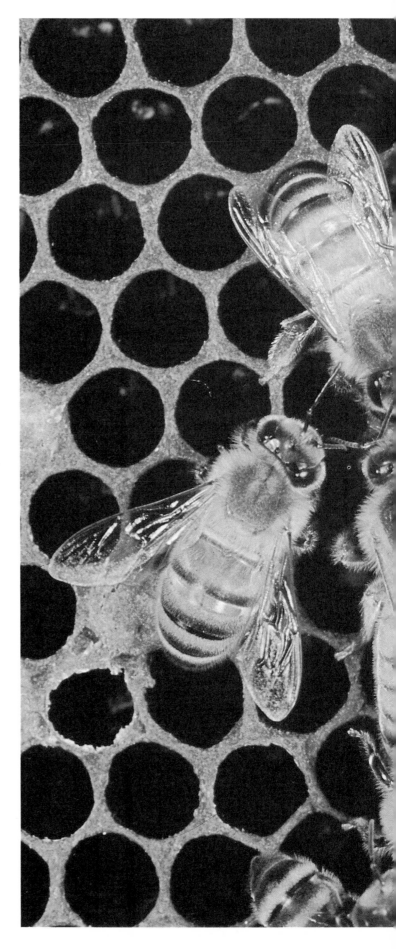

A queen honeybee (below) is rarely seen by anyone except a beekeeper who watches closely over the hives, because she spends nearly all her life in the dark interior. There she is fed by worker bees (left). Her first flight from the hive occurs when she reaches full growth. As she circles high in the air, a swarm of male bees follow. One, outdistancing the others, reaches her and mating takes place. She then returns to the hive and begins laying eggs. These are placed in wax brood cells, which are sealed off by workers (bottom).

twenty-two muscles into play, and once the barbed sting sticks in the victim, it is torn from the bee's body as the insect leaves, and the resulting damage causes death.

The order of insects to which bees, as well as wasps and ants, belong is Hymenoptera ('membrane wings'); the only one in which genuine stingers are found. The stinger actually is the modified ovipositor (the egg-laying organ) of the female worker; obviously the males (drones) do not possess stingers. In early summer when a mass of bees leave their hive with a queen to find a new home, they seem quite tolerant; they almost never sting during this swarming.

Many children and even adults have the mistaken idea that all bees store honey. This is true of only a few of the thousands of species of bees. Most eat the nectar as they take it from flowers rather than use it for honey.
The true honeybee, valuable in fertilizing such plants as clover and fruit trees, is native to Europe. Members of this species were introduced to North America by colonists in the seventeenth century and have been highly valued by beekeepers ever since. If you find honeybees in hollow trees in the woods, they are swarms that have escaped from man-made hives, or are their descendants.

What Goes on in a Beehive
Many children are familiar with man-made beehives, which are built to house bee colonies in order to take advantage of the bees' production of honey. This kind of hive usually has one lower story in which frames are used both for the brood and for the honey that the bees need in winter. There are more upper stories with extra frames for storing honey.

As they would do in a natural hive, the bees house their brood in the lower section; then they work hard filling the top part with honey. Beekeepers remove the upper frames as they are filled. Small sections of each frame, containing about a pound of honey, are taken out and sold in the frame. Honey removed from the larger frames is sold as liquid.

To store honey honeybees manufacture cells from a wax produced by certain glands in their bodies. Bumblebees also produce wax for the cells, but many species make their cells of wood, leaves, or earth. The making of a honeybee comb is an amazing example of cooperative effort. A group of the

▷ Bees have the remarkable ability to communicate with each other by means of special dances. In this way, one bee that has found a good food source can pass on the information to the workers of the rest of the hive.

The basic dance follows a figure-eight pattern and is performed on the vertical side of the honeycomb. As the bee flies back to its hive from the source of nectar, it notes the position of the sun relative to the food and the hive. It then transfers this information into the form of the dance. If the honey source is directly south of the hive at noon, then the bee performs its dance vertically on the honey comb (1). By afternoon the sun may have moved some 60° relative to the food and hive, and so the bee also moves its dance by an angle of 60° (2). If the sun makes an angle of 120° with the food source, then the 60° dance is reversed (3).

These dances are only used if the food source is at some distance from the hive. If it is close by, the dance is a circular one which does not indicate direction. The figure-eight dance can also tell the bees the distance between the source and the hive. The faster the bee wags its abdomen while dancing, the closer the food source.

▽ This modern hive, made of wood or aluminum, has largely replaced the old wickerwork beehives that were considered unhygienic. Rectangular frames are slotted inside the hive and can be easily removed for inspection or when full of honey.

▷▷ The beekeeper, examining a frame covered with bees, is wearing the protective clothing essential for his work. The special hat has a netting skirt which guards his face while allowing him to see through it. The gun (right of hive) produces smoke which slows the bees down so that they are less likely to sting.

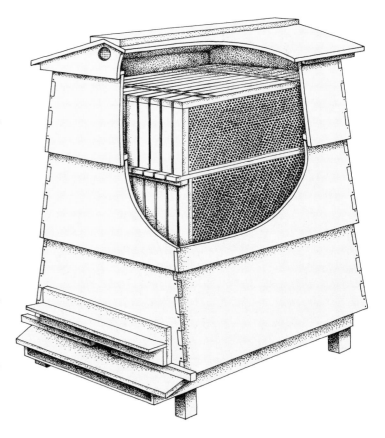

hive

food source

hive

60°

food source

hive

120°

1

60°

2

3

120°

bees will form a living curtain of their bodies, each one holding on with its forefeet to the hind feet of the bee above. After they have remained in this position for some time, little plates of wax appear on each insect's abdomen. They then chew the wax and form it into a comb.

The nectar that the bees take from flowers becomes honey in a part of their bodies known as the honey stomach. This is not involved in ordinary digestion; in the honey stomach the nectar mixes with secretions from certain glands, thus causing chemical changes. The cane sugar of nectar, for example, is changed into the fruit sugar of honey – a form of sugar that humans can digest more easily.

Insect Oddities

Insects provide many of nature's most remarkable oddities. You have discovered one of them when you observe a curious bump, or ball, on a plant stem or flower. It looks like a large nut growing on a tree branch, but if you cut one open you will discover an insect larva at its center. It is known as a gall, the home of a growing creature that will develop into a small wasp, fly or moth.

The young nature observer is likely to be puzzled by the imprisoned larva. 'How does it get in there? I don't see any opening from the outside.'

Actually the larva does not get in; its home has grown about it. Let us follow the life cycle of one of the common gall insects, choosing a very small wasp responsible for a gall known as the oak apple. In early spring the wasp deposits its eggs on the leaf of a scarlet oak. When one of these eggs develops into a legless and almost colorless larva, there is an immediate change in the leaf. Vegetable fibers start to grow, radiating out from the little grub; as this process continues, a thin smooth crust forms around the outer edges. This is now known as the oak apple, and the insect larva is completely surrounded by food, as well as protected by its globular house. Inside the gall the larva eats, completes its growth, changes to a pupa, and at last emerges as a wasp, no more than a quarter of an inch in length.

The oak apple is but one of the many kinds of gall. You may see two different types on goldenrod stems. One of them, made by a grub that becomes a fly, is spherical in shape; the other, which is spindle-shaped, develops into a tiny moth. There also is the willow cone gall, produced by a little gnat. It lays its eggs on the tip of the bud of a twig. This stops the further growth of the twig and stunts the leaves into small scales, which overlap in rows around the larva. The very pretty galls often found on wild rosebushes resemble small chestnut burs; they are pink and green when young, but later they turn brown.

Grasshoppers and Their Music

Grasshoppers are divided into two groups – the short-horned and long-horned families. The horns (really the antennae) are considered long if they are nearly as long as or are longer than the insect's body. Katydids belong to the long-horned group.

Katydids have become so closely indentified with their name because of their insistent refrain *Katy did, no she didn't,* that people sometimes forget that these insects are really grasshoppers. People hearing them on a summer night may refer to their 'singing.' However, 'fiddling' is a better word for their music. A male katydid – the females do not 'fiddle' – rubs its left wing over the right wing. On the left wing is a filelike row of ridges; on the right wing is a hard little scraper just behind the shoulder where the wings overlap. The scraper rubbing over the ridges produces the fiddling sound. It is the broad-winged katydid that plays its name with insistent repetition. The large oblong-winged species has a refrain of *zzzzzz-ipswich.* The work-tailed bush katydid plays a slow *zeep-zeep-zeep.* The common meadow katydid fiddles several soft *zees* in a row, each faster than the one before, then holds a higher-toned *zee.*

A short-horned grasshopper has a different fiddling technique. Its long hind leg forms the bow; a coarse outer wing is the fiddle. It may play one leg at a time or both sides together – a kind of 'one-man duet.' However, little actual music is created by these efforts, and the resulting rasps can be heard no more than a few feet away.

Both male and female grasshoppers have large hearing organs. You can see what looks like an oval window on each side of the first abdominal segment under the wings. This is the outer part of what might be referred to as the grasshopper's ears.

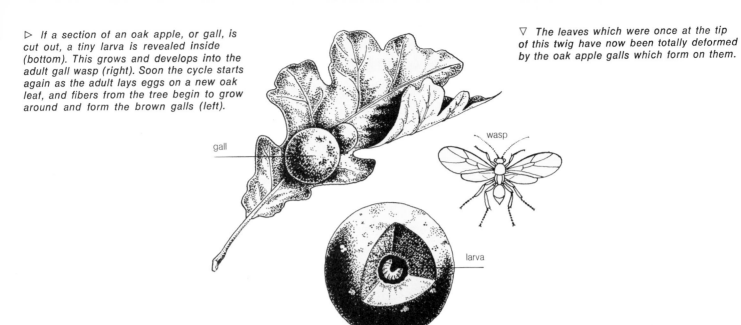

▷ If a section of an oak apple, or gall, is cut out, a tiny larva is revealed inside (bottom). This grows and develops into the adult gall wasp (right). Soon the cycle starts again as the adult lays eggs on a new oak leaf, and fibers from the tree begin to grow around and form the brown galls (left).

gall

wasp

larva

▽ The leaves which were once at the tip of this twig have now been totally deformed by the oak apple galls which form on them.

Chirpy, Cheery Crickets

It may seem that katydids dominate the summer serenades of the insect world but crickets also contribute their share to the melodious performances. They produce music with their wings in the same way that katydids do. The tune of the common snowy tree cricket begins as a musical *waa-waa-waa,* played at first by each individual on his own but soon they join forces and play as if they were following a conductor's baton.

The performance of the snowy tree cricket seems to be directly related to the temperature: by counting the number of notes it produces every minute, you can estimate what the temperature is. A hundred chirps to the minute indicates that the temperature is 63 degrees. The tempo increases as the temperature rises and slows down when it gets cooler.

The common black crickets, with their clear chirping, are the first insect musicians to be heard in the summer. Often you may discover them if you turn over a log or a stone. They run fast, but despite their muscular-looking legs, they do not imitate the grasshopper's high-jump tactics. The European cricket, now quite well established in the eastern United States, is a persistent fiddler. Unfortunately once these musicians find their way indoors, they do not limit their activities to making music; they may get into food and eat holes in everything made of cloth.

The Indestructible Fly

There are many species of flies, but probably the most familiar to us is the common housefly. It is easy to understand the problem of keeping this insect in check once we are aware of the rate at which they reproduce. The female lays a mass of from twenty-five to a hundred eggs at a time. In less than a day these hatch into tiny white maggots about the size of a pin point. These maggots, or larvae, mature in four or five days and then enter the pupa stage, which lasts about another five days. The full-grown fly now emerges. Within a few days the females of this brood may lay another mass of eggs, and produce young of their own. During warm weather generations follow each other from within two weeks to a month. Adult flies, eggs, and larvae are destroyed by cold weather, but pupae survive in their protective shell, remaining inactive during the winter. With the onset of warm weather they develop quickly, and the same process begins again. The average life of an adult is from two to three weeks. Some live considerably longer.

If you have ever watched a fly cleaning itself, you must have wondered at its reputation for being dirty. Its grooming is remarkably thorough. First it rubs its front feet together briskly so that the hairs on one leg act as a brush for the other. Then it nibbles at its front feet with the rasping disk it has in lieu of teeth. Next it gives its whole head an energetic scrubbing, and then it pulls forward its middle pair of legs one at a time and brushes and nibbles them. Finally its hind feet are used to clean each other and to brush the wings and most of the body.

This careful grooming, however, is of no use in protecting our health, for flies can breed in manure. The odor of fermented and decayed plants and animals also has a special attraction for them. Therefore harmful germs often cling to their feet, and these may easily be deposited on food. Typhoid fever and amebic dysentery are among the many diseases they help spread.

Flies differ from most other adult insects in having only a single pair of wings instead of two pairs. (Dragonflies, mayflies, and some other insects with the word *fly* in their name are not flies at all.) Nevertheless, with their single pair of wings they seem able to remain in the air indefinitely. Instead of hind wings they have short stalks, or knobs, which help to balance them as they fly.

You may observe how a fly crawls up walls, windows, and across a ceiling as easily as it walks across the floor. Two tiny claws on the last segment of each foot are an aid in this. It also has on each foot two small flat pads covered on the lower side with tiny hairs; these hairs give out a sticky fluid, which effectively holds the insect on slippery surfaces and in an upside down position. It is on these hairs that innumerable germs can be carried.

The Bloodthirsty Mosquito

Of all flies the mosquito is surely the most troublesome to humans. There are many hundreds of species, and they live almost everywhere on earth. Nearly all have one habit in common: sucking blood, which they need in order to thrive. Apparently in most species the female must have one meal

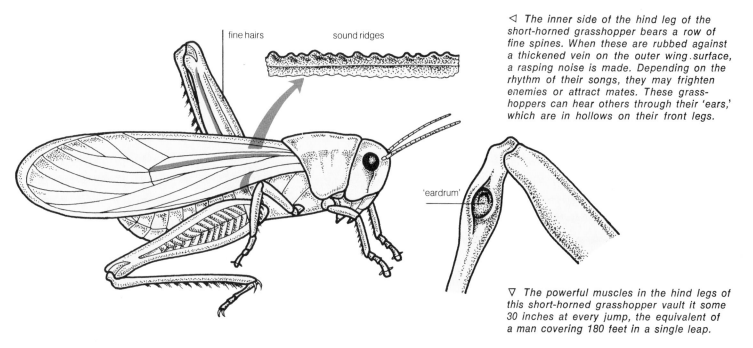

◁ The inner side of the hind leg of the short-horned grasshopper bears a row of fine spines. When these are rubbed against a thickened vein on the outer wing surface, a rasping noise is made. Depending on the rhythm of their songs, they may frighten enemies or attract mates. These grasshoppers can hear others through their 'ears,' which are in hollows on their front legs.

fine hairs

sound ridges

'eardrum'

▽ The powerful muscles in the hind legs of this short-horned grasshopper vault it some 30 inches at every jump, the equivalent of a man covering 180 feet in a single leap.

of blood before she can develop eggs. Some species seek the blood of animals, but the common house mosquito seems to prefer human blood.

The females, like female bees, are the troublemakers for human beings. They have piercing, sucking mouth parts. Some males have what is somewhat like an elongated beak, but it is not suited for piercing skin; they live on the juices of fruits and plants. It is the females, too, that give out a high-pitched whine by vibrating thin hard projections that lie across the breathing pores.

Mosquito eggs hatch only in water. Small puddles are fine breeding grounds for them, and even if the eggs have been laid on dry land, a hard rain may provide sufficient moisture for them to develop. The water must remain long enough – from two to three weeks – for egg, larva, and pupa stages to be completed.

Often a child believes he has discovered a giant mosquito when he sees a long-legged, gangling creature awkwardly drifting through the air. Most likely it is a crane fly, an absolutely harmless insect. In spring and autumn swarms of crane flies dance in clumsy, blundering flight a few feet above the ground or water.

Praying Mantids

I know of a girl for whom the praying mantis will always seem a curiosity if only because of the way she first became acquainted with this insect. On a summer evening one of them alighted on the windowsill at her New York City apartment. It would be hard to imagine a more unlikely intruder in a large city than this queer creature with its pointed, elfin face and big round eyes. The child managed to get it into a box and took it to the American Museum of Natural History in the belief that she had something on the order of a visitor from Mars. There she learned the true nature of her captive. In natural surroundings mantids are great hunters, capturing by stealth such lively insects as butterflies, mosquitoes, grasshoppers, beetles, and flies. The mantis lies in wait with its front legs upraised in a prayerlike pose, and when its prey approaches, it snatches at the victim with lightning speed. The prey has little chance of escaping the rows of sharp spines on the second and third joints of the forelegs.

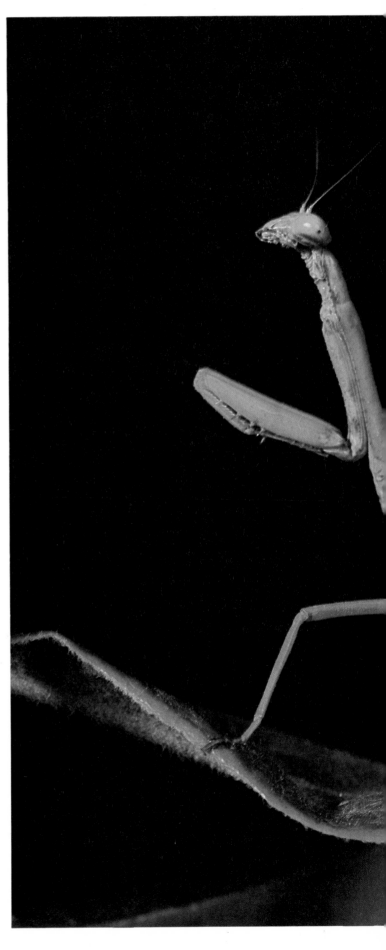

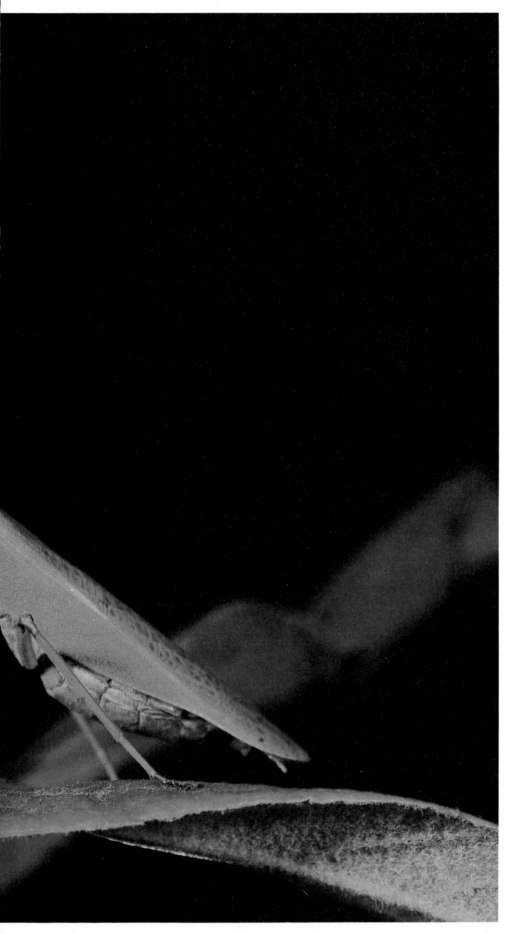

◁ Two different spellings may be seen in the name of the mantid: praying and preying. Both are appropriate because the insect assumes a prayerful attitude as it waits for victims, and it is a flesh-eater, preying on various insects that come near. Some mantids are native to the United States; others were imported and have now become widespread. This species is native to South Africa.

△ The individual above shows its wings extended. Though they are heavy-bodied, mantids are excellent fliers.

During the winter, mantid's brownish egg cases, about the size of walnuts, may be collected from weeds and bushes. In the spring at least a few hundred babies will emerge from one of them.

Mantids of the southern United States are native to that area, but a species found commonly in northern regions originally came from China and Japan; there is also a species from Europe. At first they were introduced from abroad by accident. Later more were imported for their value in destroying insect pests. However, since they also eat ladybugs and other insects valuable to farmers, they are not entirely beneficial. In China they are sometimes tied by a silk thread to a bedroom windowsill where they trap flies and mosquitos.

Dragonflies – Beautiful and Useful

Although the dragonfly is one of the most beautiful of all insects, and harmless as well, any child may be frightened by some of its common names and the fables from which these names originated. 'Devil's darning needle' recalls the ancient superstition that the insect sewed up children's ears. 'Mule killer' is a reminder that it was once believed to kill livestock. The name 'snake doctor' was inspired by the weird notion that it resuscitated dead water snakes.

All of these stories and the names derived from them are ridiculous, of course, but one name, that of mosquito hawk, is well deserved. In their nymphal stage (spent in the water) dragonflies eat great quantities of mosquito larvae. As an adult a dragonfly catches all sorts of insects – flies, honeybees, butterflies, and even other dragonflies smaller than itself. The nymph has a long underlip that folds back between its front legs. When it approaches a victim, this lower lip shoots out rapidly and grasps the prey with two claws that form a pair of pinchers at the end. This interesting insect neither stings nor bites people.

If you are an early riser, and especially if you are camping, you may some day enjoy the memorable sight of a dragonfly emerging from its nymph. You would have to be at the edge of a pond about six o'clock of a summer's morning and watch carefully. When it happens, the nymph crawls out of the water up a tree trunk, water plant, or some other support. Sure of this support, it then strains at its armorlike

covering until the skin of its back splits along its length. Then very carefully it begins to pull its soft body from the shell. This accomplished, two pairs of transparent, glistening wings expand and harden. They are beautifully tinted in blue and brown. The insect has an elongated body, and its great compound eyes cover almost the entire surface of its head.

To distinguish a dragonfly from its close relative the damselfly is not easy. They are alike in many ways; yet the dragonfly has a larger body and is a stronger flier. The dragonfly always holds its wings outstretched when resting; a damselfly holds its wings together over its back.

Water Insects

Summer outings are a lot of fun for your children if they make acquaintance of some of the odd little creatures found in ponds and streams. One of the most easily observed is the whirligig beetle, which you may see spinning in circles on the water's surface.

Whirligigs are usually found in groups, sometimes made up of hundreds of individuals. If alarmed, they make a sudden dive. They prefer shade to bright sunshine and may sometimes be found on the water, resting on sticks or rocks. The whirligig's eyes are worth special mention. Each is divided so that the upper half looks into the air while the lower half looks down into the water. Its legs are also specialized; the middle and hind legs are broad and oarlike, while the front pair are long and slender. Another strange feature of the whirligig is that if you hold one in your hand for a time, you will find that it gives off a white milky fluid that smells something like ripe apples.

Water striders, usually found in fresh and brackish water, have long, slender middle and hind legs. It is difficult to capture them, because they skate away with great speed. The middle pair of legs propels the insect over the water while the hind pair steers. The color is dull dark-brown above with a silvery white underside.

Another water insect, the back swimmer, is named for its habit of swimming on its back, which is shaped like the bottom of a canoe. You may see one as it hangs head downward in the water, but when alarmed, it propels itself

The children's rhyme 'Ladybug, ladybug, fly away home, your house is on fire, your children are gone' has a firm basis in fact. The ladybug larvae—its 'children'—are scattered all over the fields just when farmers burn back the stubble of the past year's wheat crop. Without doubt, many are killed in this way, but far more survive to continue eating insect pests, thus endearing themselves to farmer and fruit grower alike.

The life of the ladybug: an adult female lays her eggs on the underside of a leaf (below). Up to 200 eggs may be laid, in several batches. After about a week, each egg hatches into a larva, which immediately begins to feed hungrily. Its favorite food is aphids (right); thus, ladybugs are much liked by farmers, for aphids are a great danger to crop plants. After about three weeks, the larva becomes a pupa, from which hatches the adult insect (bottom of page). The fine wings of the ladybug can be folded neatly under its colorful, spotted wing cases. The close-up photograph opposite shows the wing cases lifted up as a ladybug lands clumsily on a flower.

swiftly away – bottom side up – pushing with its hind legs. The more common species are about half an inch long, and they have enormous compound eyes. The back, which you do not see when it is swimming, is pearl-colored. The underside, which you do see, is darker.

Among the fascinating creatures of ponds and streams are some which, like the dragonfly, spend their early life in the water; and later, as adults, live on land and in the air. Check out shallow pools for one of the most interesting of these water insects. At first you may see what appears to be a stick, one or two inches long and half an inch around. If it starts to move along the bottom of the pool or up the stem of a plant, you know it is animal rather than vegetable. It is the larva of a small mothlike insect called the caddis fly.

Many caddis fly larvae make coverings out of pebbles, sticks, or other materials as a protection for their caterpillarlike bodies. Those that use sticks for their coverings are said to construct 'log cabins.' More commonly they use sand or bits of vegetable matter. This is made to adhere to their bodies with silk, produced by certain glands.

Welcoming Ants Indoors

The ant is one kind of creature that may be collected with a clear conscience. These insects exist in such tremendous numbers that people usually are more concerned with destroying than with caring for them. However, a colony of ants, properly housed, is an appealing hobby.

The ants' living quarters may be constructed as a do-it-yourself project, or a colony may be bought in a hobby shop, complete with the insect residents. If you are collecting your own ants, of course it is important to know the best species to look for and which members of a colony to take. The abundant cornfield ant is a good choice of species.

If you can capture a queen (recognizable because of her larger size), and also gather a number of larvae and pupae, you have the makings of the entire life cycle of a colony, from eggs to adults. Even without a queen, the workers are fascinating to watch. You may see them constructing a central hall, excavating a system of tunnels, grooming themselves with tongue and front legs (something they do repeatedly), or lying down to sleep, legs pulled close.

Caring for a colony is quite simple. About once a week water should be inserted into the soil, and tiny bits of apple, banana, lean cooked meat, and dry bread crumbs provide a good diet. Their need for sweets is satisfied by a drop of honey every few days.

To encourage their activities, the ants must be sheltered from bright light. If the home you provide for them has glass sides, these should be kept covered except when you are making observations.

Caring for Crickets

In nature not many crickets survive the coming frost. However, if they are taken in as pets, they will often live through the winter. You can make a cricket cage simply with a flowerpot full of earth and the chimney of a kerosine lamp. Sink the chimney into the earth to a depth of two inches and cover the top with mosquito netting, held in place by a strong rubber band. Or you can make an attractive home with an aquarium, also covered with mosquito netting, with soil and plants set on the bottom, to make the cage as attractive as possible.

After you catch a cricket, place it inside its cage with bits of cabbage leaf and other greens, and fasten the mosquito netting top. Aside from providing leafy food, it is a good idea to occasionally drop a little corn meal saturated with water into the cage. Periodically the inside should be sprayed gently with water to keep the atmosphere moist. It is not practical to keep more than one cricket in a cage; frequently they will fight savagely.

Growing Your Own Butterflies

Some years ago butterfly and moth collecting were popular hobbies. But now that so many people populate the earth and wildlife of all kinds is diminishing, collecting, as a rule, should not be encouraged. Instead you may have a new hobby; that is, actually raising butterflies.

Butterfly gardens can be bought at some hobby shops or by mail order. A garden kit includes a container equipped with caterpillars about half grown, as well as enough food to take care of their needs. After they become chrysalides, they are moved into the actual garden – an enclosure suitable for their emergence into winged adults.

A closeup of an ant lion shows the fine tracery of its wing veins. With its long, narrow body, this insect looks somewhat like a dragonfly, but it does not live near water. The name comes from the habits of its larva, which preys on ants with its huge pincerlike jaws. In the southern states the larvae are also known as doodlebugs.

Colors for Defense and Warning

Animal colors are a source of endless fascination, and few animals are more famous for them than the butterflies and moths. The bright, cryptic, or contrasting patterns exist to help insects survive in a world where many birds and other animals consider them good eating.

Camouflage is the most straightforward use of color patterns. Combined with special shapes, it reaches peaks of perfection in the angel-wing butterflies, which imitate leaves in the 'green marvel' moth that seems to merge with the tree bark, and in the small moths that actually look like the scattered white spots of bird droppings. The caterpillars, too, make an art of camouflage. The inchworms, famous in song and fable, can resemble twigs so closely that even when they smother a bush or tree, they are hardly noticed.

Camouflage alone is not enough for some types of moths. They employ 'shock tactics' known as flash coloration. They have camouflage colors on the upper wings, so that they blend into their usual background. But if an enemy is not fooled and comes too close, the moth suddenly pulls forward the top wings to reveal very bright colors on the bottom ones, often enough of a surprise to an inquisitive bird to frighten it away. Adding to this trick, other species of moth have large eye spots on their lower wings, so that the intruder is fooled by eyes that look big enough to belong to one of its own enemies.

Such color schemes are bluff—they simply shock an enemy to scare it away. In contrast, many moths and butterflies advertise themselves with bright, clashing patterns of red, yellow, and black. But these are intended to warn hungry birds that they are not good to eat. The brightly colored monarch butterflies, for example, have poisonous blood. The swallowtails and the spectacular tiger moth are also poisonous and unappetizing.

But not all moths and butterflies that seem to be advertising their poison are really doing so. Some boldly colored but unrelated species merely imitate the nasty ones, thus sharing the protection of their colors. Once a bird has had an unpleasant experience when it tries to eat—for instance—a monarch butterfly, it will certainly hesitate before trying to peck a viceroy butterfly. The latter looks just like a monarch, but contains no poison.

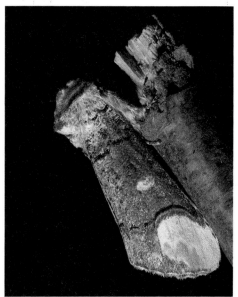

Well camouflaged by the colors of its top wings, a red underwing moth (opposite, above) rests on a tree trunk. When alarmed (below), the same moth tries to scare the enemy by flashing its bright lower wings. The same shock tactics are improved by an io moth (this page, bottom), which has eye spots on its lower wings. The colors of the burnet moth (left) are a poison-warning, while the harmless buff-tip moth (below) is disguised as the tip of a twig.

Welcoming Ants Indoors

Keeping ants at home is an interesting and educational hobby. An ant home (known as a formicarium) is easily made with the aid of a wooden mold, some plaster of Paris and some oblong sheets of glass, together with a little plasticine. The mold may also be made of an old shoe box coated with vaseline (petroleum jelly). There are two basic do-it-yourself types of formicarium. (The glass-walled types are best bought complete with occupants from a hobby shop.)

For the first type, which is a 'closed' home, have the glass cut 1″ narrower and $\frac{1}{2}$″ shorter than the mold's inside measurements. Lay the glass on a sheet of celan card. Press the plasticine into a sheet $\frac{1}{8}$″ to $\frac{1}{4}$″ thick and cut three or four circles from it, the largest around $2\frac{1}{2}$″ in diameter. Press them on the glass and connect them with 'worms' of plasticine of the same thickness. Place a $3″ \times 1″ \times 1″$ block of wood, smeared with vaseline, near one end (see diagram), and connect it with two more 'worms.' Finally, place the wooden mold over the glass so that it is centered, with the end opposite the wooden block flush against the wall of the mold.

Mix a large bowl of plaster of Paris: add the powder to the water (not the other way round) until it resembles thick cream after careful mixing. Pour it slowly over the glass in the mold to a depth of a couple of inches, tap the sides to level it off nicely, and leave it for twenty-four hours. After this time, turn it all over, take away the card (using a knife if needed) and trim away any excess that stops the glass moving back and forth, or that overhangs when the plasticine is removed. You now have a wood-lined block of plaster with the living rooms for the ants and an accurate glass roof.

Some experts maintain, however, that this type of formicarium is a 'prison' for ants, and prefer a more open type. This is molded in the same way but with only one large compartment for the ants and an unconnected rectangle for keeping up the moisture level. This type should be placed on a small stand (a slab of wood with big nails for legs is ideal) with the legs standing in bottle-tops filled with DDT (10 percent) to prevent escapes. A hole is bored from the living quarters to the outside, and food and drink supplied in the manner shown. Some ants prefer a combination of both types, in which this design is given several rooms.

When you have collected some ants (see opposite) tip them into a bowl of water to which a couple of drops of detergent have been added. They will sink. As soon as they have stopped moving, strain them off with a tea strainer and put them in a cell of the nest. They will soon recover, none the worse for their experience. At all times when not observing the ants in any type of formicarium, keep a piece of card over the glass so that the ants are in the dark.

The ants will feed quite well on sugar or honey solution, freshly killed insects, and scraps of meat of fish. This should be placed in the square compartment of the closed type, and in a matchbox or similar container in the open one. Keep the plaster slightly moist in both by adding a little water to the squared compartment.

Catching the ants presents few problems. If they are the type that lives under stones, replace their stone with a flat slate, wait two or three days, and return on a sunny afternoon. Using a square tin can, the lifted slate can be scraped clean of many ants. Not all species can be taken in this way, so the glass jar catcher, known as a pooter, illustrated, comes into its own. It is simply a glass jar, couple of pieces of glass and rubber tubing, and *very important,* a piece of muslin over the shorter tube. Simply point the flexible tube at the insect to be collected, and suck sharply. This is a good method for selecting the essential queen ant, recognizable by her large size.

insect collection jar

filter

insect in

food

water

DDT

open formicarium

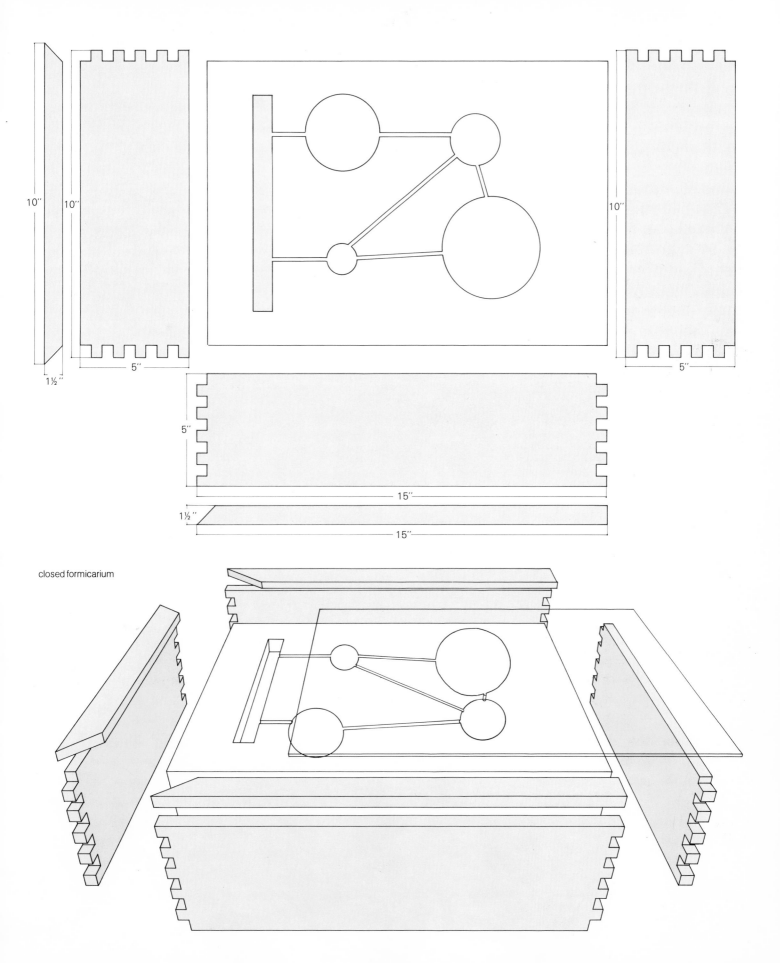

10''

10''

1½''

5''

10''

5''

5''

15''

1½''

15''

closed formicarium

Plants, Trees, and Flowers

Children are likely to find animals more interesting than plants. It seems to them that plants are inactive or even inanimate, whereas animals are lively and do all sorts of unexpected things. Yet if people, young or old, stop to think about it, they soon realize that plants produce the food on which all animal life – including human life – depends. They also produce all the exquisite flowers and abundant leaves that add beauty to the world. Certainly plants are anything but inactive.

Like animals, plants are made up of living cells. Like animals, they feed, breathe, grow, and reproduce themselves. They are also capable of motion, such as those that shoot their seeds and those that close their flower petals at night and open them in the morning. Such observations may stimulate a young mind to wonder: 'What is the difference between plants and animals?'

The one vital difference is in the way they feed themselves. Animals must secure their nourishment from organic materials; they cannot take the necessary elements out of inorganic compounds in nature. By contrast a plant produces its own food by turning nonliving (inorganic) matter into living matter. This wonderful process is made possible by the green substance known as chlorophyll.

Chlorophyll is often called leaf green because it is found chiefly in leaves. When this substance is activated by sunlight, chemical changes occur that transform inorganic matter into life-giving and life-sustaining matter. Animals do not have chlorophyll; they cannot manufacture food from raw materials, air and sunlight. Without plants, therefore, animal life could not exist.

If you examine green leaves, you will notice that generally they are darker on the upper side than underneath. The reason for this is that the chlorophyll-bearing cells on the top surface are packed more closely, thereby catching as much sunlight as possible. The manufacturing cells are protected on the top and bottom surfaces by a skin, or epidermis, which is perforated with innumerable tiny holes. Each hole is surrounded by two guard cells, the only surface cells that contain chlorophyll. Through these the leaf constantly takes in and gives off oxygen, carbon dioxide, and other gases as well as water vapor.

The Leaf Factory

Before manufacturing begins, a leaf also requires another item – a watery solution, containing many substances, that originates in the soil. This solution enters the plant roots, works its way up the stem, and then enters the leaf. Within each leaf carbon dioxide is separated into carbon and oxygen. In the same way, water is broken down into oxygen and hydrogen. The leaf cells combine the carbon with the hydrogen, and add oxygen to make a form of sugar that will nourish the plant. Chlorophyll accomplishes this remarkable feat, but it can take place only when sunlight, or artificial light approximating sunlight, shines on the plant.

Youngsters find it interesting that plants often change the position of their leaves according to the direction of the source of light, and that as the stem grows, its new leaves bend in order to avoid the shade of surrounding leaves.

Plants release oxygen in the daytime, and this helps to purify the air we breathe. But at night they give off carbon dioxide, a gas that is poisonous in considerable quantities. This explains why a room with many houseplants should be well aired at night.

A Flower's Workshop

Because flowers are such lovely creations, it might seem to a child that they are produced for the one purpose of bringing beauty to the world. That, however, is not the reason for their existence; they are necessary for the existence of the particular plant on which they grow.

The interested child who learns this is sure to wonder how this occurs. An over-simplified explanation – the production of seeds – may seem a satisfactory answer for a short time. But a more comprehensive explanation, which involves the description of a flower's working processes, is quite complex. This is especially true because there is considerable variation among flowers.

There are some factors that are applicable to all flowers. A pistil is one important part of what may be called a flower's workshop. At the bottom of each pistil is an ovary in which tiny seeds, called ovules, are formed. (Some ovaries contain a single ovule, others have many.) Each ovule contains an egg cell. When an egg cell is touched by a tube that grows

◁ *It would be a dull world if there were no plants to brighten the scene. Nature's way with flowers is to mix a brilliant jumble of colors and shapes, as in this summer alpine pasture.*

▽ *Man's way with plants is usually a little more orderly: in a family garden, the gardener will select plants carefully, according to their color, size, and growing season.*

▽ ▽ *In a formal garden, plants are often arranged to grow in geometric designs, such as this well-known symbol formed by succulent, fleshy-leaved desert plants.*

from a pollen grain, the ovule begins to grow and develops into a seed. Seeds remain in the ovary until they have ripened. Another important part of a flower is the pollen-bearing stamen.

In some types of flowers the parts that work together to make seeds are quite easily seen. However, in some flowers you need a magnifying glass, and in still others you could never see all the working parts in a single blossom. A lily is an example of what is called a perfect flower – that is, each blossom has a pollen-bearing stamen and a pistil with its ovary. But in some types of plant one flower has only the stamen while another flower bears only the pistil. The flower with the stamens is called the male flower, and the one with the pistil and ovary is the female flower. Within these two types there are also a number of variations in the way the seeds develop, in the way the seeds are nourished and protected, and in the manner they are scattered.

A Flower's Crowning Glory

As you study a flower, you will enjoy being able to name its more colorful parts. There is the corolla (a term meaning crown) which is composed of the petals. In many flowers it is made up of separate petals. In others, as in a squash flower, the petals are joined together so that only their points are separated. In some, as in the petunia and morning glory, the corolla is completely in one piece without any separation of petals.

In all these variations the petals are encircled by sepals. All of the sepals together make up the calyx, which serves to protect the flower, especially in its budding stage. Sepals are really specialized leaves. They vary in different kinds of flowers in size, shape, and number. Often they are green, as in roses. Sometimes, for example in tulips, they are the same color as the petals. On certain kinds of plants sepals fall off as soon as the flower opens. On many, such as apple blossoms and roses, they remain attached even after the seeds have ripened.

The Travels of Pollen

Pollen may be blown by wind from the stamen of a flower to stigmas which the sticky, broadened tips of pistils are called. More commonly, however, an insect going from one blossom to another in search of nectar gets pollen on its body, and later these grains rub off on stigmas. Once a pollen grain has become attached to a stigma, it quickly forms a tube which forces its way downward; the lifegerm of the pollen then goes through the tube to fertilize the egg cell within an ovule.

Because a fully developed seed is the embryo of a new plant, it must have a supply of stored food that can be used whenever conditions are right for the new plant to begin growing. In some seeds, such as peas and beans, the food is stored within certain parts of the embryo. Other plants develop elaborate structures about their seeds, which are called fruit. Apples and pears are familiar examples of these. When a scientist speaks of a fruit, he is usually referring to the ripened ovary of any kind of plant, from the pod of a pea or a hard nut to a juicy tomato. There are many opportunities for examining seeds when you are preparing dinner. To the diner, peas, beans, and corn are food. To a nature explorer they are seeds.

Flowers and Insects

When a child learns that pollen is transferred from one flower to another by messenger insects, he may wonder what attracts an insect to the flowers. Is it the sweet scent or the color of their petals?

For years it was a generally accepted theory that the chief value of color in flowers was to attract insects. Then a study was made of the insect's pollinizing role. It was found that bees and other flower-visiting insects have poor vision but a well-developed sense of smell. It was also demonstrated that in addition to the colors people see, some flowers emit ultraviolet rays. Although these rays are not visible to human eyes, insects can see them as well as, or even better than, the colors that the human eye perceives. It was concluded that color is, at most, only incidentally responsible for bringing insects to flowers.

Since then innumerable observations and experiments have shown that insects are attracted by the scent of flowers. One demonstration was made by the great botanist Luther Burbank, who worked for a long time to develop a petunia that would have fragrance. He knew that he had succeeded at last when he saw several bees hovering over one of the plants in a large bed of his experimental petunias.

The beautiful blossoms of fruit trees (below) attract many insects. These insects are essential to pollinate the flowers; only if the seeds are fertilized by the pollen will they develop into edible fruit, which is simply the fleshy covering of the fully-mature fertilized seeds. The flowers have both male and female parts, so any one of them can produce a fruit. This is not so for the hazel tree. Here the pollen is produced by the male, yellow catkin (left). This pollen is light and dry and is carried on the wind to the tiny female flower, which bears a tuft of red hairs that traps the pollen. Only the female flower can develop the hazel nuts.

The Travels of Seeds and Spores

Nature's own gardening techniques are interestingly varied. Among seeds alone there are numerous ways of planting new crops. Probably the most commonly observed distribution system is by wind, because seeds can be seen sailing through the air. On maple trees two seeds grow side by side and each has a thin, paperlike wing extending from it, so that a small but perfect flying machine is formed. After one has been carried by wind and has settled on the earth, if conditions are right, in time the seeds begin to germinate. Dandelions and milkweed are other plants that depend on wind. After their flowers have gone to seed, the silky tufts attached to the seeds are caught by passing breezes. Sooner or later, like tiny parachutes, they settle on the ground.

Waterborne seeds are a distinctive type. Probably the most noted example is the coconut: a seed has an outer fibrous husk with a waterproof coat. As the trees often overhang water along the borders of tropical shores, the fruit can drop into it. Buoyant because of many lightweight fibers inside its husk, the seed may drift for many miles before reaching land. After a while the hard covering cracks open, leaving the seed free to sprout and produce a new tree.

Some plants have both water and wind working for them. In both the American lotus and Egyptian lotus, for example, the flower is borne on a stiff stem which projects a foot or more above the water. Seeds develop in depressions in the flat upper face of a top-shaped receptacle, and they cannot fall out because the cavities open upward. However, when the wind blows hard enough, the receptacle is shaken by resulting waves, and the seeds are thrown out to begin their travels on the unquiet water.

Quite different are methods employed by plants on which hooks or spines develop on the outside coverings of seeds. Here a partnership between plants and animals is required, because the hooks or spines must become entangled with hair or fur, then be transported a distance away from the parent plant and brushed free. Of course they can catch on to a person's clothing with the same results. Other partners of plants are birds and mammals that eat fleshy fruits containing indigestible seeds. After eating, the animals travel about and eventually the seeds pass through their bodies falling on new growing grounds.

◁ ◁ *A bee is an important aid to plants in the dispersal of pollen. On this honeybee, baskets attached to the legs may be seen, in which masses of pollen are carried.*

◁ ▽ *Dandelions depend on wind for scattering seeds, which can easily sail away as moving air catches the silky tufts.*

◁ *A bullfinch enjoys a feast of honeysuckle berries. The seeds within the berries will pass through the bird's body, undigested.*
▽ *Burdock seeds travel by catching on to fur, hair, or clothing.*
▽ ▽ *A mushroom hit by a drop of water expels a cloud of spores.*

Some birds hide or store seeds. The blue jay, for one, will tuck away certain nuts or other fruits. The tufted titmouse inserts pine seeds into the bark of trees. A number of these eventually are eaten, but others reach the earth, perhaps by being washed down by rain. Even more than birds, rodents stow away seeds of the type commonly called nuts, placing many in situations favorable for their germination. The gray squirrel is an outstanding gardener in this way, for although the nuts are hidden to be used at a later time, many are never dug out. Squirrels, chipmunks, and mice are credited with the planting of many nut-bearing forest trees.

One of the most simple devices for scattering seeds is that of explosive fruit. Here the seed capsule of a plant bursts open and the seeds literally explode out of it. Violets, wild geraniums, and many members of the bean family use this method. When the ripened ovary of a sandbox tree bursts, it makes a noise like that of a pistol shot, and the seeds are scattered far and wide.

Long before seeds are ripe and ready for dispersal, insects and wind are helping plants to produce them: for seeds to be created, grains of pollen must get from stamens to pistils. Sometimes stamen flowers and pistil flowers are on the same plant and the pollen easily falls from one to the other. Sometimes, however, it is necessary for the pollen to be carried by wind; and often it is a busy bee that acts as a carrier. As this insect travels, pollen catches on its body hairs and so is carried from one flower to another. There are also special hairs that form tiny pollen-holding baskets.

With the great importance attached to seeds, it is almost startling to realize there are many successful plants that produce no seeds whatever—such plants as mushrooms and other fungi. These flowerless forms of plant life have, instead, microscopic spores. In the fruiting body of a mushroom, spores develop in fantastic numbers. When conditions are favorable, a spore rapidly grows out in the form of a thread and from this other threads develop, forming a mass called the mycelium. The bundle of threads is the true plant. It may grow for weeks or months, then finally is ready to produce a new fruiting body; and that is when a mushroom is said to spring up overnight. The sole purpose of the fruiting body is to produce new spores. As with seed dispersal, wind again comes to the aid of the fungus, carrying spores to countless locations, many of which will prove suitable for growth.

◁ Amid the ferns and fallen leaves of autumn, a gray squirrel buries a sweet chestnut. Of the thousands of nuts a squirrel buries or stores, it returns to eat only a few. In this way, it plants new trees and bushes.

▽ The dried central husk of a flag iris splits to reveal bright red seeds that attract birds to disperse them.

▽ ▽ The winged seeds of both sycamore and maple trees are carried, whirling like miniature helicopters, on the wind.

221

Plants Without Flowers

Anyone who has been studying flowers, and the seeds that they produce, may find it startling to realize that some plants do not produce flowers. How then, do those species continue to exist?

Flowerless plants have their own special kind of seed. Microscopic in size, it is properly called a spore. When a spore lands in a favorable growing place, it develops rapidly into a threadlike form. From this a whole mass of threads grows for weeks or even months until there is enough tissue to produce a fruiting body. Then with surprising suddenness a new plant appears.

Mushrooms and mosses are two well-known plants that produce spores. The moss spore grows a branched green thread on which leafy buds appear. These develop further into leafy stems, which in turn produce rootlike projections – not true roots. Some of the plants bear eggs at their leaf tips, and others produce sperms. Wind or the water from dew or rain may bring sperm and egg together. Then the egg is fertilized, and it develops delicate upright stalks on which spore cases, full of green spores, form.

Where to Find Moss

In late spring you can often see mosses in all stages of development. Although mosses are usually found in essentially moist places and on woodland floors, as well as on rocks and tree trunks where sunlight does not penetrate, what is probably the best-known species grows also in open fields and meadows. This species is known by several names, including pigeon-wheat and haircap moss. It flourishes in North America, Europe, and Asia. Rather a large moss, it has stems a foot long, and in fall or winter the stems become a bristling greenish brown mass. By summer new growth adds vivid green to the tips of the stems. During dry spells the small leaves shut lengthwise into mere threads, and these huddle against the stem to prevent their moisture from evaporating. After rain they open up again.

Ferns, Fronds, and Fiddleheads

Although lacking colorful petals, ferns are favored for gardens and home decorations because of their gracefully shaped fronds, or leaves. They are a delight to the eye from the time they come out of the ground, uncoiling like a watch spring, until the divided leaves are fully developed.

A characteristic sign of late summer is the appearance of mushrooms and toadstools. They grow very quickly—often during the night—and may be found in such places as on rotten tree stumps in a wood (opposite, top), among fallen leaves (opposite, below), or in damp grassy meadows (this page). They are often very attractive in color and shape, and some are good to eat; but it is difficult to tell simply by their appearance whether they are poisonous or edible.

Ferns, like mosses and mushrooms, produce spores. Some species also have an underground stem, called a rootstock, which pushes forward and sends up new fronds each year. One species is known as the walking fern because new growth starts where the tips of the fronds come in contact with the ground or with rocks.

If you look closely at a Christmas fern in early spring, you will notice on the underside of some of the leaflets a double row of circular raised fruit dots. They look somewhat like pale blisters. Later they turn brown, and by the middle of June masses of globules the size of pinpoints push out from under them. Each of these is a case packed with spores so tiny that even under a magnifying glass they look like yellowish powder. By July the brown covers have shrivelled into irregular scrolls, but they still cling to the ferns.

Several hundred million years ago, ferns and their relatives were the principal land plants on the earth. Century after century massive, but weak, fern trees fell, gradually filling swamps and marshes. Later the pressure of overlying mud that oozed over these regions turned the fern masses into coal. Occasionally the outline of a fern was imprinted in the slate or rock that formed from the muddy deposits as they pressed against the vegetation that was turning into coal. These ancient prints reveal that the appearance of ferns has not changed much in millions of years.

Plants Without Leaf Green
Considering how vital leaf green is to the growth of plants, it seems rather extraordinary that mushrooms and other fungi develop without a trace of green. No wonder that generations ago, when not much was known about plant life, people were in superstitious awe of magic toadstools. The plant apparently sprang out of nowhere, some being edible and some poisonous.

Lacking leaf green, mushrooms are unable to manufacture starch, sugar, and other elements. They must absorb these from dead wood, withered leaves, or soils enriched by the remains of green plants. They are a kind of fungi known as saprophytes ('living on decaying or dead matter'). They are valuable because they prevent forests from becoming choked with dead wood. As the fungi absorb tissue from stumps and old logs, the wood softens and falls apart.

Other kinds of fungi take their food from the cells of living things. Anything which lives on the tissues of another animal or plant – the host – without giving food or other materials back, is known as a parasite. These are often destructive to the plants and animals on which they grow. It is a parasitic fungus that causes potato blight. Another is responsible for the costly disease known as wheat rust. Some simple forms of parasitic fungi can cause serious diseases in animals.

Trees and How to Know Them
'Fun to climb!' 'Good to swing on!' These comments are likely to be the first appreciation children show of trees. But before long they may have a more serious understanding of the importance of trees. They witness an area flourishing with trees suddenly laid bare to make way for home developments or a shopping mall. They quickly see, then, how the area's beauty is destroyed; and in summer they discover that the surroundings are hotter than before, in winter more desolate. Such observations can prepare them for a broader appreciation of the value of trees, and the need to preserve them.

A few generations ago trees were one of the most important of natural resources. They furnished power in factories before coal and oil were available. They powered railroad trains and ships. The wood was used to manufacture houses, furniture and fences, and homes were kept warm with logs. Gradually this changed, and early in the nineteenth century an iron age began. By then vast forests had been destroyed and there was a significant tree shortage. Few people, however, gave attention to such a situation and ignored what was happening to the land, while the reckless waste of trees continued.

Later, after great farms had been destroyed by dust storms and other areas ruined by flood, federal programs were begun to save the soil. The importance of trees was soon made clear: their roots grip and hold soil firmly in place, the leafy canopies of forests have a beneficial effect on the soil under them and the air around them. Without the protective covering and the food supplies provided by woodlands, animal life – mammals, birds, reptiles and insects – would soon disappear and the land would rapidly become a desert with little chance of recovery.

▽ *Tightly furled young fern fronds show a characteristic 'fiddlehead' shape in spring (top). Gradually the fronds spread out to catch the sunlight (bottom), while on their undersides the powdery spores develop in the small brown spore capsules.*

The Underground Life of a Tree

Besides understanding the fact that trees are indispensable to life, young people can find enormous pleasure in learning about their composition and the nature of their growth. Underground, where the root system is concealed, is a good place to begin. This system is extensive. The roots of some species grow almost straight down. Other species have roots extending outward, close to the surface of the ground. Some have both types. Certain oak trees have been found with roots two or three times as widespread below ground as their branches above it.

Roots that have pushed partly above the earth's surface may help children picture the extent of a root system. An uprooted stump to which roots are still attached is also an aid in understanding the extensiveness of a root system. Or they may happen to see work being done on pavements, or watch the installation of pipes under sidewalks which uncovers or cuts into the roots of shade trees. It is impressive to realize the amount of abuse that trees will take, yet there are limits to the damage that a tree can withstand. Often the injured roots require treatment. Sometimes it is enough to trim away the ragged edges; in other cases the broken sections must be removed completely.

How Trees Are Nourished

The feeding of a tree begins at the roots as minerals dissolved in water are drawn into tiny root hairs. From these root hairs food travels up through the larger roots into sapwood and through the branches and twigs to the leaves. In the leaves are many veins that serve as channels for spreading the water and minerals. From these raw materials, with the help of sunlight and carbon dioxide from the air, the leaves produce a sugary liquid that travels back to the trunk, and through the fibers of the innermost layer of bark, to all parts of the tree in order to nourish it, and to provide the food for growth of the tree.

The process of making food and distributing it goes on throughout the spring and early summer. By midsummer the tree has achieved most of its growth for the year, and it begins to store extra food in its trunk, branches, twigs and roots. During the winter the tree rests. The following spring the reserve food is available to help buds open and new leaves begin to grow.

Tree Rings – Signs of Growth

You can see the record of a tree's growth in a trunk that has been cut across, because in the wood are rings that mark each year of its life. To add to its girth, a tree depends on a layer of cells called cambium, which lies between the protective bark on its outer side and a layer of wood on its inner side. During spring and early summer when conditions for growth are most favorable, wood cells develop.

During late summer and early fall, new but somewhat smaller wood cells are still produced. During the winter growth stops entirely. When growth resumes, with 'spring wood' growing next to 'fall wood,' the contrast between the two produces a line around the trunk. This line is known as the annual ring.

In a sense the annual rings are the biography of the tree – wide spaces between rings indicate good growing years, and narrow spaces are evidence of seasons of drought or other climatic conditions unfavorable to growth. A series of rings with little space between them at the center of the trunk, changing to wider-spaced rings toward the bark, might also be a clue to improved growing conditions. The thinning out of surrounding trees, for example, would provide more sunlight and the roots would have less competition for the water and minerals of the soil.

Annual growth rings are common to most of the trees that grow in temperate climates. But in some regions, such as the rainy tropics, there is no distinct growing season. As a result tree growth is constant; there are no annual rings, and the wood is unmarked. When these trees are sawed into boards they do not show an intricate grain. The grain is simply the texture of the wood revealed by the annual growth rings when the wood is sawed lengthwise.

If in wintertime you were to open a bud from the tip end of a branch, you would find tiny but perfectly formed stems, leaves and perhaps clusters of flowers. Some trees produce all these in the same bud; others have twigs and leaves in one type of bud and flowers in another. The buds, folded neatly and tightly, are protected by scales that overlap like shingles on a roof. In the spring you can see the buds open as the scales are cast off and the new twigs appear in response to the season's warmth.

On these pages, a single year in the eastern part of the United States shows its four different faces. At left, the blossoms of spring—in this case, a dogwood tree—are scattered among the fresh green leaves of the forest.

As spring gives way to summer (opposite, top), the bright warm sunshine enlivens all the colors, and grasses and flowers seem to bloom on every inch of ground. The same scene (below) turns to a deep gold in autumn, as the leaves change color.

By midwinter, everything looks completely barren; bare branches and trees seem to sleep under a white blanket of snow. However, in spite of the harsh weather, the new life of spring is getting ready. A bud on the dogwood tree (this page) is covered in an icy case, but in a few weeks it will burst into flower, and the whole cycle will begin again.

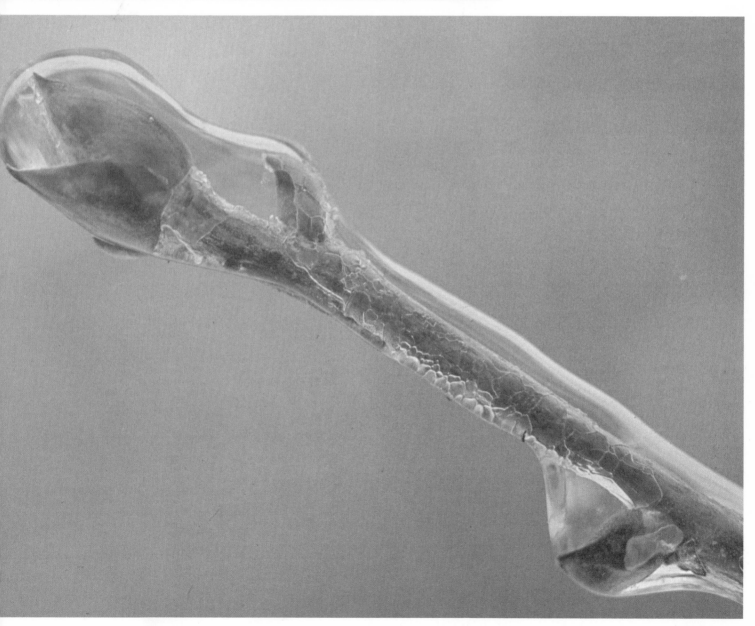

An observant child may notice that while young trees have smooth bark, that of older trees is furrowed and frequently sheds untidily. This is also caused by growth; as the girth of the trunk increases, pressure causes the bark to split. A special layer of cells in the bark forms new corky layers that patch the damaged parts, but these new layers do not smooth the wrinkles that have formed.

Why Leaves Change Color and Fall

As children first notice the reds and yellows around the time of the first cold snap, they often conclude that frost causes the leaves to change from green to bright autumn colors. Frost is not the cause, however, though lower temperatures do have some bearing on the change. With the coming of colder weather the earth starts to harden and the trees can no longer easily draw water from it.

Lacking water, the green pigment of the leaves begins to fade and is gradually replaced by yellow and orange pigments that have been present in the leaves all along but in smaller quantities than the green. Red coloring has a different origin. It is formed in the cell sap by the same kind of dye that colors red cabbage and beets. Lovely reds are displayed on sugar maples, white oaks and sumac. Poplar, hickory and linden are some of the trees that have golden yellow coloring. The green pigment of evergreens (as reflected in the name of this type of tree) is so hardy that it is not affected by winter conditions.

While the leaves are changing color, a thin corklike layer of cells develops between the leaf stems and the twigs to which they are fastened. This layer of weak tissue reduces or shuts off completely the flow of sap to the leaf, not only contributing to the death of the leaf but also weakening its attachment. Consequently it will fall from a slight breeze or even from its own weight.

Knots and Knotholes

Children often have the opportunity to watch trees being pruned in city parks or on suburban lawns. But they may be surprised to learn that trees growing under natural conditions are also pruned; the trees accomplishing this themselves. In one process, called natural pruning, lower branches become undernourished because excessive shade prevents their leaves from manufacturing food; as a result

these branches die and drop off. In some trees, layers of weak tissue are formed somewhere along certain branches – sometimes at their base. After a while the branches break off, even though many fresh leaves may still be attached to them. This process is known as self-pruning.

When a branch is lost to a tree by pruning, the remaining short stump of branch eventually becomes overgrown by the trunk. If the tree is felled and cut for lumber, the end of the branch shows up as a knot. In cases where the branch was quite dead when it dropped from the tree, the knots are also dead and fall out readily, leaving the knotholes that are often seen in board fences.

How to Identify Trees

Nature explorers are sure to experience additional pleasure in observing trees if they know them by name. It would be an overwhelming task to identify all of the earth's trees, but it is certainly possible to learn the species that grow in one's own neighborhood. They may be recognized by their bark, twigs, leaves, flowers and fruit. A tree's general silhouette is often an aid in revealing its species – for example, the slender birch, the widespread oak, and the cottonwood with its massive trunk that divides near the ground.

Sometimes, however, there are variations in the same type of tree caused by the conditions in which it grows. When a sugar maple has enough room in which to expand, its trunk is short and its head of branches oval-shaped. But in a forest where it must reach up to obtain sunlight, its trunk may be a hundred feet or more in height so that its leaves are not deprived of sunshine by taller neighbors.

Certain characteristics give various species their popular names. The red maple has red buds in winter and early spring. Its flowers are usually red, and in summer the color of the leaf stalks is red. In the autumn its leaves turn a beautiful crimson. Silver maples have two-toned leaves – pale green above and silvery white below. As a result, when they are blown by the wind, their color may seem to change from green to silver.

North America has a number of native species of maple, but one species of maple that is greatly enjoyed for ornamental planting is the Norway maple. The leaves of this tree

In summary a tree operates as a factory for the production of sugar and starch. Carbon dioxide gas is absorbed from the air through holes in the leaf's surface. Water moves up the plant from the roots and combines with the gas, using the energy of the sun to make the sugars. This food then travels throughout the tree in the sap.

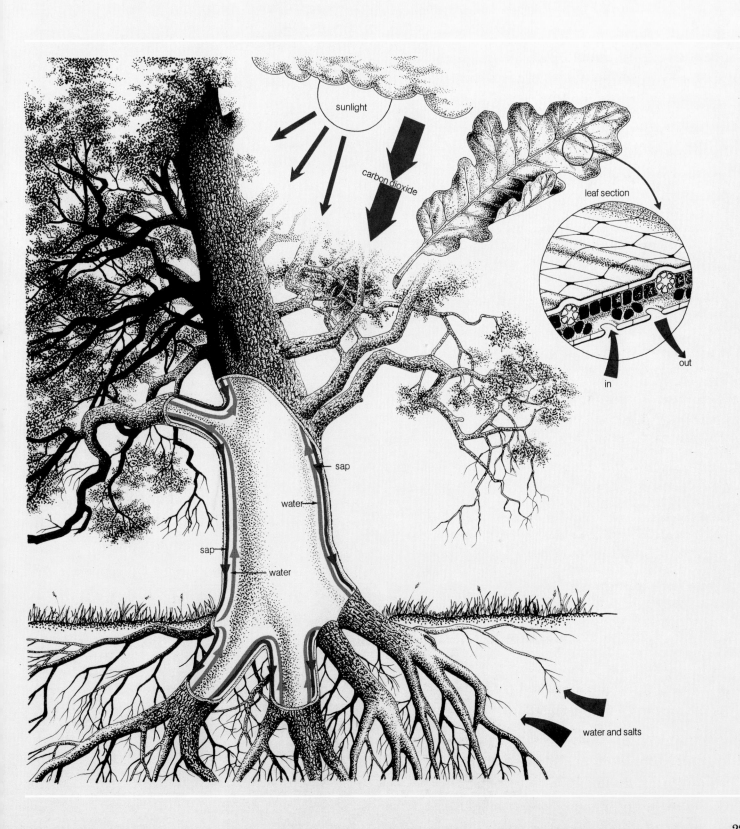

sunlight

carbon dioxide

leaf section

out

in

sap

water

sap

water

water and salts

are much like those of the sugar maple, but they are broader than they are long. Its bark is dark gray and fairly smooth.

The Horse Chestnut – a World Traveler

While certain trees are common to only one continent or one country, the horse chestnut has become well known in many areas. It had its beginnings in southern Asia. It was introduced to Europe in the eighteenth century, then later brought to North America. It flourished everywhere. Its profusion of leaves and snowy white flowers give beauty in the spring. In the fall it has fruit consisting of reddish brown glossy nuts, borne within prickly green husks. One explanation for the name horse chestnut is that these nuts were once used to make medicine for horses (they are terribly bitter to the taste). Another claim is that the name results from the shape of the scars left on twigs when leaves break away; the scars resemble the print of a horse's hoof, with the broken veins marking the nails of the horse's shoe.

Oak Trees and Maidenhairs

The majestic oaks are certainly among the most beautiful, useful and well known of trees. Who has not quoted the ancient saying, 'Great oaks from little acorns grow!' Altogether there are about three hundred species, which are variously found in Europe, America, Asia and Africa. They are divided into two classes: white oaks and black oaks. A number of differences may be noticed in oaks, such as the shape of the leaves, style of branches, type of bark and acorn. The red oak's large acorns are set in flat saucer-shaped cups making them enjoyable toys for young children. Oaks are comparatively slow growing trees and can sometimes thrive for centuries. Some species do not produce acorns until they are about twenty years old.

A far more specialized tree is one known either as the maidenhair tree or the ginkgo. It is native to Japan and China but was imported to other parts of the world because it grows well in poor soil, and is not harmed by the heat reflected from city pavements. It also responds well to pruning; it can be trimmed to shapes that are suitable to narrow streets. As a result it gives welcome green touches to many areas that would otherwise be barren. The name maidenhair was suggested by its leaves, which are shaped like the leaflets of the maidenhair fern.

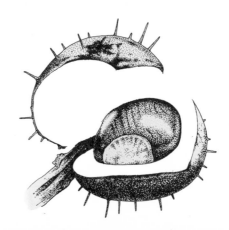

The sticky brown scales which protect the horse chestnut shoot in winter split open in spring to reveal the pale leaves inside. Soon the tree is covered in flower spikes and large palm-shaped leaves, which offer welcome shade in summer. Come the fall, these leaves turn golden yellow, and the prickly green cases of the chestnuts drop, releasing the glossy brown seeds within.

231

Gardening is nature exploring with something added, for children and their parents become partners with nature as they plant and tend seeds. Furthermore, the excitement of actually being involved in growing the modest flowers or vegetables of a home garden is likely to be more satisfying than viewing the spectacular specimens that are displayed at flower and garden shows.

Seeds are easily obtained at florists, supermarkets and variety stores and the packages usually carry instructions about the methods and appropriate time for planting each variety. However, because of the great choice available, it is important for a new gardener to make plans before shopping for seeds. As concerns a flower garden, a color scheme might be desirable – for example, an all-yellow display could include marigolds and nasturtiums; or a red, purple and white combination of salvia, petunias and baby's breath would be very attractive. There are also many other important considerations. How much space is available for the garden? (The mature plants should not crowd or overshadow each other.) Does the space receive much or little sunshine? (Certain plants flourish only with great amounts of sunlight, others do not require much light.) Will it be more interesting to arrange some tall and some short plants? (If this contrast is chosen, the tall plants should be arranged at the rear, or in the center, of the short varieties.)

Fortunately gardening is not limited to those who have growing space outdoors. There are many possibilities for gardening activities indoors. A wide windowsill or a table placed in front of a sunny window can be the setting for a small but colorful garden, with some of the same plants that are good choices for outdoors, such as marigolds, nasturtiums and petunias.

Petunias, which bloom profusely in bright sunshine in widespread areas of the world, furnish an interesting example of how new varieties of plants can be developed from an original species. Less than a hundred and fifty years ago some long-tubed white flowers were taken from South America to Europe. Shortly afterward the seeds of another species of plant that had small, broad-tubed red-purple flowers were sent from another part of South America to Glasgow, Scotland. There, botanists crossed the two species, and the crossing resulted in petunias as we know them today.

Youthful gardeners are sure to enjoy producing pansies. Each flower is beautifully colored, and its markings often suggest an appealing face. The dark spots at the bases of the side petals and the lines radiating from them suggest eyes and eyelashes, and the opening of the nectar tube makes up a nose. The spot near the base of the lower petal passes for a mouth. There is another intriguing and useful feature: the more often the flowers are picked, the more abundantly they appear. If seeds are allowed to ripen, the plant will bloom for only a short time. Picking the blooms, on the other hand, ensures new buds and blossoms.

An Easy-to-Grow Vegetable

Turning from flowers to vegetables, a young gardener can do no better than to plant radishes as a first crop. For one thing, they develop quickly; for another their progress is easily checked. Indoors the seeds may be planted in potting soil in a flat wooden box or a flowerpot at least seven inches across. They need only a light covering of soil. They should be kept close to a sunny window and given plenty of water. In a few days tiny plants should push through the soil. If they are very crowded, they should be thinned by pulling up some, so that there is at least an inch of space around each plant. Within a few weeks the roots should be rounded and large enough to eat. If a plant is left to grow, it will produce small white or purple flowers for several months.

Bulbs and Other Plantings

A somewhat different kind of gardening can be enjoyed with bulbs. Bulbs are actually buds compacted with a stem surrounded by leaves. The leaf layers are fleshy, since they contain food that was stored during the previous season. Tulips are among the most popular of bulb plants. The bulb may be put in the earth in the fall, placed so that the tips point upward and the tops are level with the surface of the soil. After growth starts in the spring the roots, which form a thick white tassel at the bottom, will bring minerals and water up to the bud within each bulb. When a new bud appears above ground it is protected by three sepals. As the bud stretches upward and becomes larger, the green of the sepals changes to the color of the petals; when the flower opens, there is no noticeable difference between petal and sepal. The sepals, standing out below the petals, give the flower a triangular shape. When the sun is not bright, the sepals partially close about the flower.

Producing flowers indoors is extremely simple with certain bulbs; one good example is the narcissus. These do not need soil; they may be supported in a shallow dish with pebbles or bits of broken shell and given just enough water to show through the pebbles. At first the plant should be kept in a dark cool place until its roots have formed. Usually this requires only a few weeks. It should then be gradually brought into sunlight, meanwhile kept away from drafts. In two or three weeks flowers should appear. Indoor gardening need not be limited to bulbs and seeds. There is also a choice of plants that grow directly from roots, such as the sweet potato; or from stem cuttings, such as geraniums, cacti and begonias; or from certain fleshy leaves, such as those of the African violet.

A small wooden box will serve to give stem cuttings their start. Bore holes in the bottom and spread pebbles or chips from broken flowerpots over them. Then fill the box with clean sand to within half an inch of the top. Moisten the sand and press it down firmly. Make a hole in the sand (a pencil makes a good tool for this purpose) for each stem cutting. Place a freshly cut stem in each hole, making sure that at least two nodes of every stem have been buried. (Nodes are the juncture points where leaves have been removed.) The little garden should be kept moist in a cool place.

A good arrangement for propagating African violets from leaves may be made by using two flowerpots, one an eight-inch shallow pot, the other a three-inch pot. Cover the hole of the larger pot with a piece of crockery and partly fill the pot with sand. Close the hole of the smaller pot with a loose-fitting cork and place this pot inside the larger one. Fill the space between their sides with more sand. If the small pot is always filled with water, the sand will be moist at all times. Set the base of a few violet leaves in the moistened sand.

The Wonderful World of Plants
Young explorers who become involved with the world of plant life have a lifetime of fascinating discoveries awaiting them. As a matter of fact, the plant kingdom is so vast and complicated that too much information about it, acquired too quickly, can discourage further interest. For this reason simple gardening projects are usually the best means to begin learning of the wonders of the plant world; a world that encompassed the earth long before animal life.

Although there are thousands of wild flower species, each one is different in form and has its own individual beauty.

▽ The petals of the mountain laurel, a legally protected flower, are arranged to suggest a five-sided trumpet shape.

▽ ▽ The brilliant yellow head of the dandelion is formed of hundreds of tiny fingerlike petals in a cluster.

▷ The simple red petals of the wild poppy are silky to touch, and so fine that they are almost transparent.

▽ The ball-shaped head of a clover flower is made up of many little tube-shaped flowerets, each containing a tiny drop of nectar. Bees are especially fond of these sweet flowers.

▽ ▽ The wild rose has five well-separated petals; but by careful breeding, gardeners have cultivated new types of roses with many full, overlapping petals in rich colors.

▽ ▽ ▽ The spiky petals of the water lily give a brilliant starry effect on the surface of the water, contrasting with their flat circular leaves. Water lilies may be white or yellow.

Seeds, Roots, and Storage

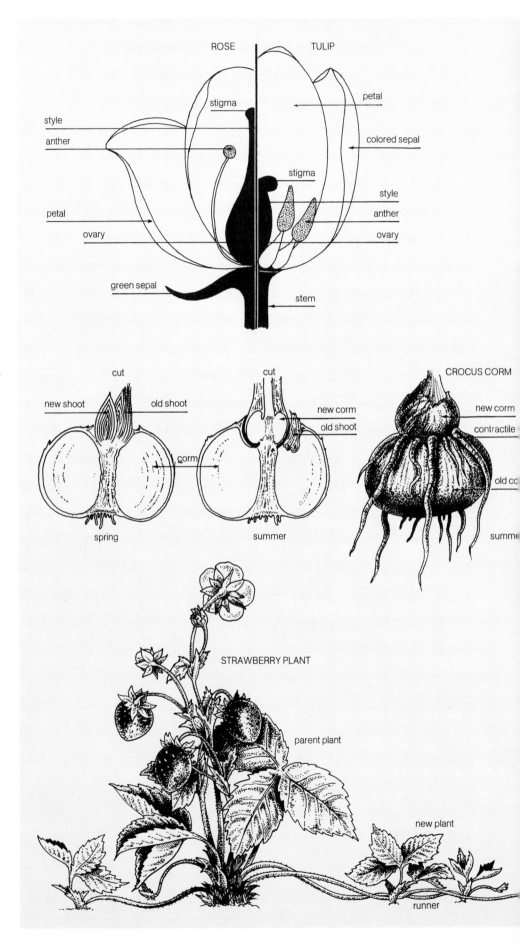

ROSE   TULIP

stigma

style
anther

petal

colored sepal

stigma

style
anther
ovary

petal

ovary

green sepal

stem

The life of green plants is devoted to two main tasks: to reproduce their own kind and to survive the seasons. The ways in which the plants function with regard to these tasks are varied and interesting. Some of them can be seen in the common plants and their products illustrated on the right.

The creation of seeds begins the cycle. Insects are attracted to flowers by bright petals and strong perfumes. Inside the flower, they transfer pollen as a fine dust on their bodies, from the anthers to the sticky stigma. From there, the pollen grains extend inside the style to reach the ovary, where they will fertilize future seeds. The basic plan of most flowers is similar, as can be seen in the cutaway halves of the rose and the tulip. Seeds are not the only method of reproduction. Some plants, like the strawberry also send out runners above the ground. These root at intervals, making new growths. Seeds do, however, serve another vital function: they are one of the ways in which plants overcome the cold, shortened days of winter. Plants that last only a year – the annuals – ensure that the species will reappear by leaving seeds. Each one of these contains the germ of a plant, together with a food store to support its growth the following spring. If you halve a seed – a bean is a good example – it is easy to see the future shoot and root between its specially food-packed leaves, the cotyledons, protected by a tough skin, the testa.

The plants that live more than a year, known as perennials, survive the winter with various other types of food stores. In spring, all the food made by their leaves produces flowers, then seeds to scatter new plants. Afterwards, any surplus food is stored in the warmth and safety of the earth. Among the most familiar of these stores are the corms, bulbs, and tubers.

Corms, such as those of the crocus plant are the bases of stems swollen with food. Because the new corm forms partly above the ground, strong roots connect it to last year's corm and contract to pull it in to the protection of the earth. Bulbs are the swollen bases of leaves that overlap around the new shoot. Both hyacinths and onions are produced from bulbs. A neat cut down the center of one of these bulbs will reveal the leaf layers and the new shoot. The one in the illustration is just beginning to make its journey upwards in spring. Even the familiar potato is a type of storage organ for its plant, known as a tuber. It is formed by the swollen tip of an underground stem. When it is planted new shoots sprout out of the 'eyes.'

cut

new shoot   old shoot

corm

spring

cut

new corm
old shoot

summer

CROCUS CORM

new corm

contractile

old co

summe

STRAWBERRY PLANT

parent plant

new plant

runner

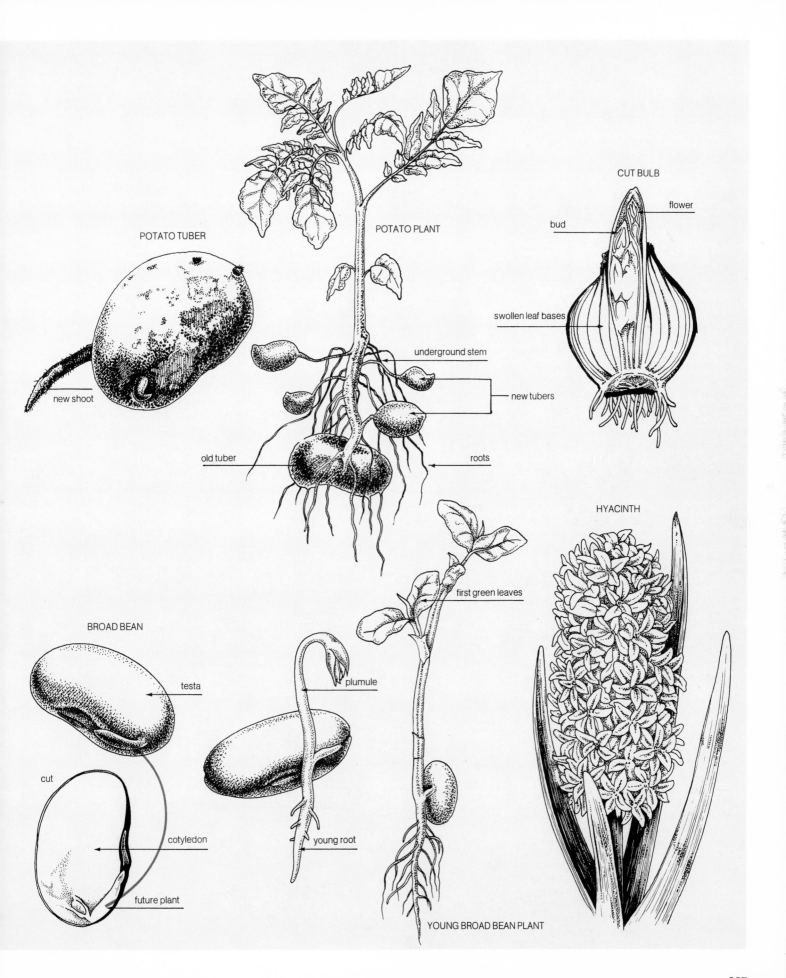

POTATO TUBER

new shoot

POTATO PLANT

underground stem

new tubers

old tuber

roots

CUT BULB

bud

flower

swollen leaf bases

HYACINTH

first green leaves

BROAD BEAN

testa

cut

cotyledon

future plant

plumule

young root

YOUNG BROAD BEAN PLANT

Index

Numbers refer to the text on the page indicated, italic numbers refer to illustrations on the page indicated.

ACORN, 230
Adder, *117*
African violets, 234
Alligators, 126
Amphibians, 132
Animal tracks, mammals, *64/65*
Ants, 184; 190; *193*
    keeping, *212/213*
Ant lion, *209*
Antennae of the insect, 184
Antlers, 62
Apes, 136; 138
Aphids, 206
Aquarium, *104/105*
Archerfish, *92*

BACK SWIMMER, 204; 208
Baltimore orioles, 14
Bats, *11*
Beaks of birds, 16; 18; *21*
Bears, *46; 57;* 61
    in the zoo, *149*
Beavers, 52; *54/55*
Bees, *194;* 196; 198
Beetles, 188; 190; 204
Birdbath, 24; *36*
Bird calls, 32
Bird house, *38/39*
Birds as pets, 168; *170*
    baby, 34
Black widow spider, 174
Boa constrictor, *116/118*
Bombardiers, 190
Budgerigar, 168; *171*
Buds of the tree, 226
Bugs, 182
Bulbs, how to grow, 232
Bullfrog, 7
Butterflies, *7; 186*
    development, *187*
    breeding your own, 208

CADDIS FLY, 208
Camels, 140; 145
Camouflage, 6,
    birds, 14; *18*
    crabs, 72; 75
    fish, 90
    toads and frogs, 134
Canaries, 168
Caterpillars, 182; 186; 188
Cats, 156; 158; 159
Centipedes, 180
Chameleons, *127;* 128
Chart for fish, 104
Cheetah, *55*
Chestnut trees, *226/227*
Chickens, 14; 16
Chimpanzees, *54;* 138
Chlorophyll, function of, 214

Clams, 73
Climbing perch, 100
Clover, 234
Cobra, 118
    African cobra shedding skin, *110/111*
Communication of animals, 48; *49*
    colors of insects, 210/211
Copperhead snake, 113
Coral snake, 113
Corals, 71; *74/75*
Cormorant, *17*
Crabs 73, 75
    hermit crab, *79*
Crickets, 184; 200
Crocodiles, 126

DADDY LONGLEGS, 180
Damsel fly, 204
Dandelions
    flower, *234*
    dispersal, *218*
Deer, 44; *48; 53;* 62
Dogs, 160; 163
Dogwood trees, *227*
Dolphins, 68
    bottlenose, *70*
Donkeys, *165*
Dragonfly, 204
Ducks, *22/23*

EAGLES, *28*
    African fish, *35*
Ears
    birds, 19
    cats, 159
    dogs, 163
    fish, 90
    grasshoppers, 184; *201*
    insects, 184
    snakes, 108
Earthworms, 180/181
Eels, 97
Eggs
    ants, 190
    birds, 34
    butterflies, development, *186/187*
    earthworms, 181
    flies, 200
    frogs, 132
    mosquitoes, 202
    ostriches, 152
Elephants, *56; 141;* 138; 140
Evergreen trees, 230/231
Eyes
    birds, 18
    cats, 158/159
    chameleons, 132
    fish, 90
    insects, 184
    snakes, 108

FEATHERS OF BIRDS, 14–16; *19*
Feeding birds
    baby birds, 34–36
    in winter, 24
Feet of birds, *24/25;* 168
Fennec, *56*
Ferns, 222; 224
'Fiddleheads', 222, *225*
Fighting among mammals, 43–44, *52*
Fins, *84;* 86; 88
Firefly, 188
Fish, study of, 84
Fish hatcheries, 104
Fish scales, 93
Flies, 200
Flight methods of birds, 19; 21; *26/27*
Flowers, study of, 214; 216
Flying fish, 100
Flying hours of birds, 22
Foxes, *47; 56;* 61; *169*
Frigate bird, 35
Fronds, 222
Fruit, 216

GALL INSECT, 198
Garden for the child, 232
Garter snake, *115*
Geese, migration, 30–31
Gerbils, 167
Gibbons, 138
Gila monster, *110–111*
Gills of fish, 86
Ginkgo trees, 230
Giraffes, *55;* 140
Goldfish, *85;* 88; 90
Gorillas, 138; *141*
Guinea pigs, *166;* 167
Grasshoppers, 198
Grass snake, *107*
Gulls, *29*

HAMSTERS, *166;* 167
Hares, 168
Hibernation
    caterpillars, 188
    ladybugs, 188
    snakes, 106
Hippopotamus, *44, 143;* 140
Honeycombs, how made, 196; 198
Hornets, 193
Horse-chestnut trees, 230
Horses, 164; *165*
Hummingbird, *27;* 155
Hydroids, 71

INSECTS, pollination by, 216
Insects, study of, 182–208

KANGAROO, 150; 152; *153*
Katydids, 184; 198

King snake, 123
Knots and knotholes, formation of, 228
Koala, *152*

LADYBUG, 188; 204–206; *205*
Leaves of the tree, 228
Lions, *46;* 144; *147*
Lizards, 128
Lobsters, 75

MAIDENHAIR trees, 230
Mammals
  family life, *54–57*
  hunting, *46–47*
  tracks, *64–65*
  winter living, 44
Maple trees, 228; 230
Marmot, *48;* 61
Marsupials, 150
Martens, *33*
Mermaids, 66; 70
Metamorphosis of the insect, 182
  dragonfly, 182
Mice, 48; 50
  as pets, 167–168
Migration
  birds, 21–24, *30/31*
  butterflies, 186
  eels, 97
  fish, 93
  geese, *30/31*
  robins, 21
  salmon, 18
Milk snake, 123
Millipedes, 180
Moles, 58; *63*
Mollusks, 73
Molting process
  birds, *15;* 16
  snakes, 108
Mongoose family killing cobra, *118*
Monkeys, 138
Mosquitoes, 200; 202
Mosquitofish, 94
Mosses, 222
Moths, 186
Mountain laurel, *234*
Mushrooms and toadstools, *222/223;* 224
Muskrats, 52

NASTURTIUMS, 232
Nests
  ants, 190
  mice, 50
  moles, 61
  sparrow, *37*
  squirrels, 44; 48
  swallow, 37
  wasps, 193

OAK TREES, 230
Orangutans, 138; *104/141*
Ostriches, 152; 155
Otters, 52; *53*
Owls, *18/19*
  as pets, *169*
Oysters, 73

PANDA, 149
Pansies, 232
Parrots and parakeets, 168; *170*
Peacocks, 155

Penguins, *154;* 155
Persian cats, 159
Petunias, 232
Pigeons, *13;* 168; 170
Pine cones, 230
Plants, 214
  roots, *236/237*
  pollination and dispersal, 216; *218–221*
Poison spiders, 172
Ponies, 164; *165*
Poppies, *234/235*
Porcupine, 44
Prairie dogs, 62
Praying mantis, *202; 204*
Prosimians, 138
Pythons, 118

RABBITS, *7;* 48; 168
Raccoons' tracks, 62
Radishes in the garden, 232
Rats
  muskrats, 52
  pet albino Norway rat, *166*
  as pets, 167
Rattlesnakes, *117*
Ravens, *169*
Reptiles, 106; *107; 110/111*
Rhinoceros, 140
Root-system of the tree, 225
Roses, dog, *235*

SALAMANDERS, *134/135*
Salmon, 98
Sea anemones, 71
Sea cow, 71
Sea lions, 136
Sea horses, 100
Seals and sea lions, *68/69*
Sea urchin, *78/79*
Seasons, change of, *226/227*
Seaweed, *78*
Seeds
  flowers, how they start, 214; 216
  how scattered, 218; *218/219; 220/221*
  trees, planting of, *7*
Sharks, 94; 97
Shellfish, 71; 73; *81*
Shells as a hobby, 76; *82/83*
Shrimp, 77
Siamese cat, 159
Skunks, 44
Snails, *10*
Snakes
  cold blood, 106
  collecting them, 125
  fact and fiction, 106
  feeding, *114/115*
  harmless ones, 118
  how, when and what they eat, *113/116*
  killing of their food, 113; *115*
  life of, 110/111
  motion, 108/112
  poisonous, 113
  rattles, 116
  reproduction, 113
  senses, 107
  shedding of skin, 107; *110/111*
  water snakes, 123
Songs of birds, 32–34
  canary, 168
  white-throated sparrow, 32
  robin, 32

Spawning migration
  eels, 97
  salmon, 98
Speed of birds in migration, 22
Spiders, 172–180
  web-making, *178/179*
Sponges, 71
Spruce trees, 230
Squirrels, 44; 48; *50/51; 220/221*
Starfish, *78; 81*
Stargazer fish, 100
Sting of the bee, 194; 196
Storks, 155
Sunfish, 93–94
Swimming methods of fish, 84; 86
Sycamore seeds, *221*

TADPOLE, 132
Talking sounds of mammals, 43; *48/49*
Tarantula, 172; *175*
Termites, *189;* 193/194
Tern, *29*
Tigers, *40/41;* 145; 147
Toads, *9;* 139
Tortoise, Galápagos, giant, *121*
  wood, 126
Tracks, identification of
  mammals, 62
  snakes, 108/112
Tree biography, how to keep, 226
Tree rings, 226
Trees, identification of, 228; 230
  planting of, *7*
Trout, 97
Tulips, 232
Turtles, *122/125*

VEGETABLES IN THE CHILD'S GARDEN, 232
Viper, *117*

WALKING FISH, 100
Walruses, 149
Warfare among mammals, 43–44
Wasps, 193
Water insects, 204; 208
Water lily, *235*
Water spiders, 176; 180
Weasel, *46*
Whales, 66
Whirligig, 204
Wildcat, *42/43*
Wild horses, 164
Wildflowers, 234–235
Wintertime
  birds, feeding in, 24
  mammals in, 44
  fish in, 93
Wolfspiders, 172; 174
Wolves, 61
Woodchuck, 62

ZEBRA, *54;* 164
Zoos, 136

Acknowledgments

b = bottom, c = center, l = left, r = right, t = top.

P. Abbink cover c, 3bc, 29, 235c. Artis Bibliotheek, Amsterdam 133; Bavaria Verlag/Dr. F. Sauer 87b; Heather Angel/Bio Fotos 12, 79t, 80r, 80l, 81tl, 81tr, 81br, 107, 111t, 219br, 233; Tony Ayling 101t. Bruce Coleman Limited/Helmut Albrecht 54b; G. F. Allen 217b; Des Bartlett 69tl, 115b, 130; Jen and Des Bartlett 30/1, 129t, 211b; S. C. Bisserot 11t, 78bl, 111b, 175b, 209, 210t, 210b; C. Bonington 11b; Rod Borland 35b; M. and R. Borland 118; Mark Boulton 114t, 114b, 115t; Bill Brooks 225t; Nicholas Brown 201; John R. Brownlie 191b; Jane Burton cover b, 7, 10, 17, 18, 20, 21t, 42, 46tl, 47t, 47b, 53t, 72b, 75, 74t, 76r, 78tl, 78c, 79b, 81bl, 82, 83tr, 85, 87tr, 88, 90b, 91tc, 91b, 92b, 94, 95t, 95c, 95b, 97, 110b, 124c, 124b, 125, 126, 131t, 135, 155, 158t, 159t, 166tr, 166 tl, 168l, 168l, 170b, 170t, 173, 181b, 184, 185b, 189t, 191t, 192t, 197, 199, 206tr, 206tl, 206b, 211tl, 217tl, 218t, 218b, 220, 221b, 231b; Colin G. Butler 193; Clara Calhoun 128b; Bruce Coleman 67, 160; Neville Coleman 83tl; Rex Coleman 163b; Gerald Cubitt 146b; Davies 181lt; L. R. Dawson 49t; A. J. Deane 25, 211tr; Jack Dermid 192b; Nicholas Devore 163tl; Francisco Erize 154b; Inigo Everson 69b, 154t, 163tr; M. P. L. Fogden 189b; Jeff Foott 53b; Neville Fox-Davies 221t; Sven Gillsater 149t; Dr. Gualco 145; Karel Hofland 83b; David Hughes 8/9, 122/3; John Koopman 74b; G. Langsbury 26; G. Laycock 35t; A. P. Mann 230b; John Markham 24, 39, 205, 219l; Derek Middleton 117b; Norman Myers 56b, 110t; C. Ott 15, 27, 54; Nelly Peter 215tr; G. Pizzey 153; G. D. Plage 54/5t, 147t; S. C. Porter 219tr; Allan Power 76r; Prato 194t, 194b; Mike Price 112;

Hans Reinhard 19, 49b, 53, 54t, 63, 134, 158b, 161b, 164tr, 166b, 168r, 185l, 234c; H. Rivarola 131b, 185t, 202; Dick Robinson 146t; Leonard Lee Rue 7, 14t, 51tc, 55b, 117t; W. E. Ruth 14b; Toni Schneiders 215tl; Harold Schultz 189, 203; James Simon 55t; Norman Tomalin 69tr, 70; Simon Trevor 142/3 all; John Wallis 152; D. Washington 117. Pieter van Delft 2, 3, 7, 50, 51tr, 51b, 157, 161, 215b, 222t, 222b, 223t, 230tr. Piet Eggen 22, 28, 33, 64, 65, 68, 72t, 84, 91tr, 92t, 104/5, 109, 178, 196, 231t, 236/7. Mary Evans Picture Library 175t. Otto van Eersel 217tr, 225b, 226/7 series, 230tl, 230tc, 234t, 234b, 235t, 235b. Sally Foy 223b. Jens Ploug Hansen 98b. Frank Lane/Ralph Thompson 97. N.H.P.A./Anthony Bannister 100; Stephen Dalton 37tl, 37bl, 183, 187 series, 207; Brian Hawkes 33b; James Tallan 67b; Philip Wayne 51tl. Norwegian Tourist Board 98t. Oxford Scientific Films 102t, 102b, 103t, 103m, 103b. PAF/124t; Karsten Mortensen 164l; Gunvor Jørgsolm 171, Picturepoint 23b, 74. Seaphot/Dick Clarke 89, 96b; J. Lythgoe 90c; Perez 96t. Spectrum/Tony Boxall 37tr, 37br; T. F. Holland 13. Dr. D. P. Wilson 87tl. World Wildlife Fund/Paul Barruel 4, 26; M. Boulton 46tr; Helmut Diller 1, 57, 139, 148t, 150, 151; E. Flipse 46b; W. Hoffmann 146l; Peter Jackson 147b; E. Schumacher 18b, 21b; K. Scriven cover t; Urs Woy 120/1; C. Zuber 55b. Zoological Society, London 41, 45, 56t, 128t, 141t, 141l, 136r, 137, 144t, 144b, 148b, 149b, 164tl.

We would also like to acknowledge the valuable help of Sally Foy, John Hoskin, Charmian Murley, and Paddy Kuhnen in the preparation of this book.